A Critique of Monetary Policy

A CRITIQUE OF MONETARY POLICY

Theory and British Experience

J. C. R. DOW AND I. D. SAVILLE

CLARENDON PRESS • OXFORD
1988

Oxford University Press, Walton Street, Oxford OX2 6DP
Oxford New York Toronto
Delhi Bombay Calcutta Madras Karachi
Petaling Jaya Singapore Hong Kong Tokyo
Nairobi Dar es Salaam Cape Town
Melbourne Auckland
and associated companies in
Berlin Ibadan

Oxford is a trade mark of Oxford University Press

Published in the United States
by Oxford University Press, New York

British Library Cataloguing in Publication Data
Dow, J. C. R.
A critique of monetary policy: theory and British experience
1. Chicago school of economics — History
2. Economics — Great Britain — History — 20th century
I. Title. II. Saville, I. D.
332.4'941 HG 220.G7
ISBN 0-19-828599-X

Library of Congress Cataloging in Publication Data
Dow, J. C. R. (J. Christopher R.)
A critique of monetary policy: theory and British experience/
J. C. R. Dow and I. D. Saville.
p. cm. Bibliography: p. Includes index.
1. Monetary policy — Great Britain. 2. Interest rates — Government policy — Great
Britain. 3. Monetary policy. 4. Interest rates.
I. Saville, I. D. (Iain D.) II. Title.
HG939.5.D68 1988 332.4'941—dc19
ISBN 0-19-828599-X

Printed in Great Britain
at the University Printing House, Oxford
by David Stanford
Printer to the University

Preface

I was Economics Director at the Bank of England from early 1973 until early 1981, and for the next three years performed the same role as Economic Adviser to the Governor. Thus, I saw in, and slightly outstayed, Lord Richardson's ten years as Governor of the Bank, and saw events from within the Bank for most of the period covered by this study.

The book is a co-operative effort by myself and Iain Saville. He was formerly a member of the Bank's Economic Section, and was granted leave of absence by the Bank in accordance with its policy of encouraging its staff to move for periods to work outside. However, he returned to the Bank when the work was half done; its completion and revision thus had to be carried out without his full assistance, and the drafting is mostly mine. Nevertheless, this study of monetary policy is very much a joint result of our collaboration, and represents our shared conclusions. The essence of the argument is contained in Chapters 2, 3, 4, and 11. These especially are the product of close discussion between us and repeated exchanges of drafts, to the point where, as with all successful collaborations, it is impossible for either to feel sure what each contributed. After Iain Saville left Robert Anderton acted as research officer, and we are both indebted to him for his help with the task of completing the work.

Our analysis leads us to the conclusion that the ten-year experiment with monetary targets was pursuit of a false trail. Grounds for some disillusion were apparent as early as 1973 when the Corset was imposed. Since then, the difficulty of controlling bank lending has become increasingly obvious, and our work may be seen essentially as an analysis of the implications of that observation. That, however, is not the same as saying that we felt or knew at the time what we feel or think we know now.

The advice we offered, and the views we held five or ten years ago, cannot, then, be inferred from what we say now. That may not be obvious and may easily be ignored, and I will cite one illustration. Although the book implies various objections to the idea of monetary targets, when targets were announced in 1976 I was among those most in favour of the innovation, which many then doubted. My reason was, admittedly, not that it would be counter-inflationary; rather that, in face of an evident tendency by the Bank simply to accommodate to events, it would lead the monetary authorities to define their aim and thus have a policy.

One would like to think one changes one's views because one learns more. In the first postwar decade, monetary policy was usually thought to have a minor role, and in my previous book I could see only a small place for it in the management of the economy. Contrary to this impression, when I went to work at OECD (which I did for the ten years from 1963), it seemed that in other countries monetary policy was nevertheless influential, and I was persuaded that it must be more important than I had thought. The present book suggests that its true role is, as of old, the management not of demand, but of the exchange rate.

In their confrontation before the Macmillan Committee, Montague Norman is usually depicted as hopelessly out-manœuvred and wrong, barely able to grasp what Keynes was saying. I now wonder whether it was not Montague Norman who was right, inarticulate though he was on that occasion; and whether the large impact on activity that Keynes attributed to changes in the short-term rate of interest (on which so much has since been built), though clever and ingenious, was not simply mistaken, and Norman right to be puzzled. The use of interest rates for domestic purposes rather than the exchange rate may come to seem one of the greatest aberrations of the half-century since.

The present book is not what was first intended. The aim was originally a broader study of the issues raised by current economic policy, in which monetary policy would have only a section. Of that wider study, only part has been completed; chiefly, the econometric study by Iain Saville and Kevin Gardiner of the causes of recession and inflation in the United Kingdom since the early 1970s, a summary of which has been published in the *National Institute Economic Review* for August 1986. It was soon clear, however, that monetary policy and monetary theory would require a separate book. The subject was too complex for anything less, discussion of it at all levels too diffuse and too various, the role that monetary policy had come to be allotted in economic strategy too dominant, and the handling of what would have to be an involved argument too demanding on authors and readers alike.

The book is based throughout on published sources, and in view of our different connections with the Bank, we wish to state that the Bank of England has no responsibility for it. Somewhat as a court jester is licensed to voice unpopular truths, an economic adviser is paid to give honest advice. To examine critically the policies followed by the Bank, as we here do, is thus not to criticize the Bank; and is better seen as an act of possible utility than of disloyalty to an institution in whose work we have taken part.

The world has moved on as we were writing, and in this country monetary targets have been largely abandoned. Some proclaim that this kind of monetary policy is dead; for others, perhaps, there has been an uneasy forced retreat. Our view, as it has developed, is that it ought never to have been believed either possible or useful in the first place. Since we have found it difficult to set out the argument fully and clearly, and since after a decade of living with monetary targetry it now seems to be time to take stock and consider what other line of policy to pursue, we hope that the book may contribute to a discussion in this and other countries which will no doubt continue. Our thesis in some respects runs counter to prevailing economic theory, and is perforce addressed largely to economists. The argument is however of general importance, and we have tried to make it, at least in outline, intelligible more generally. We hope, then, that the book will interest various sorts of reader, including those now responsible for the conduct of monetary policy, and — among those who formerly were — the Governor, whom those of us who worked with him knew we were lucky to serve, and who, with his own great mastery and style, presided over the monetary events of that decade.

We have to thank Michael Artis, John Fleming, Andrew Britton, and an anonymous critic who read and commented on the whole of the draft, and Brian Henry, Bryan Hopkin, and Christopher Allsopp who read parts. I have also to thank my son James for help with two passages. A book such as this, dealing with a broad theme and touching on many fields where a vast amount has been written, inevitably exposes the authors to risks of faults of both omission and commission. We are conscious that huge deficiencies must remain, but without these critics the book would certainly have been worse.

The study has made been possible by grants from the Nuffield Foundation, the Leverhulme Trust, and the Gatsby Charitable Foundation. We acknowledge our debt to these bodies, and also to Sir David Scholey of S. G. Warburg & Co. for his friendly offices in getting the project started. The National Institute of Economic and Social Research agreed to administer the grants and provide a home for the project, and for this purpose kindly made me a Visiting Fellow. No base could have been more congenial, and we owe much to Andrew Britton and Kit Jones, the Director and Secretary of the Institute, and all who assisted our work. In particular, we thank Julia Salisbury, our secretary and assistant, for lending her talents with such willing grace.

Christopher Dow
National Institute of Economic and Social Research
31 March 1987

Contents

List of Tables

List of Figures

1

Introduction

This book is an essay in theory, and a study of monetary policy in practice. It is an examination of how monetary policy has worked, or failed to work, in the United Kingdom in the 1970s and 1980s. This involves questions of monetary theory; the book is theoretical more than historical, and bears on the general question of the effects to be attributed to monetary policy at any time.

The point we start from

This study has its origins in observation of how the operation of monetary policy looks to those working in a central bank, and is an attempt to make sense of that experience. The central bank is only one operator among many in financial markets, and those responsible for conducting monetary policy are invariably fully aware of the strength of market forces and their limited power to influence the outcome. The actual financial operations conducted by a central bank are trivial in scale compared with the monetary and financial aggregates it seeks to influence. On the face of it, it seems unlikely that small-scale actions should be capable of profound and decisive consequences for national output and the general price level.

These perceptions contrast with the powerful effect attributed to monetary policy in political discussion and in monetary theory. Despite the limited scale of their operations, the power of the authorities to affect the behaviour of financial markets — at least within a range — is nevertheless clearly considerable. Among the questions to be explained is how that power arises, and how deep it goes, i.e. how far it extends beyond financial markets, and thus has important repercussions on the working of the economy as a whole.

These questions were raised by observation of events in the United Kingdom, more especially since 1971. The removal in that year of ceilings on bank lending, which in stricter or looser form had existed since the war, marked at least in intention a clean break from one type of monetary policy to another. For most of the period since then, the authorities have been concerned to control the rate of growth of the monetary aggregates, a concern expressed from 1976 onwards in the yearly announcement of targets for the rate of monetary growth in the year ahead. The study thus is concerned most directly with the type of monetary policy that seeks to control the rate of monetary growth. The possibilities of policies with a different orientation are discussed at the end of the book.

Our initial aim was to take a close look at the different methods of monetary control used by the authorities, and to examine the effects they could be expected to have on monetary conditions and on the economy generally. It was quickly obvious, however, that that required a prior account of what it was that the authorities were seeking to control, namely, an account of the nature of monetary growth. Since most of what we call broad money consists of the liabilities of the banks, we needed a fuller account than appeared to be available of the dynamic aspects of the behaviour of the banking system as a whole. We have therefore sought to explain the forces that, within the setting of the rest of the financial system, cause the collective balance sheet of the banking system to expand in an economy where nominal incomes tend to grow progressively.

Our broad strategy thus has been, first, to try to provide an account of the behaviour of the financial system in the absence of official intervention or control, and then, as a second stage, to superimpose the effects of official acts of control. That is what Parts I and II in turn attempt.

Some comments on our general approach

Since the argument of successive chapters is interconnected, it will probably be helpful at the outset to give a foretaste of the argument and make some general comments about it.

Our analysis treats lending by financial institutions as the driving force of monetary growth. It is convenient for much of the time to concentrate on lending by banks. Since this is broadly matched by bank deposits, which are the main component of sterling M3 (£M3; after 1987 called simply M3), we give emphasis to that aggregate, which we refer to as 'broad money' — and which, perhaps for somewhat different reasons, has been the focus of policy in the United Kingdom. Deposits with building societies are, however, close substitutes for time deposits with banks, and are likely to become closer as building societies provide fuller banking services. Much of what we have to say about bank lending therefore applies also to lending by building societies; and we also give emphasis to a wider aggregate including deposits with building societies, which we refer to as 'very broad money'. (This we take to be roughly represented by PSL2 — after 1987 called M5 — which includes cash and all bank deposits together with relatively liquid building society deposits and the small amount of money-market instruments that is held by the non-bank private sector.)

In most theoretical discussion, and in most macroeconomic models that incorporate money, the supply of 'money' is treated as exogenous, i.e. as determined not by the working of the economic system but from outside, by decision of the monetary authorities. The assumption is that the central bank can readily control the volume of bank deposits. The banks, it is assumed, maintain reserves in the form of balances at the central bank; the reserves they need to maintain are assumed to be related to the size of their deposits; and the central bank can determine the size of their reserves. Hence the central bank decides the size of their deposits, and if it supplies the banks with an increase in reserves, bank deposits will expand by a multiple of that increase.

In our analysis of monetary growth, our strategy is to look first at the factors determining the growth of bank lending on the assumption that the authorities make no attempt to control the process. At this stage therefore we also assume that the authorities follow an accommodating policy with regard to banks' reserves, and allow the banks themselves to decide, in the light of the costs and advantages as seen by them, what balances to hold at the central bank. Only later do we examine the consequences of monetary-base control. To those accustomed to the standard analysis, this procedure will appear perverse in omitting what to them will appear an essential element.

The reasons justifying our procedure are these. In the first place, this treatment is realistic; for in fact, the authorities have always stood ready to provide liquidity in the form of balances at the Bank of England, in essentially unlimited quantities though at a price of the authorities' choosing. They have not allocated a predetermined quantity of reserves at whatever price was required to clear the market, but rather have varied the price at which banks were permitted to replenish an insufficiency of reserves. In the second place, it is questionable whether base control could provide effective monetary control. Since the effects of such control are difficult to analyse, the argument is best presented, as we have laid it out, in two stages. We hope that, to those willing to wait till the end of the argument, the initial assumption of an accommodating policy will appear a legitimate device.

The terminology used in discussing money creation itself may carry theoretical implications. For those who see the money stock as being easily controlled by the control of bank reserves, the demand for money derives from private preferences, but the supply of money is an official decision. The stock of money allowed by the authorities is regarded as the money 'supply', and is often called by that term; and an excess of 'supply' over demand can be seen as in 'injection' of money into the economic system, from which further important consequences are traced. In our exposition we avoid the term 'the money supply' because of its connotation of exogeneity, and speak simply of the money stock;

we use the term in inverted commas only in referring to other analysis where that connotation is intended.

Our account of how the money stock is determined is coloured by the developments that in fact occurred, and is meant to explain them. In fact, it early became clear that the main difficulty in controlling monetary growth lay in controlling bank lending. The course of sterling bank lending and of broad money is shown schematically in Fig. 1.1, which shows bank lending and broad money as ratios of GDP. Expressed in these terms, there was a surge in bank lending after the removal of lending control in 1971 that continued through 1972 and 1973. In the years 1974–80, when the Corset control was intermittently in force, there was first a contraction and then a more level trend. After 1980 there was again a fairly rapid rise.

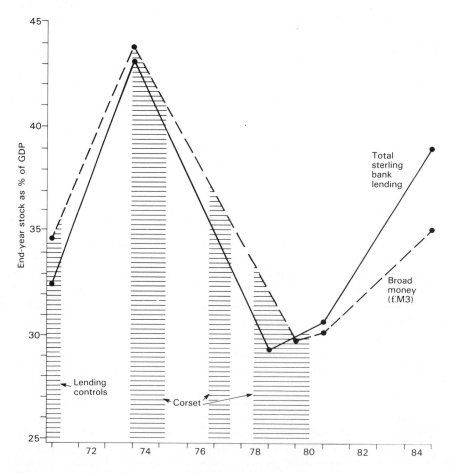

Fig. 1.1   *Bank lending and broad money, selected years, 1970–1984*

We clearly have to give weight to the influence of direct controls before 1971 and of the Corset; but how much influence one ascribes to them depends in part on how one sees the system working without them. Our initial approach was to regard other types of monetary policy not as determining the pace of monetary growth, but as one influence among others which modified an endogenous process of money creation by the banks. It is mostly by variations of central-bank rate that the authorities sought to influence monetary growth; but closer analysis suggested that it neither was nor could be expected to be effective for that purpose. Thus, despite our initial presumption, we conclude that, apart from the possible influence of direct lending controls, the historical growth of the aggregates was largely endogenous and was determined primarily by bank lending.

We see banks rationing the size of loans to individual customers not out of inertia, but as an equilibrium response; and we argue that the rules of thumb adopted by the banks in determining loans are related to their customers' prospective incomes. Hence (provided lending criteria remain unchanged), aggregate bank lending to the private sector will grow with nominal GDP. It is for this reason that we present historical developments in the form of ratios of the aggregates to GDP, and, with some reservations, interpret a change in the ratios as evidence of a change in the banks' lending criteria. We see lending criteria as fairly stable and subject only to gradual change; but it is difficult to make sense of what occurred without supposing that large shifts occurred. We see banks as able to vary their lending, however, only within limits set by the availability of substitute channels of lending. Thus though banks have some freedom to vary lending and hence the stock of money, this is true only within a certain range.

In much macroeconomic theory, the twin assumptions of exogenous money 'supply' and stable money demand mean that money 'supply' controls the price level — either continuously except for temporary divergencies (as in monetarist models); or in the equilibrium long term (as in other macroeconomic models). If, as on our view, the money stock is largely or wholly endogenous, it cannot provide a nominal 'anchor' that controls the price level. To this basic question we revert in our two final chapters (and there give reasons why we do not discuss many propositions stemming from the postulate of rational expectations that have figured in recent discussion).

For this reason we see the development of output and prices as largely dependent on factors other than the rate of monetary growth. As noted above, we see banks within certain limits being able to vary bank lending at choice, and we see the expenditure made possible by such variations in bank lending as influencing output and prices, but not being a dominant influence. For these reasons, in relating the course of the financial aggregates to that of nominal GDP, we take the course of output and prices as largely given, influenced only marginally by the pace of bank lending, and confine ourselves to an analysis of how banks behave in this given environment; we have not regarded it as essential to our task to provide an explanation of what determines that environment. Had we been constructing a model of long-term equilibrium, we would probably have taken bank lending in the long term to be completely endogenous, dependent on the course of output and prices, and the latter as determined entirely by non-monetary factors. This general approach appears similar to that of Kaldor (1980).

We have also had to be concerned with interest rates. For the authorities have tried to control monetary growth largely by changes in what used to be called Bank rate and which we call central-bank rate. Most theoretical discussion of interest rates has been in equilibrium terms and relates to the long term. To supplement this, our purposes forced us to propose our own account of the various influences, including that of central-bank rate, that determine the general level of interest rates in the short term.

In the long term, the (real) rate of interest is usually seen as determined by the marginal productivity of the stock of capital and the desire by consumers to hold wealth. In such a theory there appears no room for interest rates to be directly influenced by central-bank rate. To provide room for that we argue that, within a range, interest rates are indeterminate in terms of the factors that figure in long-run equilibrium theory; these however remain important, in that they set bounds to the short-term fluctuation of interest rates. Within this range, we argue that market opinion about future interest rates can be influenced by central-bank rate, which is nevertheless an instrument of limited capability; if pushed too far, it would cease to seem to market operators a credible policy, and thus would lose its grip over market forces. Our account of the determination of exchange rates, which we have also to discuss, is in broadly analagous terms.

To see the system as (within limits) indeterminate in this sense may seem unduly to play down the market-type relationships on which economists typically build. But it is not a dismissal of rationality, which is the basic postulate of economic theory. The rational response to large uncertainty about the future may result in a loose-jointed economic system in which the ultimate equilibrium point is a range that does not rigidly fix current prices and quantities.

Various forms of uncertainty have an important place at most stages of our account. Not only is money held as a hedge against uncertainty; its creation, via the granting of new loans, depends on the attitudes of banks towards the creditworthiness of borrowers, which is impossible to assess objectively. Because of uncertainty, both capital markets and exchange markets are, we argue, in some broad sense imperfect. That produces a range of indeterminacy in both interest rates and the exchange rate, and consequently also gives scope for the authorities to influence them. Within this range, the course of interest rates and exchange rates is determined by the guesses of markets regarding the uncertain future evolution of policy, of economic events, and of other participants' views.

Our discussion is not couched in algebraic terms, primarily because it did not appear necessary for the kind of arguments we wished to make. This is partly because of the kind of reality we are describing. While mathematical treatment is legitimate where 'risks' can be quantitatively evaluated, it is certainly more difficult in the case of the more elusive types of 'uncertainty' which seem in fact to prevail (Knight 1921). An illustration of the limitations of mathematical treatment is the failure of econometric work on the exchange rate to model the risk premium, noted later in Chapter 5 (Section 4).

To the extent that this study is novel, there is the question of how firmly based it can claim to be. It would be difficult to find full empirical verification for propositions of the sort we advance. There is, however, wide disagreement among economists on all aspects of economic theory. Econometric research, too, is no better based than the theories it tests. Though our conclusions must clearly be tentative, they are based on close observation and analysis and may appear worth critical examination.

The potential scope of this study being large, it may be helpful to note what we have not attempted. In describing the macroeconomic working of the financial system and the influence of monetary policy on it, we have discussed only those aspects of the microeconomic behaviour of financial institutions that appeared essential for that purpose. We have not sought to provide a picture of all aspects of the behaviour of a typical individual bank, or to discuss in detail the behaviour of different financial markets. For our purpose, therefore, only part of the extensive literature (reviewed for instance in Cuthbertson 1985) appeared relevant. The most important propositions we advance are not such as to be capable of econometric testing, and we refer to econometric results much more briefly than for instance Spencer (1986). On questions where there has been recent debate, we have not attempted a full review of the discussion, but confined ourselves to points (for instance on buffer-stock money) where we had something to add, or where this would clarify the implications of the view we were putting forward.

A detailed history of monetary policy in this country since the mid-1960s would have required a different sort of book, and we have tried to give only a brief outline of the high points. Fuller accounts are to be found, for the early period, in Blackaby *et al.* (1978); and for later years for instance in Artis and Lewis (1981), in Gowland (1982), in the collection of material from the *Bank of England Quarterly Bulletin* (in

Bank of England 1984), and (though this is part only of their aim) in Goodhart (1984) and Spencer (1986). A particular reason for not attempting a fuller historical account here is that it is in fact difficult to write of what the authorities did without either appearing to endorse the intentions of policy and the theory on which it was based, or inserting frequent disclaimers of a sort that tend to make the account seem pointless. To unravel how policy really operated, deeper analysis is needed than can be embodied in a chronological narrative.

The plan of the book

The bulk of the study is concerned with analysis of how the financial system behaves, and the effect on it of intervention by the monetary authorities. It is only in the last chapter that we are concerned with policy prescription; elsewhere it is touched on only incidentally.

The study has three main parts, discussing, respectively, how the financial system behaves, how policy impinges on it, and finally, the implications of the analysis for theory and for policy. The first three chapters of *Part I* contain the essential features of our analysis. For simplicity, that is first set out in terms of the reactions of the private sector (abstracting from government transactions) and of a closed economy (abstracting from transactions with other countries):

- *Chapter 2* discusses the behaviour of the banking system as a channel for the flow of funds between ultimate lenders and ultimate borrowers.
- *Chapters 3 and 4* discuss the behaviour of interest rates.

The following two chapters extend the analysis to include the effects of government transactions and transactions with overseas. That modifies the analysis only in minor ways; these chapters are thus to some extent digressions from the main line of argument:

- *Chapter 5* considers the effect on interest rates of external influences, involving a general discussion of the determinants of floating exchange rates.
- *Chapter 6* considers the impact of public-sector financial operations, and in particular of public-sector borrowing from the banks.

We are then in a position to examine in *Part II* the impact of policy.

- *Chapters 7–10* analyse the impact of the various methods of monetary control that have been attempted since 1971 or, in the case of monetary base control, seriously considered.
- *Chapter 11* draws on the earlier analysis to offer a broad

explanation of monetary developments in this country since the 1960s.

Part III then concludes as follows:

- *Chapter 12* examines the general theoretical implications of the analysis.
- *Chapter 13* considers the implications for monetary policy in future.

The analysis in the study casts doubt both on the possibility of controlling the rate of growth of broad monetary aggregates by anything short of direct controls, and, more generally, on the rationale of a policy couched in the terms of the aggregates. The most important conclusion of Chapter 13 is that monetary policy should aim not to control the aggregates but to secure a fairly stable exchange rate.

PART I

The Behaviour of the Financial System

2

The Macroeconomic Behaviour of the Banking System

This chapter analyses how, in an economy with rising money incomes, the stock of money tends to grow. This analysis is required as a basis for our later discussion of monetary control, which can be regarded as modifying the working of the market forces that cause the money stock to grow. The discussion will be mostly in terms of broad money (£M3 — after 1987 called simply M3), or of very broad money, including deposits with building societies (of which we take PSL2 — after 1987 called M5 — as an indicator). Deposits with building societies are very like deposits with banks, and building societies are here regarded as a specialized type of bank. Although the discussion in principle embraces both sorts of institution, for convenience we will often refer only to banks.

Broad money (or very broad money) consists for the most part of deposits with banks (or banks and building societies). The counterpart of such deposits mainly takes the form of lending to the private sector. What this chapter attempts therefore is a general account of the behaviour of the banking system in response to the preferences of borrowers and lenders in the private sector. Most of the remainder of bank lending (nowadays much the smaller part) is to the public sector. The scale of such lending is essentially under the authorities' control (with qualifications noted later) and will be discussed not in this chapter but in Chapter 6, along with other questions about the management of public debt.

The banking system provides a major channel of finance between final lenders (who are predominantly in the personal sector) and final borrowers. (Among private borrowers companies formerly predominated, but persons have now become equally important.) Banks' operations involve them in risks of various sorts, including the risk of withdrawals of deposits; to guard against these latter risks, banks need to hold reserves of relatively liquid assets. Balances at the central bank are, together with cash, the most liquid asset available. Treatment of the money stock as within the control of the authorities may seem justified by the fact that the authorities can influence the size of balances at the central bank, or at least make them more costly to the banks. But (for reasons explained in Chapter 1) the analysis in this chapter will assume that the banks are left free to choose the level of their reserves, and that penal interest rates are not imposed when the central bank provides reserves as necessary. (The operation and consequences of official action to put pressure on the banks' reserves is discussed later, in Chapters 8 and 9.)

In the following discussion (for reasons also noted in Chapter 1), we take the growth of real output and the pace of inflation as given and try to give an account of why, against this background, there is likely to be a progressive expansion of banks' balance sheets, and hence of the stock of money. There is a considerable literature on the behaviour of individual banks in a static environment, but no generally agreed description of this collective dynamic process; the argument in this chapter is thus necessarily tentative. We have tried to give an account that includes the broad considerations to which theory would point, and also gives due emphasis to factors that seem to have been important.

Section 1, after noting the scale of banks' activities in the context of the whole financial system, goes on to discuss some features of the role of banks that are important for their collective behaviour; Section 2 discusses what determines the scale of bank intermediation; and Section 3, to exemplify the working of the system, examines the effects of an exogenous change in bank lending behaviour. Section 4 then discusses in greater detail the relation between banks and the wholesale money markets. As will be apparent, this chapter provides only a first statement, which will leave much to be filled in in following chapters.

1. THE PLACE AND FUNCTIONS OF BANKS

Most money consists of bank deposits. At mid-1985, the stock of broad money held by the public (£M3) was nearly £120 billion, of which notes and coin amounted to only about £12 billion (Table 2.1). Notes and coin are in effect an interest-free loan to the government, and, if thus considered a liability, are a liability of a body 'outside' the financial system. Bank deposits, on the other hand, are the liability of institutions 'inside' it, namely the banks. What we have on this distinction been taught to call 'inside money' (Gurley and Shaw 1960, 73) amounts to nearly nine-tenths of the total. The relative importance of bank deposits has been increasing (from somewhat over 80 per cent of broad money in 1970 to over 90 per cent in 1985). The stock of very broad money (PSL2 — which includes most deposits with building societies and some other relatively liquid assets) was just over £200 billion at mid-1985, two-thirds as much again as broad money.

The total of financial assets of all sorts is many times larger. On the classification adopted in Table 2.2, the total at the same date was nearly £1,900 billion; if one nets out financial intermediaries, the total was about £900 billion. Table 2.3 shows in greater detail the major items among the financial assets and indebtedness of the main sectors.

TABLE 2.1. The stock of money, mid-1985

	Holdings of sterling assets by non-bank public		
		£b	% of annual GDP
Narrow money (M1)		56.4	$18\frac{1}{2}$
Notes and coin	12.4		4
Sight deposits at banks	44.0		
Time deposits at banks		62.1	
Broad money (£M3)		118.5	39
Persons	70.4		
Companies	48.1		
Deposits with building societies and other items included in PSL2[a]		86.1	
Very broad money (PSL2)		204.6	$67\frac{1}{2}$

[a] For definition of PSL2, see Table 11.1.
Source: CSO, *Financial Statistics.*

TABLE 2.2. UK financial assets and capital stock, mid-1985
(£ billion)

	Net financial position			Stock of real capital[a]	Total wealth
	Assets	Liabilities	Net		
Persons	590	185	405	275	680
Non-financial companies	235	435	− 200	280	80
Public sector	70	190	− 120	370	250
Total excluding financial intermediaries	895	810	85	925	1010
Financial intermediaries	995	1020	− 25	45	20
Whole economy	1890	1830	60	970	1030

[a] Net stock at replacement cost.
Source: CSO, *Financial Statistics* and *National Accounts.*

Over time, the value of the stock of financial assets has tended to grow, along with nominal national income and the value of the capital stock. Excluding the duplication represented by financial intermediaries, the value of financial assets of various sorts at mid-1985 was about equal to the (variously owned) value of real capital (Table 2.2). Non-financial companies have typically borrowed to buy real assets; persons have built

TABLE 2.3. Selected financial assets and liabilities by sector, mid-1985 (£ billion)

Financial assets		Financial liabilities	
FINAL LENDERS AND BORROWERS			
Persons			
Total	591	Total	187
of which:		*of which:*	
Value of pension and		Loans from banks	56
insurance rights	240	Loans from bldg societies	89
Bank deposits	62		
Government debt	51		
Equity (etc.) of non-			
financial companies	71		
Non-financial companies			
Total	234	Total	435
of which:		*of which:*	
Bank deposits	35	Value of equity and	
Inter-company debt	80	debentures	211
Overseas assets	81	Loans from banks	65
		Inter-company debt	80
		Overseas liabilities	57
Public sector	68		189
Total	894		810
FINANCIAL INTERMEDIARIES			
Banks			
Total	574	Total	574
of which:		*of which:*	
Lending overseas	399	Deposits from overseas	416
Lending at home	175	Domestic deposits	128
Building societies			
Total	110	Total	110
of which:		*of which:*	
Mortgages	89	Deposits	97
Other financial institutions			
Total	309	Total	335
of which:		*of which:*	
Government debt	63	Clients' pension and	
Equity of UK companies	128	insurance rights	240
Overseas assets	68	Loans from banks	40
Total	993		1019

Table continues p.17

Table 2.3 continued

Financial assets		Financial liabilities	
TOTAL	1887	TOTAL	1829
of which:		*of which:*	
Corresponding to		Liabilities to:	
liabilities of residents	1303	Residents	1303
Overseas assets	584	Non-residents	526

Source: CSO, *Financial Statistics.*

up stocks of real assets (largely houses) and also have claims on companies and government, having lent to them; and the public sector owns real capital considerably in excess of its net debt. Including financial assets held and liabilities owned by financial intermediaries, total financial assets are worth double the real capital stock. Since the middle of the last century, the value of the capital stock has about kept pace with that of national output (Matthews, Feinstein, and Odling-Smee 1982). The value of the stock of financial assets has grown somewhat more rapidly (Goldsmith 1969), with the rise of both corporate enterprise and financial intermediaries.

This picture of a growing stock of financial assets, in a growing economy with prices also tending to rise, needs to be kept in mind in analysing the behaviour of the banking system. Within the total of financial assets, the stock of broad money has grown at varying rates, but over the last century it has very broadly kept pace with national income (Capie and Webber 1985).

Lenders' risks and banking conventions

Banks typically do not stand ready to lend as much to a potential borrower as the borrower might wish to borrow at the prevailing rates charged by the banks on loans. Rather, they attach limitations to the scale of his borrowing that are related to his circumstances; and this we refer to as rationing. This behaviour implies that banks' lending rates are not such as to clear the market, and that there will in general be an excess demand for bank loans. There is perhaps some agreement that this behaviour on the part of the banks is the result not of inertia or frictions, which delay the attainment of equilibrium, but of factors that persist, so that banks' rationing is 'equilibrium rationing'. There is less agreement on what these factors are, and various explanations have been proposed, some of which we note before indicating what appear to us the main factors.

We see banks over a large part of their lending as being price-setters, with the rates charged by them for loans being set and varied only at relatively infrequent intervals; and we refer to bank lending rates over this large part of the field as being 'administered rates'. This perhaps was never true of bank lending to large firms, where the terms have long been negotiable, and it appears to be becoming decreasingly true. Large firms have long had the alternative not only of fairly ready access to the capital market, but of the more flexible alternative of issuing bills that (with the bank's acceptance, or guarantee) are readily saleable in the money markets. More recently, markets have developed in short-term commercial paper, issued by large firms and (with only its issue underwritten by a bank) sold on the money market on terms comparable with the cost of a bank loan. Bank lending rates to large firms therefore are not administered rates, but market-related.

Most previous explanations of equilibrium rationing start from the general assumption of a von Neumann–Morgenstern world in which agents are able to assess the degree of risk attaching to particular acts, and to engage in riskier acts when the return obtained is great enough, in their view, to compensate for the additional risk. (The compensation required for risk will be higher if agents are generally risk-averse than if, as may be assumed as a simplifying case, they are risk-neutral.) The question then is why, in such a world, banks do not charge more for riskier loans instead of rationing.

One earlier account (Jaffee 1971) had it that credit rationing arises because banks are restricted (by law, as earlier in the United States, or by social convention) from charging high enough interest rates on riskier loans to compensate for their riskiness. Stiglitz and Weiss (1981) offer a different rationalization: the reasons why banks do not charge more for riskier loans are that, first, if they did so only riskier propositions would be put to them (adverse selection); and, second, to charge higher rates would encourage borrowers to select riskier projects (the adverse incentive effect). While not entirely rejecting explanation on these lines, we doubt that it captures the central factors.

In our view, banks are not able to make precise estimates of the risks attaching to particular loans, and consequently (even apart from possible adverse selection and incentive effects) they could not protect themselves by charging more for riskier loans. They are partially protected by the fact that they lend to many customers, so that the risks are pooled. But this is not enough; putting quantitative limits on how much they lend to individual customers is a further way of limiting the risk of loss. The reason why banks seek to avoid risk is primarily that, to engage in banking, a bank must retain the full confidence of its depositors as to the safety of their deposits. Such confidence is potentially fragile, for depositors have little to go on but the reputation of a bank. Banks therefore attach overriding importance to appearing safe.

An additional consideration is that, given the emphasis on risk avoidance, the capital that prudence (or bank supervisors) requires a bank to maintain is small in relation to the deposits it takes. Serious miscalculation and bad debts could well result in inadequate capital to carry on business on the previous scale, and could force a bank to make a multiple contraction of its balance sheet. (The Midland Bank's ill-starred acquisition of its Californian subsidiary, Crocker National — subsequently disposed of — had something of this effect.)

In order profitably to employ money deposited with them, banks are nevertheless bound to take limited risks. Banks would not incur risks in lending to the private sector if their customers could offer secure collateral against the loan; then, if a customer got into unforeseen difficulty, the lending bank could hope to recover all its money and any additional costs by sale of the borrower's assets. Such a condition however is far from being met in the case of lending either to firms or to individuals. Traditionally, firms borrowed to finance stocks of materials and work in progress. Although stocks of materials have a market price, it is often volatile; the price at which finished or semi-finished products can be disposed of in a forced sale is even more problematic. The same is true of industrial and commercial buildings, and even more so of plant and machinery, where the second-hand market is highly imperfect. The expected profits of a firm typically depend greatly on the skill and experience of its management, so that the break-up value of its assets is generally a great deal lower than its value as a going concern. This means that it is reasonable for a bank to extend loans to the firm on the basis of a general assessment of its creditworthiness, even though the formal security the firm is able to offer is limited.

The reason why it is not possible for banks — or other lenders — to make an accurate assessment of the risks to which they are exposed by lending is that the borrower himself is unable to accurately predict the future course of his income or profits, and that the lender has to judge this at one remove. Banks have to judge on indirect indications such as the reputation of the borrower, or the knowledge they have acquired of the working of a firm (which is one reason why they value a continued working relationship). Assessment of creditworthiness cannot be an objective procedure; lenders cannot hope to obtain enough information to assess prospective borrowers' prospects in each probable future state of the world, or to calculate the probability of each state; nor, consequently, are they able to summarize the result of their evaluations in terms of the probable expected distribution of returns on possible loans.

In general, the risks of lending to an individual borrower are likely to be less the smaller the loan extended to him. Though that provides a rationale for credit rationing in general, it still leaves the question of how to decide how much credit to allow an individual borrower. As with other decisions that have to be made in face of great uncertainty, banks, for want of anything better, are driven to apply rules of thumb in making such decisions. This feature of banks' behaviour is a matter of direct observation, and is the starting point for our subsequent analysis. Even if the reasons for it suggested above were not accepted, it would appear a reasonably firm starting point.

Our account of banks' behaviour over time rests on the argument that many of the criteria by which banks determine the scale of their lending are related to their customers' past and prospective income, and thus are likely to rise as aggregate nominal incomes rise.

For firms, the criteria applied include the customer's debt/equity ratio, and his prospective profits in relation to debt service charges. For unsecured personal bank loans, which have grown rapidly in importance in recent years (and for which banks charge considerably higher rates), lending limits are related to a customer's wealth and income. In the case of lending on mortgage, whether by banks or by building societies, the value of the house provides considerable security, but some risk remains: repossession of the house of a customer in difficulties involves a cost, and what the house will fetch on the market is uncertain. Here too, therefore, lending institutions apply limits to the scale of loans. These relate in part to the proportion of the purchase price that will be advanced, and in part to the customer's income and hence his ability to service the loan.

Apart from limitations on lending imposed by the banks, the customer's willingness to borrow will be limited by considerations on his part very similar to those that motivate the banks; the customer's willingness to abide by such rules will indeed be a factor in the banks' assessment of his creditworthiness. The aggregate demand for loans is thus also likely to rise with nominal income. Customer restraint however is likely to be less restrictive than the bankers' constraint, for borrowers typically rate their prospects more favourably than those asked to risk their capital with them. It is because of this dichotomy between the views of lenders and borrowers that borrowers are likely to want more than banks will lend, and that there is likely to be persistent excess demand for loans, or an 'unsatisfied fringe of borrowers'.

Mechanisms that have an effect similar to credit rationing by banks operate also in the financial markets that are the effective alternatives to bank intermediation. Subscribers to equity issues necessarily accept greater risks than purchasers of debt; but firms are constrained as to how much equity they seek to place, not only because a larger issue would in the present entail a lower price and a higher cost of finance, but also because that would reduce their credit standing in future. Purchasers of debentures, Eurobonds, or commercial paper have to make much the same assessment of a firm's creditworthiness as do banks, and find it no easier to do so; they appear to react in much the same way by following conventions that limit the scale of issues. How much a firm can raise on the money or capital markets at any time is thus fairly narrowly circumscribed.

The implication is that, although interest rates in money and capital markets are flexible and market-determined, and although these are markets where the price mechanism appears to operate, the prices established are not market-clearing prices. Borrowers' power to borrow in them is subject to limits similar to those restricting their access to bank finance. The ability of the banks to maintain rationing of credit is thus not undermined.

Factors affecting the growth of bank lending

Our general picture is that banks follow established rules of thumb in lending decisions and that their lending criteria are fairly stable. A factor contributing to this result is that the internal organization of the large retail banks is not highly centralized: managers of individual branches or regions are not given detailed instructions, but are left to follow accepted rules (see further Chapter 11, Section 2). In consequence, aggregate bank lending tends to grow as nominal GDP rises. It is, however, difficult to interpret historical developments over the last decade and a half without supposing that there have been changes in banks' attitudes to lending which have caused major changes in lending and thus in the money stock. This will become clearer in Chapter 11 when we examine the historical course of the aggregates.

One reason for the relative conservatism of banks is that it is important for each bank to keep in step with fellow banks. A bank's business involves maturity transformation, i.e. rolling over a sequence of short-term deposits to fund longer-term loans. Banks need to rely both on the continuance of their customers' deposits and (since these are somewhat erratic) on being able to make good any deficiencies by borrowing on the money markets. Short-term funding of either sort will become hard to obtain if doubt becomes established about the quality of the banks' loans. The maintenance of confidence is thus vital, and this entails pursuing lending policies similar to those of other banks. Following a lead set by the authorities is one way in which such co-ordinated change may occur. It will be argued later (in Chapter 11, Section 4) that what may be called the general supervisory climate may thus be a more potent influence than might at first appear.

This account implies that the banks, at least in many cases, face an excess demand for loans, and that, if they collectively decide to expand their lending, they can in many circumstances do so. That, however, does not mean they could do so without limit. At any point in time, one must envisage that there is an equilibrium size of the banking system beyond which it could not profitably expand. (A closer definition of that concept will be given in Section 2 below.) The framework of ideas about banking set out above is similar to that developed by Gale (1982). In various respects, it will need to be amplified or qualified in later discussion.

Both for their own prudential reasons and to satisfy the requirements of supervisory authorities, the banks need to maintain adequate capital–lending ratios. Provided that banks remain sufficiently profitable, they should be in a position to increase their capital as needed, either out of undistributed profits or by new issues. The attractiveness of the services offered by banks in competition with other channels of finance must in general limit the profits to be earned in bank intermediation. If expansion of bank lending is constricted by considerations of capital adequacy, therefore, this may be seen as one way in which the forces determining the equilibrium size of the banking system work themselves out.

It is our impression that considerations of capital adequacy have in practice not been a great constraint on bank lending, and its rapid expansion in the 1980s supports this view. The rise in lending by UK banks to less developed countries in the mid-1970s, and these countries' subsequent difficulties in servicing the loans, has however been accompanied by increased concern by official bank supervisors about capital adequacy. This may have begun to put some restraint on bank expansion. (How far the requirements of bank supervisors in this respect could be used to put a greater restraint on the expansion of banks will be considered in Chapter 10, Section 3.)

The analysis given in this section relates to the operations of the banks *vis-à-vis* the private sector, and has sought to show that it was the element of risk in lending that led banks in effect to ration their lending to any individual customer. This does not apply to bank lending to the public sector, on which the banks incur no comparable risks. (Indeed, holdings of short-term government debt provide them with readily disposable assets, and such reserves may well facilitate their lending to the private sector.) Bank lending to the public sector is thus not constrained in the same way as lending to the private sector; it may, with some qualification, be treated as a separate factor, additional to whatever the banks lend to the private sector, determining the scale of banking activities. (This will be discussed further in Chapter 6.)

The analysis in the following section will be concerned with two types of financial assets/debts, and the relation between them:

1. deposits with, and loans by, deposit-taking financial institutions (of which banks and building societies are the main two), on which interest rates are administratively determined;
2. marketable financial assets of various degrees of maturity, whose price and yield is flexible and market-determined.

Since government borrowing is not to be discussed until later (Chapter 6), for present purposes marketable financial assets will be taken to comprise corporate debentures and equities. The analysis will be in terms of final lenders and borrowers — which here means persons and companies. Although banks and large companies lend to each other via the short-term financial markets, such transactions in the present context net out and will be ignored in Section 2 (but will be discussed in Section 4). Holdings of corporate debentures and equities by the non-deposit-taking institutions (pension funds, insurance companies, and unit trusts) will be treated as holdings by the personal sector.

2. THE EQUILIBRIUM SIZE OF THE BANKING SYSTEM

One agent's financial asset is another agent's liability, and those who hold financial assets in effect lend to those whose debt they are. The two sides may then be called lenders and borrowers. The financing may be direct, or indirect if a financial intermediary such as a bank intervenes between final lenders and final borrowers. The potential scale of bank intermediation depends on its being a channel of finance that final lenders and borrowers prefer, or find convenient or economical, as compared with alternative channels.

It may be helpful to define here two senses of the concept of the equilibrium size of the banking system. The first may be thought of as the size that final lenders and borrowers would prefer (and for which they would pay the banks the going return on their capital employed) if the banks themselves were willing to extend loans and accept corresponding deposits on this scale. This we will call the 'potential equilibrium point'. We have argued above that in many circumstances the banks will stop short of making loans on the full scale the market would be willing to pay for, leaving an unsatisfied fringe of borrowers. The second sense of equilibrium may be thought of as the scale of intermediation which the banks themselves, given their conventions about risk-taking, think it worth their while to provide. This we will call the 'operative equilibrium point'. The following paragraphs will argue that in a growing economy both the theoretical limit and the operative limit to the size of the banking system are likely to rise progressively. We start with the static concept of the equilibrium scale of the banking system, and then consider the equivalent dynamic concept of its equilibrium rate of growth.

The potential equilibrium scale of banking

Banks match loans and deposits: there can be no growth in one side of their balance sheet unless the other grows as well. At any point in time there must, in principle, be a limit to how far the banking system can profitably expand its operations, the limit being set by the preferences, on the one hand, of depositors and, on the other, of borrowers. The concept of an equilibrium scale of banking derives from portfolio theory.

Taking first the deposits side, deposits are one type among others of financial assets that the public holds. The qualities of different types of financial asset are usually analysed in terms of their liquidity (ease of conversion into money), the relative certainty of their capital value, and the relative certainty of their yield. The price and yield on each type will reflect holders' preferences with respect to such characteristics. It will also depend on the quantity of each, and prices and yields must be supposed to adjust in such a way as to make asset-owners willing to hold the existing stock of each type of asset. If the public initially holds the stock of bank deposits it wants, it will be willing to hold a larger stock only if deposit rates are raised relative to the yield on alternative assets.

On the lending side, bank lending is for many borrowers one of a number of sources of finance to which they can resort. Each source of finance has its own conveniences and inconveniences, and if borrowers had initially borrowed from banks as much as they wanted, it must be supposed that (the cost of alternative finance being unchanged) they would be willing to borrow more from the banks only if the rates charged on bank loans were reduced.

The main alternative to bank finance is finance by the issue of stock exchange securities (bonds and equities). At any point in time, assuming that final lenders' net lending and final borrowers' net borrowing is unchanged, an increase in bank intermediation means on one side that bank loans displace some finance obtained through the issue of securities, and on the other side that the holding of bank deposits takes the place of some of the securities held by the public. The further the scale of bank intermediation is extended, the narrower is the margin likely to be between what banks have to pay for deposits and what — if they charged what the market would bear — they could obtain on loans. Thus, as Tobin (1963b) has it, 'there is a natural economic limit to the scale of the commercial banking industry. . . . Marshall's scissors of supply and demand apply to the "output" of the banking industry, no less than to other . . . industries.'

Banks must therefore be seen as part of the wider financial system. An account of how, at any point in time, the public distributes its total portfolio as between different types of financial asset explains at the same time how relative interest rates on different assets are determined. Thus, if for example there had at any point in time been more bonds in existence, and less of some other financial asset, it must be supposed that the relative price of bonds would have been lower and their relative yield higher. What determines the general level of interest rates is to be discussed in Chapter 3: for present purposes it is sufficient to take the general level as given, and to deal only in terms of relative interest rates.

In a growing economy, the economic scale of banking is likely to rise progressively. As saving proceeds, the public's wealth will be rising. As incomes and expenditure grow, so will the demand for transaction balances, so that the public is likely to hold a proportion of its increase in wealth as deposits with banks. On the side of the borrowers, with such growth persons are likely to wish to borrow more; and companies, as investment proceeds and profits rise, are also likely to want to extend their borrowing — much of it in both cases from banks. If nominal incomes rise because of inflation, though the details of the process will be affected, the general result will be the same.

Corresponding to the equilibrium scale of banking at any point in time, it is then reasonable to conceive of an equilibrium rate of growth of banks. This rate of growth will depend on the evolving preferences, on the one hand, of depositors, and on the other, of private borrowers. Along this path, which traces the moving equilibrium point, the preferences of depositors can be seen as determining the supply of deposits to the banks, which they are then able to on-lend, and the preference of borrowers, as determining the demand for bank loans. As national income rises, both the supply and demand in this sense will rise; and, in the absence of financial innovations, the rise seems likely to be in rough proportion to the rise in income. Reasons have already been given (in Section 1) for supposing that the banks will not wish to expand fully up to the potential equilibrium level. But it may be supposed that the level up to which they prefer to expand is also likely to grow with rising national income, for reasons that must now be set out.

The operative equilibrium scale of banking

The operative equilibrium point was defined above as the scale of bank intermediation that the banks themselves find it worthwhile to provide. The element of risk in lending and the difficulty of measuring it will ensure that banks retain quantitative restrictions on their lending. But at this point, banks will have expanded to the point where they have made all the loans they judge profitable to make. From their own point of view, the banks will then have eliminated excess demand, though from the point of view of the borrowers, an unsatisfied demand for loans may well remain. Where this point lies will depend on the criteria that govern banks' lending behaviour at any time. It should perhaps thus be described as a quasi-equilibrium point, which is movable but may be stable. If banks' lending conventions remain unchanged, the operative limit to the size of the banking system will be given. A change in banks' attitudes to risks, or in their methods of appraising risks, or in the information on which appraisal is based, will lead to a change in the operative equilibrium scale of banking.

The conventional rules of thumb that determine the scale on which banks (or building societies) are willing to lend are framed (we have argued) with reference to the expected income of would-be borrowers. With unchanged lending criteria, banks and building societies are thus likely to be willing to increase the scale of their lending as nominal incomes rise. Given rising incomes, the desire to hold deposits with banks and building societies is also likely to grow. To some extent, then, there seems likely to be a harmony between the two sides of lending institutions' balance sheets, with the demand for loans and for deposits to hold both growing together. How close the harmony is, however, will need to be looked at more closely (Section 3 below).

An account of banking behaviour on these lines appears to provide a framework for interpreting monetary trends in the last one and a half decades. As will be shown in more detail in Chapter 11, bank balance sheets have expanded roughly in line with money national income for some of this time. But there were two periods — the years 1971–3, and the years following 1980 — when bank lending, and also building society lending, grew markedly more rapidly than money national income. In each case the upsurge followed the removal of direct controls on bank lending; and in each case there is some evidence that both banks and building societies significantly relaxed their lending criteria, and began on an increasing scale to exploit lending opportunities from which they had previously abstained.

Our analysis above of the behaviour of the banking system relates to conditions as they were in the 1970s and the first half of the 1980s. This period has seen a continuous process of innovation in financial markets, and we need to consider how far our analysis has to be modified in the light of that process.

Various aspects of this process are noted at various points, in this and later chapters, and may conveniently be listed as follows (see also Mayer 1986, Rose 1986, and Goodhart 1986). One important development that occurred in the 1960s was the emergence of the wholesale money markets. This greatly facilitated the first rapid expansion of bank lending in the early 1970s. The high inflation in the latter period prompted the development of (medium-term) variable-rate borrowing (in place of fixed-rate borrowing). Greater competition from the building societies led banks themselves to enter the mortgage market and, in order to protect their retail deposits, progressively to extend the payment of interest on sight deposits. The wave of innovation in the 1980s saw a rapid development of new financial instruments. From the point of view of the banks, this resulted in new substitutes for bank loans and for wholesale bank deposits — the provision of which, however, was typically arranged by the banks in return for a fee. Large companies found themselves able to place their own paper more cheaply than could the banks themselves. Bank lending has, accordingly, been increasingly concentrated on smaller companies, and the pricing of such loans has become increasingly competitive.

Greater competition in financial markets has stimulated financial innovation, and that in turn has made for greater competition. What we have described as a relaxation of banks' lending criteria may be regarded as a response of the banks to this more competitive environment (see further Chapter 11, Section 2). One result has clearly been to diminish the relative importance of bank intermediation. But although conditions are more competitive, this has not resulted in a situation where markets clear: it is still not the case that a borrower can borrow from banks (or in financial markets) on an unlimited scale if he pays above the going rate. The process of financial innovation, therefore, does not appear essentially to invalidate our analysis of banks' behaviour, and in particular our emphasis on the importance of rationing by banks.

3. THE EFFECT OF A RELAXATION OF LENDING CRITERIA

We have so far discussed in general terms the forces determining the equilibrium scale of the banking system in static terms or, by extension, in terms of the moving equilibrium position that would obtain in an economy with steadily growing nominal income. To give a more precise description of the nature of the equilibrium position, it is useful to look at the path to a new equilibrium if the system is somehow moved away from equilibrium.

For this purpose there are various shocks we could look at. We could, for instance, consider the effects of an increase (or decrease) in investment or export demand. However, it seems more illuminating for present purposes to look at the effects on the financial system of a relaxation in banks' lending criteria, leading to an expansion of bank lending. We do not see lending criteria as being highly unstable, but some major gradual changes do seem to have occurred and to have been important. Our aim here is primarily methodological; this illustration offers a way of throwing more light on how the limits on banks' power to create money arise, and how quickly they operate.

It is not necessarily the case that people borrow more only in order to spend more: they may borrow more in order to hold more money, and in Chapter 11 (Section 3) we will suggest that this has been important. But here we will assume that the increased lending leads to higher total expenditure. That means assuming also that there is underemployed capacity to start with. (That assumption is not crucial: we could equally well look at the effects of a tightening of lending criteria, leading to a contraction of total demand. The general assumption we make here is thus that Keynesian unemployment can occur, and that total activity can change in response to changes in total demand.)

Suppose that the increase in bank lending results in higher investment. That will initiate a cumulative expansion of output and income which will increase savings, and lead to an increase in total holdings of financial assets (or a faster rate of increase than would otherwise occur). Analysis of the effects must then allow not only for changes in the composition of asset holdings, but also for an increase in the total stock. This makes the process more than a static portfolio adjustment. Elucidation of the effects of a relaxation of banks' lending criteria requires an analysis of the financial counterparts of the stage-by-stage multiplier expansion of incomes and expenditure which will be set in train by the increased spending made possible by the increased bank lending.

For simplicity, assume a closed economy, without a government sector, in which productivity is not increasing, and with stable prices; and suppose that an increase in investment to a higher steady rate is made possible by an increase in the rate of bank lending. What happens in the early stages of expansion differs from what happens in later stages.

The increase in investment first leads to an increase in incomes. The multiplier is not instantaneous but takes time. Those who receive additional income require time to recognize that incomes have increased, and to adjust their spending to their higher level of income. The saving ratio of those who receive additional incomes thus will be temporarily increased; and as a result, they will acquire financial assets on an unusual scale in the early stages of the expansion process. But after a lag, the increase in incomes will lead to increased spending — which again, initially not spent, later leads to a further increase in spending. *Ex post* investment equals saving at each stage, with the *ex post* saving rate remaining higher than normal till the end of the process. The expansionary process ceases when income has risen to the point at which the saving required to finance the higher investment has come back to the normal relation to income.

The additional bank lending will create additional bank deposits; and it may, for simplicity, be assumed that these are the only additional financial assets to be created. While the process is running its course, those to whom the increase in incomes accrues, since their *ex post* saving is unusually high, will be acquiring financial assets at an abnormal rate; and it is they who at first will hold the additional bank deposits. The extra financial balances are acquired essentially because their recipients have had insufficient time to perceive their higher permanent level of income and adjust their spending to it. This means also that it is likely that they will wish to hold them in liquid form, and will willingly hold them, at existing interest rates, as bank deposits. (Some recipients of higher incomes may wish to repay existing bank debt, but this is likely to be only a minor offset to the effects considered here.)

The new pattern of financial assets that emerge at the end of the process will contain an abnormally high proportion of bank deposits. As time goes on and the public adjusts its spending to the ultimate higher level of income, it will (given previous relative interest rates) wish to revert to a more normal distribution of its (higher) stock of financial assets. Some of those holding more financial assets will try to buy non-monetary assets, such as bonds and shares. The result will be that the price of such assets will be bid up to the point where the stock of bank deposits in existence is willingly held. (It is perhaps only the richer minority who would consider shifts of this sort. But they will be the larger holders of financial assets, and movement by only a minority will be effective.)

This shift in relative interest rates may in the later stages of the expansion process prompt a further adjustment in the composition of the stock of financial assets. The yield on long-term assets will now be lower than before in relation to the cost of bank loans. Some of those who have taken bank loans will now wish to issue debt or equity to the public at a price that will tempt people to buy, and will repay loans out of the proceeds. This process may (by analogy with public debt operations) be regarded as 'funding' by the private sector of its shorter-term debt. It represents a process of disintermediation, perhaps of a more fundamental sort than disintermediation into money-market instruments (to be discussed in Section 4), from which it needs to be distinguished. If this occurs, some of the earlier expansion of banks' balance sheets will be reversed. It is only if such funding occurs that the stock of broad money can fall back to a lower level. (This will clearly be an important point when we come to consider the logic of monetary control.)

The analysis has, for convenience, been in terms of banks, and little has been said of building societies. The building societies are not usually regarded in the literature as credit-creating bodies, but much of what has been said above about banks applies to them. If building societies relax their lending criteria and increase their mortgage lending, this will lead to a higher demand for houses, and in turn to more house building (though in practice not on a scale commensurate with the increase in mortgage lending: see Chapter 11, Section 3). House prices may also rise, perhaps making existing owners feel richer and spend more. Either will initiate a multiplier process and will lead to a general expansion of incomes, in just the same way as will an increase in company investment financed by bank lending. As a counterpart to their additional lending, the building societies must, like banks, obtain larger deposits. From many points of view, banks and building societies can be treated together as one type of institution.

The above discussion has been concerned with the effects of a change in lending institutions' criteria. Similar effects must be supposed to follow an economic upsurge resulting from other factors, such as a rise in export or investment demand. That can be expected to be accompanied by a rise in prospective profits, which — even without any change in lending criteria — is likely to increase the banks' willingness to lend. This would have the same multiplier effects, and the same financial counterparts, as the case just examined. (An expansion initiated by a relaxation of lending criteria may indeed be somewhat difficult to distinguish from one initiated by other factors. Our grounds for making the distinction have been set out in general terms in Sections 1 and 2 above and will be elaborated in Chapter 11. We rest partly on the evidence that the ratio of lending to GDP has shown some distinct shifts and that there are grounds for supposing that lending criteria did in fact change at these times.)

An old controversy about the power of banks to expand

It is useful at this point to come back to Tobin's (1963[b]) article, which was about the old dispute as to whether banks have it in their power to expand the scale of their activities simply by deciding to lend more. The view frequently taken by practical bankers is that they lend only the money entrusted to them, and hence are restricted in what they can lend. Elementary economic texts have long dismissed this view as myopic, on the grounds that, by concentrating on a single bank, it neglects what happens to the banking system as a whole. The argument is that, if one bank gives a loan to a customer, this results in a credit in his account. When he spends the loan, the extra deposit will be transferred to the accounts of those he buys from, and, though quite probably kept at other banks, remains within the system; other banks thus have extra deposits which they can lend. If all banks are expanding their loan books, each individual bank will on average gain extra deposits equal to its extra lending. (If an individual bank is short of deposits, it can borrow through the interbank market from other banks which have excess deposits: see Section 4.)

Thus, so the argument goes, the process can continue indefinitely. Like the widow and her cruse (in Tobin's phrase), the more banks lend, the more will the supply of deposits to them be replenished. (The argument is usually presented along with the proposition that there is a minimum ratio of banks' reserves to deposits, and that the authorities fix the size of the reserves. Since in that case the banks could, it is argued, expand credit by a multiple of an increment in reserves, it is often described as multiple credit creation.)

Tobin criticizes the view that the banks can act in this way essentially on the grounds set out in Section 2. The size of the stock of loans the banks can profitably lend must equal the stock of deposits the public will wish to hold; that depends on the preferences of borrowers for bank loans as against other sources of finance and of lenders for banks deposits as against other financial assets; and these set an economic limit to the size of the banking system and of the money it creates. For realism, the argument needs to be set in a context in which bank lending may start a process in which the total stock of assets is increased (as is done above, and as Tobin briefly allows). If at the end of the process bank loans are funded, that validates Tobin's objection to the 'widow's cruse' view: what the banks earlier decided about the scale of lending gets reversed by the decisions of non-banks.

But important qualifications must immediately be made; for funding bank debt is an uneven, uncertain, and slow process. The major qualification is that it is only for some classes of borrowers that funding bank debt is a practical option. Small firms and personal borrowers have little or no access to the stock exchange, and thus little or no opportunity to convert bank loans to other forms of indebtedness; disintermediation via security markets must be restricted to almost as narrow a class of borrowers as disintermediation via money markets. Lending by banks to persons is now as large as their lending to industrial and commercial companies — and lending by building societies, where the same considerations apply, half as large again (see Table 11.4 below).

For the minority of borrowers for whom it is an option, there are a number of factors that reduce the attractiveness of funding. First, even if the banks relax their criteria, an unsatisfied fringe of borrowers is likely to remain. That means that borrowers would be willing to pay more for bank loans than they in fact have to. The cost of alternative sources of finance may therefore have to fall considerably before borrowers find it worthwhile to reduce bank loans by funding. The disparate attitudes on the part of banks and their customers towards the risk attaching to loans create a kind of discontinuity in the adjustment of the financial structure.

Second, the incentive to fund is that the cost of security market finance has fallen relative to the cost of bank loans. The price of securities clearly fluctuates a great deal (and with it the relative cost of finance by new issues) for reasons that have nothing to do with the funding process (see further Chapter 3 below); and such fluctuations may swamp the shifts in relative interest rates which abnormally large holdings of money should in theory produce. Uncertainty as to the durability of such effects may diminish their force as an incentive to funding.

Third, even if there is an effective incentive to fund, the response to it is likely to be gradual. Thus, the shift in relative interest rates of the sort here in question will not occur (for reasons already explained) until some time after the start of the multiplier process set in train by the increased bank lending. Furthermore, even if the funding of indebtedness to the banks then becomes advantageous, firms may take time to decide to fund bank loans; for the preparation of an issue takes time, and the absorptive capacity of the stock exchange for new issues in any period is limited. Firms will therefore need to feel confident that the opportunity for a capital issue on favourable terms will remain open for a considerable time before deciding to incur the time and cost of an issue. When all firms have funded back loans that are going to do so, the adjustments to the composition of portfolios and to the relative prices of different assets, consequent on the higher level of banking lending, will be complete. But the full adjustment to a discrete, step increase in the rate of bank lending (such as here examined) will take a period perhaps extending over years.

The picture of a readily adjusting financial structure — which underlies portfolio theory and which is sketched briefly in Section 2 above — has therefore to be heavily shaded. The kind of adjustments in question involve a substitution both between different types of financial assets on the part of lenders, and between different types of debt on the part of borrowers; and on each side there are many limitations on the ability of borrowers to substitute. This tilts back the argument in favour of the 'widow's cruse'. There are limits to the banks' power to create money. But the argument developed above clearly indicates that lending by the banks is the primary driving force in money creation, and that it is not so easy for influences coming from changes in the demand for money to make their effect on the outcome.

Much effort has gone into the search for stable demand-for-money equations, i.e. to explain the size of the stock of money as a stable function of income and interest rates (or of the relative interest to be earned on holding money as compared with that to be got from holding financial assets). The present argument retains the assumption that at the micro level there is an underlying stable demand for money. But at the macro level, abnormally high or low money holdings will not be subject to quick or complete correction. For this involves adjustments not merely to the composition of the stock of assets, but also to the structure of borrowing and liabilities — to which, as we have argued, there are many obstacles. On occasions when the banks make large additions to their lending, it should therefore be expected that any apparent normal relation between the stock of money and national income will be overridden. The previous apparent stability of demand functions for broad money broke down in 1971, precisely at the time when controls of bank lending were removed and the banks became free to lend more. This question will be considered further in Chapter 11 (Section 4).

The behaviour of narrow money (which until recently has been largely non-interest-bearing) has continued to be explicable in terms of demand-for-money functions. The reason must in part be that adjustments to the stock of narrow money do not involve the same kind of total readjustment in the asset/debt composition of lenders and borrowers as is involved in an adjustment of the stock of broad money: it involves a shift between demand and time deposits, leaving the total balance sheet of banks (and hence also of borrowers) little changed. Furthermore, if the aggregate is (at least largely) non-interest-bearing, it will be sensitive to the level of interest rates. The public's holdings of notes and coin, by contrast, appear not to be interest-sensitive (Trundle 1982a, 1982b). They have usually grown almost as fast as the value of consumers' expenditure, although since 1978 they have grown much less fast, probably because transactions through the banking system have been replacing the use of cash.

The account set out in this section of the financial counterparts to the sequential adjustments in a real expansionary process bears a close resemblance to the view that sees holdings of money performing a 'buffer-stock' function. The concept of 'buffer-stock' money has been espoused notably by Laidler (for instance Laidler 1984) and Goodhart (who however prefers the term 'disequilibrium' money: Goodhart 1984).

It is generally accepted that agents hold (non-interest-bearing or low-interest-bearing) money because future income and future needs cannot be precisely foreseen; and that how much money each individual wants to hold is not a fixed amount but an amount that he will want to hold on average — a buffer stock which, like a trader's stock of goods, can be run up or run down according to the timing of receipts and payments, both expected and unexpected. Hence, 'the windfall gains and losses which the agent experiences from time to time might well manifest themselves in unexpected variations in his cash holdings', says Laidler; and 'at certain times and places, and over certain time intervals' there may at the aggregate level be 'discrepancies between the actual and desired money holdings of individuals . . . ' (Laidler 1984, 19, 22).

In this spirit, Goodhart analyses the response of the system to changes in the supply of money.

Consider a case in which the authorities expand the monetary base and encourage the extension of bank loans. . . . Not only may the initial borrower of the loan be for a time willing to hold (part of) the extra funds from that loans in money balances, while in the process of disbursing the funds, but also, the recipient of the resulting expenditures will hold the higher balances for some period. . . . Thus, an initial shock to the supply of money is likely to be buffered, in the short run, both by a larger proportion of agents moving towards the top end of their acceptable inventory of holdings and by the delays between holdings going beyond such notional limits and decisions being taken and made effective to return money holdings to their preferred starting point, e.g. by expenditures on other assets. . . . (Goodhart 1984, 257)

Our account differs from this description in seeing the process as being, in the first place, a reaction of the system to an unusually rapid (and hence unexpected) increase in incomes, and as occurring only at such times. Rather than speaking in terms of a margin of tolerance between actual and desired money holdings that exists at all times, we therefore described the process as the result of the unusually high marginal saving that must follow an unexpected increase in income, and of a propensity to hold that additional saving in the form of money that, for a period, was higher than it would be in the longer term. Similarly, we saw the eventual increase in spending as a delayed result of the increase in incomes, rather than of the abnormal holding of money, which was the first effect of the increase in incomes. The observable results are similar to those in the buffer-stock description, though some of the wider implications are different.

4. BANKS AND THE WHOLESALE MONEY MARKETS

The scale of banking activities is affected, in somewhat complex ways, by the existence of the wholesale money markets. As usually defined, money-market instruments comprise both the large liquid deposits of large firms (which include other banks) and various other short-term instruments which for such operators are relatively close substitutes for bank deposits: certificates of deposit (CDs) issued by banks, commercial bills (issued by companies), Treasury bills, and local authority bills. Tax reserve instruments issued by the central government and local authority temporary debt are not usually classed as money-market instruments, but they offer large holders similar liquidity.

The rate of interest on money-market instruments other than bank deposits is flexible and market-determined, and varies fairly continuously. As they are close substitutes for each other, interest rates on them vary closely together. Since they are also substitutes — though less close — for bank deposits, interest rates on them tend also to remain rather close to bank base rates (see Figs. 4.1 and 4.2 below).

Transactions in money markets are conducted in large lots, which only large organizations can undertake. Access to the money markets is thus confined to banks and other financial institutions, including building societies, large industrial and commercial firms, the central government, and other public-sector bodies. The stock of assets to be classified as money-market instruments is necessarily somewhat arbitrary, and the statistics available for the main categories may not give the complete picture. But it is clear that the greater part result from transactions between banks, and that these in turn are relatively small in relation to total bank deposits (£43 billion out of £213 billion, or 20 per cent, at end-1984). The stock of other money-market instruments is, in total, probably less than interbank deposits. Of these, the largest component is commercial bills (£16 billion at end-1984).

Though the money markets are thus a relatively small periphery to the stock of broad money, they are important to the banks in two ways. First, banks' transactions with each other are conducted through such markets. Second, for other operators, the holding of other money-market assets is an alternative to holding bank deposits, and the issue of such instruments is similarly an alternative to a loan from the banks: the choice by non-bank operators between these alternatives thus affects their holding of money. These two aspects will be discussed in turn.

The use of money markets by banks

Greater lending by banks (by the processes already discussed) increases bank deposits in total. But lending by any single bank will not result in an equivalent increase in that bank's deposits — though these are likely to be increased as a result of lending by other banks. For the banking system as a whole, lending (apart from a small amount financed in other ways) must equal deposits. Individual banks, however, may find themselves either with deposits in excess of their lending, which they will wish in effect to lend to other banks; or with a shortfall of deposits in relation to their lending, which they will wish to make up by borrowing deposits from other banks.

If a bank fails to undertake transactions to make good a shortfall of deposits, then, in the case of a clearing bank, the shortfall has to be met at the daily clearing by drawing down its balance at the Bank of England; in the case of a non-clearer, it has to be met by drawing down its balances with other banks — i.e. in each case by drawing down its first-line reserves. Banks' transactions with the money markets can thus be seen as a way of redistributing liquidity between banks: individual banks undertake them in order to maintain liquidity at the appropriate level without having to obtain the Bank's help to do so.

Banks' transactions with the money markets undertaken with this purpose can take various forms. A bank can replenish its liquidity by direct transactions with other banks (taking, or failing to renew, an interbank deposit, or selling a bill or other money-market instrument to another bank); or it can issue a certificate of deposit (CD) or sell a money-market instrument to a non-bank.

Along with the removal of ceilings on bank lending in 1971, a change was also made in reserve requirements. The deposit aggregate in relation to which required reserves were specified was redefined to be net of lending to other banks. This change removed a previous discouragement to the use by banks of the money markets to match their deposits and their lending, and led to a marked expansion in the banks' holdings of each others' sterling liabilities. By 1974 the relative importance of interbank deposits and banks' holdings of each others' CDs had doubled (Table 2.4). A large proportion of interbank deposits are of short initial maturity, and highly liquid: at the end of 1984, a fifth were overnight deposits, on which interest rates reflect individual banks' very short-term need for liquidity, and tend to be highly variable (Chapter 4, Section 1).

TABLE 2.4. Banks' reliance on money-market instruments,[a] October 1971–end-1985

(£ billion and percentages)

	Share of gross sterling liabilities							
	Oct. 1971		End-1974		End-1979		End-1985	
	£ b	%	£ b	%	£ b	%	£ b	%
Gross sterling liabilities	21		44		77		243	
Liabilities to banks								
Interbank deposits	2	(9)	9	(20)	19	(24)	48	(20)
CDs held by banks	1	(4)	3	(6)	3	(4)	6	(2)
Net sterling liabilities	18	(86)	32	(74)	55	(71)	189	(78)
Non-bank deposits	17	(82)	30	(71)	54	(70)	179	(74)
CDs held by non-banks	1	(4)	2	(4)	1	(1)	10[b]	(4)

[a] Monthly reporting institutions, at last reporting day of month.
[b] Of which, discount houses (generally substantial holders of banks' CDs) held £2 bn.
Source: CSO, *Financial Statistics*

The increased use by the banks of the money markets after 1971 has frequently been represented, in official and other commentaries, as a fundamental change in the way the banks operated (see Bank of England 1984, 44 and elsewhere: also Goodhart 1984, 153–5). Previously, it is said, banks had passively accepted the level of deposits that the public provided and had only to decide how best to employ them ('asset management'). Now, with credit ceilings removed, they were free to lend, and were able to obtain the deposits required to match their lending by actively seeking them in wholesale markets ('liability management'); their new readiness to bid for deposits in this way, it is said, enabled banks to increase their deposits in total. (Such a shift in behaviour is presented also as the reason for the breakdown of the earlier apparent stability of the demand-for-money function, for which a different explanation has been offered above.)

This account appears in part erroneous. Unless existing bank loans get repaid, an increase in bank lending must necessarily increase bank deposits, and whether they be retail or wholesale deposits is largely immaterial. The removal of ceilings on bank lending in 1971 certainly allowed the banks to lend more. Their increase in total lending entailed an increase in total deposits, so that banks collectively had in fact no need to bid for deposits. But the regulatory change in 1971 may have changed bankers' psychology: they may well have come to have acquired growing faith that they could replenish shortages of liquidity by borrowing on wholesale markets. Bankers may previously have been constrained by the belief that they could lend only what the public deposited with them: after 1971, perhaps, the banking system acted more as if it knew that the 'widow's cruse' worked.

The use of money markets by non-banks

The money markets offer large non-bank depositors a way of holding liquid funds as an alternative to bank deposits. Thus, CDs (new or second-hand) provide high liquidity at the price of a degree of capital uncertainty; and for holders of them Treasury bills (now issued only in negligible quantities) and trade bills, with the credit risk insured by a bank for a fee, are close substitutes for bank deposits. Other relatively liquid instruments, not usually classified as money-market instruments, such as local authority debt or tax instruments, offer non-banks comparable rates.

Even if the latter are included, non-bank holdings of assets of these types of assets are very small. At end-1984, for instance, they seem to have amounted to only 3 per cent of the consolidated financial assets of the UK non-bank private sector. They were principally held by non-bank financial companies and industrial and commercial companies (part in the form of tax instruments). Money-market instruments have recently become rather more important as a source of funds for industrial and commercial companies. Their borrowing via the issue of bills and other short-term instruments stood at £8 billion at the end of 1984 against £41 billion of straightforward sterling bank borrowing. This was however to a considerable extent the result of the policy of 'overfunding' of the public borrowing requirement, which could possibly at some stage be reversed. (See Chapter 10, Section 2: as counterpart to the excess funding, the authorities have bought bills from the banks, which must have made the terms on bills more favourable relative to those on overdrafts than would otherwise have been the case.)

Controls on bank lending led the banks to vary the terms they offer on deposits, or charge for loans, relative to those available on money-market instruments. The resulting shifts out of, or into, bank deposits (disintermediation or reintermediation) has at times amounted to several per cent of bank deposits (Chapter 11, Section 2). This sort of disintermediation out of bank deposits into money-market instruments may be contrasted with the kind of disintermediation discussed in Section 3 above, which takes place when borrowers from banks 'fund' bank loans by issuing stock exchange securities. The second sort of disintermediation is what a policy aiming to control the growth of money must seek to bring about. The first sort of disintermediation also reduces the stock of broad money, but the effect is usually dismissed as merely 'cosmetic', and irrelevant to the purposes of monetary policy.

Companies in total are net borrowers, and the personal sector is the predominant source of saving. Neither sort of disintermediation affects the scale of lending/borrowing between the two sectors. The first, however, affects the composition of the debts of the company sector and of the assets of the personal sector. The second sort of disintermediation, by contrast, has no effect on the assets of the personal sector, which hardly deals in money-market instruments. What happens is that companies lend to and borrow from each other directly, rather than via the intermediation of the banks.

To base policy on the distinction between these two sorts of disintermediation implies that undue reliance by companies on borrowing from banks rather than via the stock exchange is in some way disadvantageous; and that is not clear. But if the proposition were valid, it would suggest that in principle broad money would be better defined to include large companies' holdings not merely of bank deposits but also of other comparably liquid assets.

The broad monetary aggregates have in recent years also been swollen by the company sector holding larger deposits (not only in absolute terms, but also relative to money national income), while also increasing the size of its bank loans (Chapter 11, Section 3). The juxtaposition in part reflects a disparity in the situation of different companies: some with small deposits borrow while others with small bank loans build up liquidity. But companies also take bank loans and leave the proceeds on deposit as a means of ensuring the availability of liquidity, as an alternative to obtaining overdraft facilities from their banks. It could be argued that broad money would be better defined to include not companies' gross holdings of bank deposits, but their net position after deduction of outstanding bank loans; but to be consistent, it would then be necessary also to include their unused overdraft facilities, which is not a clearly definable magnitude.

5. SUMMARY OF CONCLUSIONS

This chapter has examined how the banking system is likely to behave in the absence of action by the authorities to control it, and has sought to show why, in an economy with rising nominal incomes, the banking system, left to itself, is likely to expand. Although the chapter is only a first statement, it may be useful to summarize the argument so far and to indicate some of its implications for later chapters.

Since the bulk of the money stock consists of deposits at banks, the analysis has been concerned primarily with bank money. (Building societies are regarded as a specialized type of bank.) In considering the factors determining the scale of banking, it is necessary to employ the concept of an equilibrium scale of banking. Banks intermediate between final lenders and final borrowers, and the preferences of lenders and borrowers impose a limit, at any point in time, to the scale of bank intermediation.

- There are sources of finance available to borrowers other than the banks: corporate borrowers, in particular, may issue stock exchange securities, and beyond a point (given relative interest rates) would prefer other sources.
- There is a limit (given relative interest rates) to the proportion of their portfolios the public will in the long run hold as bank deposits rather than as other assets.

As lending expands, other things unchanged, the public will start to try to substitute out of deposits, bidding up the price of other assets. Beyond a point, borrowers from banks will find it profitable to issue other assets and 'fund' bank loans. The limit to banks' power to create money lies in borrowers' power to substitute other sources of finance for bank loans. In practice, however, there are important hindrances to such substitution: some borrowers have no alternative sources of finance, and for those who have, the process of substitution is likely to be slow and incomplete. This makes the equilibrium point somewhat ill-defined. As money incomes rise, the equilibrium scale of banking will, over time, shift outwards.

Because lending risks are difficult to assess, banks operate according to conventional lending criteria, related *inter alia* to borrowers' (prospective) income, and they apply quantitative limits to their lending to an individual borrower. Loans are thus not allocated to those who would pay most for them, and interest rates on bank loans are an administered price, not a flexibly determined market price. Lenders are likely to take a less favourable view of the riskiness of a proposed loan than the borrower. Hence, banks' lending criteria are likely to leave an unsatisfied fringe of would-be borrowers; i.e., the operative limit to which banks will find it worth expanding is likely, at any point in time, to lie below the potential equilibrium point. Because many of banks' lending criteria are related to borrowers' incomes, this operative equilibrium point is also likely to shift outward, over time, as money incomes rise. Assuming unchanged lending standards, therefore, broad money is likely to rise in line with the rise in national income. If the banks relax lending standards, they are able, in many circumstances, to increase their lending over and above this proportionate path.

Lending by the banks to the public sector does not involve the risks involved in lending to the private sector, and banks will feel able to undertake it even if they regard themselves as fully loaned up to the private sector. Public-sector borrowing from the banks can thus be regarded as an independent source of monetery growth.

Much monetary analysis looks only at the preferences of final lenders, and sees the stock of money as determined solely by the preferences of those who hold financial assets. Financial assets, however, are other agents' debts. Money creation involves increases more or less equivalent in both bank loans and bank deposits; in our account, it is the bank lending that sets the pace. It follows that, if the monetary authorities are to control monetary growth, they must control bank lending. If they are to do so by means other than direct control of bank lending, they must provide inducements to those with loans from banks to substitute out of them (i.e. must alter relative interest rates in a way to encourage the funding of bank loans). But even if the authorities are able to produce an inducement, it is only some classes of borrower who have access to alternative sources of finance, and who can therefore be induced to fund bank loans; and those who are able to do so are likely to be slow to respond to the inducement offered. For this reason alone, it is likely to be difficult for the authorities to get a handle over the process of money creation.

3

The Behaviour of Interest Rates: The Theoretical Background

The authorities have sought to use their influence over interest rates as a means of monetary control, and later we will have to consider how effective this can be as a method of controlling the pace of monetary growth. But we first need to disuss how the authorities are able to influence interest rates; we do this in the next chapter, and in this chapter, as background, we discuss more generally the determination of interest rates in the short term. This chapter and the next thus form a pair which have to be taken together.

What in this country was formerly called Bank rate and afterwards Minimum Lending Rate is now allotted a less public place, and lacks a convenient customary name. We refer to it generally as central-bank rate. (The technique has also changed: see Chapter 8. What once was the rate at which the central bank lent to the banking system is now the rate at which it buys bills from it.) Though the scale on which the central bank gives assistance to the banks at its lending rate is trivial in relation to the scale of purchases and sales of financial assets made by private operators, central-bank rate appears to have a direct influence on the banks' deposit and lending rates, and also seems to have a general influence on other interest rates. What these two chapters seek to explain is how interest rates in general are determined in the short term, and how it is that the authorities, without undertaking extensive financial intervention, can exert considerable influence over them.

The prevailing theoretical discussion of interest rates does not provide a satisfactory answer to these questions, because it does not aim to. That extensive literature relates to the long term, and is for the most part couched in terms of the equilibrium towards which interest rates if disturbed will converge, and of the market forces that determine that equilibrium. That kind of theory leaves no place for central-bank rate to play a role. (It is interesting that large-scale econometric models generally relate interest rates to an exogenously set and policy-determined short-term rate, though that is at variance with the theoretical literature.) This chapter explores how equilibrium theory may be modified to allow central-bank rate to influence interest rates in the short term — while leaving long-run forces nevertheless relevant as constraints on the short-run behaviour of interest rates. Three factors are identified, which leave space for other influences to operate: the delayed and weak influence of interest rates on saving and investment, the power of expectations in financial markets, and the major role played by bank intermediation.

The institutional setting is complex and its complexities are important, though much theoretical work abstracts from them in the interests of producing a manageable model. Banks are price setters, in that over a large area the interest rates at which they will lend, and which they will pay on deposits, are changed relatively infrequently and by fairly sizeable amounts: we will call these 'administered rates'. The rates charged and paid by building societies, the banks' main competitors for households' financial business, are also administered rates. This has increasingly ceased to be true of the banks' dealings with large firms, able to deal in large sums; and there is an important fringe to bank intermediation, consisting of transactions with large firms and also in the wholesale money markets, where interest rates vary continuously and sometimes by considerable amounts. Long-term borrowing takes the form of marketable securities, variations in the price of which make long-term rates also a flexible, market-determined phenomenon. Although long-term borrowing is now undertaken mostly by governments, firms raise finance by the issue of equities, which is a related market. Substitution between these forms is at least a theoretical possibility for borrower and lender alike. The subsequent discussion has therefore to be concerned with all the forces, including official influences, that affect yields on financial assets, and with the relationship between those on different types of assets.

Our account of the behaviour of interest rates focuses on the relatively short term (i.e. extending over months and years), not on the theoretical long term, in which, given unchanging conditions and perfect foresight, an equilibrium position might be reached. Since the late 1960s, high and volatile rates of inflation have been accompanied by great volatility in nominal interest rates (and probably in real interest rates), and also in exchange rates. The propositions of equilibrium theory lend themselves to exposition in terms of diagrams and sets of equations, whose tidy and logical air contrasts with the turmoil of reality. We see the forces of equilibrium only in the background, setting limits to the play of erratic expectational factors. Much of the variation in interest rates in this country has, in practice, been associated with variations in rates abroad. Although foreign influences get some mention, discussion here will be primarily in terms of a closed economy, since the main lines of our argument can be deployed in these terms. In Chapter 5 we will consider how this needs to be modified to take account of developments abroad.

In this chapter we confine ourselves to a world where all interest rates are flexible and market-determined. In Chapter 4 we will go on to consider a mixed world where there are both flexible and administered rates, the latter in practice being short-term rates; and we then seek to explain how it is that both regimes can exist side by side, and how the authorities can alter the general level of interest rates. We first set out our view without extensive reference to what others have said; then, having done so, in Chapter 4 (Section 2) we comment more fully on how our account relates to the existing theoretical discussion.

1. INTRODUCTION

Since all assets, financial or real, may be considered to be (close or partial) substitutes, it is clear that the prices and yields on all assets must be interrelated. In a stationary state one can conceive of an equilibrium in which the stock of real assets has adjusted to the wealth that the community wished to hold. Real assets would be employed in their most productive use and would be managed by those best able to employ them; they would be owned partly by those managing them and partly by others who had claims (financial assets) on the managers. The stock of financial assets would have adjusted both to the preferences of borrowers (deficit agents) and to those of lenders (surplus agents).

Equilibrium models (of which that set out in Tobin's 1981 Nobel Lecture can be taken as an example) attempt to describe the nature of that equilibrium. If one supposes for instance that there were an exogenous change in the yield of real assets, that would produce, along with other adjustments throughout the system, a rise in the yield of financial assets. In that sense, one can say that the yields on financial assets are determined by those on real assets. (This would correspond to what, since Keynes, has been called the classicial theory of the rate of interest, in which the rate of interest is determined by the 'fundamental forces' of 'thrift and productivity', 'productivity' here meaning the rate return to be made at the margin from investing in new physical capital.) In that world there would be no route for the government to influence interest rates except by transactions that would have to be on a large scale to have much effect. It could influence the general level of the rate of interest only by itself saving or investing more or less, and could affect the relative yields on different sorts of financial assets only by changing the composition of its debt or asset holdings.

The stock of capital can be changed only slowly. Hence, if equilibrium is seriously disturbed, adjustment to a new equilibrium will take considerable time. But if agents had perfect foresight as to the new position of equilibrium, the yields on all assets would immediately adjust to be in conformity with their new equilibrium values. The real world of continual change and growth can be conceived as tending towards a succession of equilibrium positions. But that alone is not a sufficient description of how the real world behaves. If one took a high view of the possibilities of foresight, one could interpret actual fluctuations in interest rates as the response to new information about where the equilibrium position is at any moment in time. We will argue, by the end of this chapter, that this picture contains an important element of truth; but on its own it idealizes unduly the perfection of the adjustment process. Expectations appear in fact to be subject to erratic fluctuations which powerfully influence interest rates on financial assets. But we will argue that fluctuations in the latter are kept within certain bounds by considerations relating to the yield on real assets.

We now consider two groups of questions more closely:

1. the consequences of the fact that the stock of capital can adjust only slowly to a change in interest rates (Section 2): this is important for our purpose since it bears on the converse question of how far yields on financial assets are determined in the short run by the equilibrium value of the yield on real assets;
2. how expectations of future yields on financial and real assets affect financial asset yields in the short term (Section 3).

2. CLASSICAL AND MULTIPLIER ADJUSTMENTS

In a stationary state, the quantity of capital that managers wish to employ, in equilibrium and given full employment, will be brought into equality with the stock of wealth that the community wishes to hold by the rate of interest. In a steadily growing economy in which the stocks of capital and saving are growing, the *rate of change* of the stock of capital and that of saving (investment and saving) will be brought to equality in the same way. In either case, the rate of interest will likewise have settled at the level required to produce this result.

The question arises whether, starting from a position of non-equilibrium and in a path towards equilibrium, full employment will in fact be maintained; and whether, if it is not, this will alter the equilibrium towards which the economy is tending, or the forces propelling it along such a path. Keynes's attack on the classical theory of interest amounted to an assertion that the level of employment would be changed, and with that result. His summary of the classical position was as follows:

this tradition has regarded the rate of interest as the factor which brings the demand for investment and the willingness to save into equilibrium with one another. Investment represents the demand for investible resources and saving represents the supply, whilst the rate of interest is the 'price' of investible resources at which the two are equated. Just as the price of a commodity is necessarily fixed at that point where the demand for it is equal to the supply, so the rate of interest necessarily comes to rest under the play of market forces at the point where the amount of investment at that rate of interest is equal to the amount of saving at that rate. (Keynes 1936, 175).

The classical theory clearly relates to real interest rates, and to simplify discussion we will assume that there is no inflation and no prospect of it, so that real and nominal rates are equivalent. It also relates to interest rates in general, not to the interest rates on particular sorts of financial assets; and to avoid having to consider relative interest rates, we will assume at first that there is only one class of financial asset.

This may be a heroic abstraction, but is not unimaginable. It is for instance as if all transactions were effected via bank accounts, bank deposits were the only class of financial assets, all borrowing were effected by bank loans, and all deposits and loans bore a flexible rate of interest. Interest would be earned for spending later rather than now, and would be purely the reward for 'waiting' — as is appropriate in considering the classical theory. Banks here would be purely intermediaries — the quantity of bank deposits equals the quantity of bank loans — and we may perhaps be allowed to appropriate to this single asset the term 'loanable funds'. By definition, an agent who spends less than his income (has a financial surplus) increases his holding of loanable funds, and one with a deficit either runs down his holding or borrows loanable funds. *Ex post*, supply must equal demand for loanable funds; *ex ante*, it may not.

The classical theory is clearly better stated not in terms of flows but in terms of stocks, and may most conveniently be illustrated on the assumption of a clear separation between 'persons', who ultimately own real assets, and 'companies', who employ them for productive purposes. Provided there is a positive rate of interest, the retention of a stock of wealth, as opposed to running down the stock to consume more now, enables persons to consume more later. The higher the rate of interest, the larger (it may be assumed) will be the stock of wealth (taking the form of claims on companies, or 'loanable funds') that persons wish to hold. Similarly, the larger the stock of real assets that companies employ, the more they exhaust profitable opportunities to employ capital, and the lower the rate of interest they will pay for additional borrowed funds to enable them to employ a marginal addition to it. If at a ruling rate of interest the *ex ante* desire by persons to retain wealth (the supply of loanable funds) becomes less (or greater) than the *ex ante* desire for loanable funds to acquire real assets, then — on the classical theory — the rate of interest will rise (or fall) to the point where the *ex ante* discrepancy is eliminated.

When stated in terms of stock, it is clear that the adjustments involved in reconciling the stock equivalents of saving and investment might, if rapid, be large and disruptive. The stock of capital normally grows only slowly; any very rapid adjustment of the stock must involve a very large increase or decrease in consumption during that short period in which the adjustment is taking place. If the classical mechanism worked instantaneously, as Tobin (1981) has noted, an increase in expected profitability that raised the expected return on real assets over the current yield of financial assets would trigger a 'virtually instantaneous jump in the capital stock', and for an instant 'virtually infinite rates of investment'. Plainly, nothing like this occurs or could occur. Not only does investment appear relatively insensitive to changes in interest rates, but so do investment *intentions*.

For this, a number of reasons may be suggested. First, since there are high risks in investment, the range of possible returns from it is wide. The average expected return embodied in the investor's diffuse expectations of future profit streams may thus have to exceed the cost of borrowing by a substantial margin for investment to be attractive; whether that can be demonstrated on theoretical grounds may be debatable, but impressionistic evidence certainly suggests that only large changes in interest rates make much difference to assessments of profitability. Second, it takes time to invest, and to make arrangements to borrow to invest. Changes in interest rates that are thought to be temporary will therefore be ineffective, and it will take time for belief to grow that a change is durable enough to be worth responding to. Third, there are costs of adjustment, which are greater if a firm extends its capital rapidly. For assets are profitable only if well managed, but management resources are limited and can be increased only gradually. That includes the capacity to assume an additional scale of risks, the appetite for which in any period is accordingly limited. For all these reasons, the response of investment to interest rate changes is inevitably slow and gradual. (That is a property of many recent applied macroeconomic models; see Easton 1985.)

It has been doubted whether higher rates may not *discourage* saving, on the grounds that people have only limited desire for income in retirement; but that seems a restrictive assumption. However, even if the response of the stock of saving to interest rates is positive, the response of savers must be held to be slow and gradual, for reasons similar to those in the case of investment. Adjusting saving (and thus consumption) to take advantage of higher interest rates involves a costly upheaval to personal spending plans, and a sacrifice of leisure in considering how best to respond. There are risks in financial investment, so that only large gains attract. Further, savers typically lack the financial expertise to take immediate advantage of the opportunities offered. The results of econometric studies of consumers' expenditure (Davis 1984; Easton 1985) are consistent with the conclusion that, for these reasons, interest rates have a relatively weak effect on saving.

The classical mechanism, if it works, cannot then be supposed to work quickly. That has important consequences, for it implies that the intentions or expectations of one or other sector of the economy will be frustrated or disappointed. It was Keynes's central proposition that such unfulfilled intentions cause adjustment to the total level of income, and that this, by altering intentions to save and invest, provides another route to reconcile saving and investment intentions.

Suppose that saving and investment are initially in balance, and that there is then a rise in consumers' desire to save and a fall in their desire to spend out of present income. Until output is cut back, goods unsold will be put into stock, so that temporarily investment is increased by as much as consumption has fallen. But the stock accumulation is unintended. There will therefore then be a curtailment of output, and hence of income, and (saving being assumed to be a function of income) at the lower level of income less will be saved. Similarly, provided there is initially an underemployment of resources, a rise in output and income will be generated if, from an initial position of balance, there is a persistent increase in the desire to invest. (What happens if there is full employment will be considered at a later stage of the argument.) This process clearly requires a certain time to complete itself; but it would appear to work more quickly than the classical mechanism must be supposed to.

The opposition between the two views may then be stated as follows. If the 'classical' mechanism works quickly, so that the capital market clears, discrepancies between *ex ante* saving and investment could not persist more than momentarily, and a deficiency of aggregate demand, or unemployment arising from it, could hardly arise. If on the other hand the classical mechanism works only slowly, the way open for an alternative mechanism in which *ex ante* saving and investment can be brought into equality by changes in the level of income rather than the level of interest rates. On the face of it, there appears room for a compromise view. We here accept that unemployment may and does arise by reason of inadequacy of demand (which implies that the classical mechanism does not operate instantaneously), and proceed to investigate the possibility that the classical mechanism nevertheless does operate but with only gradual effect, and does therefore play some part, along with income adjustments, in reconciling saving and investment.

Interest rates during a multiplier process

To consider this question we must investigate what happens to interest rates in the course of a multiplier process. For the moment, we will retain the simplifying assumptions that there is no inflation and only one class of financial asset. We must also assume that there is underemployment. We will remove these assumptions later. The assumption of a single class of financial asset removes some complications: there is no question of one class of financial asset being in short supply and others being in excess demand. The supply of that single asset can then be seen to be the same thing as the unspent income of surplus agents, and the demand for it as the spending of deficit agents in excess of their income.

Suppose, from an initial position of equilibrium, there is an increase in the profitability of investment so that intended investment now exceeds the current level of saving. According to the standard multiplier argument, that will produce a progressive expansion of income, which will proceed to the point where, at the eventual stable higher level of income, intended saving is brought up to the new higher level of investment. The increased desire to invest will mean an increased desire to borrow, and companies thus may be prepared initially to pay a higher rate of interest on borrowed funds. But at the same time their actions, by one route or another, will increase the supply of loanable funds. If they borrow more in anticipation of higher investment not yet undertaken, they will acquire an extra holding of loanable funds which on our assumption can only take the form of adding to bank deposits or repaying bank borrowing. When companies implement their plans for higher investment, the first result may be involuntary stock decumulation by other companies; though some companies might then *ex post* borrow more, others would in the event borrow less. Alternatively, the result will be to add to persons' incomes; that is likely to be unexpected, and will not immediately be matched by higher spending by those persons, so that they acquire financial assets and thus in any event add to the supply of loanable funds.

It appears then to follow that any expectation that loanable funds were going to be in short supply would be quickly corrected, and that any initial upward pressure on interest rates would then be reversed. In the course of a multiplier expansion process (which one might suppose takes a year or two or three), there might then be fluctuations in interest rates, but not consistent upward pressure. The effect of intermittently higher interest rates on the desire to save or to invest — which if large and consistent might modify the multiplier process — must then be small.

At the termination of the multiplier process, *ex ante* saving is, by definition, brought to equality with *ex ante* investment. There can then be no question of there being a shortage of loanable funds. Even if there had been pressure on interest rates along the way, any upward pressure would be finally removed. It is difficult, then, to see any significant role for the classical mechanism. The conclusion appears to be not only that the classical mechanism works sufficiently slowly for the Keynesian mechanism to be set going, but also that that removes the conditions which might otherwise have set the classical mechanism in motion.

Generalization of the argument

We must now look at the effects of removing the simplifying

assumptions with which we started. The first assumption, of no inflation, appears not to be crucial, so long as it can be assumed that the rate of inflation is given and is not significantly affected by the processes being examined. With inflation, nominal rates of interest must be higher than real rates to allow for expected inflation.

Second, we assumed a single class of financial asset. If there are many types of financial asset, relative rates of interest will be affected by the supply and demand for each class of asset. Those wishing to borrow may seek to do so in a form that does not (at existing interest rates) match the preferences of lenders. We would argue (for reasons to be justified more fully in Chapter 4) that this may affect the average level of interest rates as well as interest relativities. Thus, large issues of long-term assets by government or companies will raise interest rates on long-term assets relative to the banks' rates. We argue later that the banks' administered rates function as a pivot in the structure of rates, so that the result is a rise in the average level of interest rates. But such effects may occur at any time, irrespective of whether there is an *ex ante* discrepancy between saving and investment. Moreover, unless it is assumed that investment is particularly dependent on long-term finance (which is not the case, as we will also argue later), such effects do not appear relevant to how an *ex ante* discrepancy is closed, and thus do not affect our previous argument.

This fulcrum effect may however be relevant to a possible objection to the conclusions to which our present line of argument seems to point. The announcement or expectation of increased borrowing by a major borrower or group of borrowers appears to affect the level of interest rates, and that may appear contrary to our account. We suggest, however, that the reaction to an announcement, for instance, of a higher figure for the public-sector borrowing requirement may reflect expectations not only of higher borrowing but also about the form it will take. Thus, the expectation may be of higher bond sales, as distinct from increased borrowing from the banks. That could affect the general level of interest rates via the fulcrum effect just described. Similarly, expectations of higher corporate profits appear to affect interest rates, which may likewise appear contrary to our general contention that interest rates are not related to the profitability of investment. We would agree that higher profits will raise dividend expectations and equity yields and thus, via the fulcrum effect, interest rates in general. But that is not enough to falsify our basic argument that changes in interest rates so induced do not constitute a mechanism that helps to match saving and investment — unless, again, it is argued that investment is particularly sensitive to one particular type of finance.

We must now relax the assumption of underemployment, and consider in particular what happens if there is excess demand. This may be assumed to put upward pressure on the price level. Given that the public sector is debtor to the private sector (and public debt largely unindexed), that will erode the real value of the private sector's holdings of financial assets. We may asume that that in turn reduces private demand, and eventually eliminates excess demand. But for realism, we must suppose that prices are in degree inflexible, so that the process takes time. For a time, then, excess demand will persist and must be supposed in effect to be 'suppressed' by the inflexibility of prices (see for instance the discussion in Dow 1964, 172). There will be shortages and bottlenecks. Either private consumption, private investment, or government spending will be less than private agents or government would spend if resources were available.

In these conditions there will, in a sense, be an excess of *ex ante* investment over *ex ante* saving, and it might be supposed that this would put upward pressure on interest rates. Yet wartime experience seems to show that massive excess demand can co-exist with low rates of interest. The explanation may be that the potential excess demand for loanable funds — like excess demand for goods and services — is also suppressed. Thus the government, unable to spend all it has planned, does not seek to borrow as much as it had first intended; and the private sector, prevented by shortages from spending as much of its income as it would like, does not require the inducement of high interest rates to buy financial assets rather than goods and services.

Provisional conclusions about the determination of interest rates

We have discussed at some length the way in which saving gets matched to investment, and have concluded that the rate of interest in fact plays no significant role. From the point of view of this study, however, what we are interested in is the reverse, but related, question: whether interest rates are determined by 'fundamental' forces governing the desire to hold wealth and the return on real assets.

If the classical view were correct that intended saving and investment were brought into line by interest rates, then it would also follow that the level of interest rates had to settle at a level determined by the fundamental forces governing wealth holding and the return on real assets. We have argued that the first proposition is not correct, because neither the stock of capital nor the stock of accumulated savings that people wish to hold responds quickly to interest rates. That may perhaps be readily accepted. The converse proposition — that it is not the demand to employ capital and hold wealth that determines interest rates — may be less obvious. Our argument has been that, since the interest rate is ineffective in reconciling intended saving and investment, reconciliation is effected by upward or downward adjustments of income, and that such adjustments of income eradicate any initial discrepancy between the demand for funds to invest and the supply of saving. Given that their influence is displaced by the multiplier mechanism of income adjustments, it would appear to follow that the fundamental forces governing wealth holding and the return on real assets play no role in determining interest rates.

What we go on to argue is in fact somewhat more complicated than that. Since interest rates are not tied down by fundamental forces, this leaves them open to the play of short-run market expectations, which are liable to be erratic. But we will argue that this is true only for interest rates within a 'normal' range. Interest rate expectations are themselves subject to some constraints, because extreme outcomes will appear unlikely to market operators — for reasons to be spelt out in the next section.

3. INTEREST RATES AND EXPECTATIONS

Prices in financial markets tend to be more volatile than in markets for goods and services, for various reaons. The existing stock of financial assets is often large in relation to the flow of new assets, so that the effect of changes in their price on the size of the flows is relatively small in relation to the stock. That removes the stabilizing influence that expectations of such effects have in good markets. The views of traders are thus formed in a relatively closed world. They stand to be influenced by the views of other traders, and, by reason of this interaction, changes in prices may in the short term be cumulative. Future prices are therefore difficult to predict, and views about them are weakly held. Expectations about prices in the longer term thus exercise only a weak stabilizing influence over current prices. Interest rates are therefore dominated by market 'sentiment' and are subject to considerable short-run volatility.

The price of any financial asset of significant maturity must be largely influenced by its expected future price. The gain from holding the asset is the interest to be earned on it, plus the expected rise (or less the fall) in its price over the period for which it is intended to hold it. A change in the level of interest implies a contrary change in the capital value of the asset; and for an asset of significant maturity, the capital gain or loss associated with a change in interest rates will be large in relation to the interest rates to be earned from holding it. It follows that, if the interest rate falls, and the fall is expected to be only temporary, this 'will be sufficient to make people postpone the purchase of securities', so that 'the rate will soon be back at its old level' (Hicks 1939, 261). The rate of interest cannot therefore diverge significantly from what it is expected to be. This is most true of long-term financial assets, but expectations also have considerable influence over the price of short-term assets with a life of only months or weeks.

In practice, the price of financial assets is likely to be very erratic. As already argued, fundamental factors have little influence on them, essentially because the kind of adjustments produced by the interplay of fundamental factors take years (perhaps decades) to work themselves out, and because it is impossible to predict with any close accuracy what effect on interest rates they will have. Any observer of financial markets must be struck by the apparent triviality of the reasons that appear to occasion changes in their price. To an extent, it is to be expected that apparently minor items of news about the likely future course of events will on occasion have a large effect on current asset prices; for current prices should reflect the present value of the expected future stream of income from the asset over a long horizon, and an item of news that causes markets to reassess their expectations for a number of future dates may well warrant a large change in asset values. The process of assessment (to describe it with over-great formality) may be said to require that operators assess the information content of news, which is intrinsically 'noisy' in nature, and (with the aid of a formal or informal economic model) its impact on future earnings. In practice, neither of these operations can be carried out with any great certainty. As a result, the impact of news on asset prices is fickle and uncertain. As Keynes put it,

A conventional valuation which is established as the outcome of the mass psychology of a large number of ignorant individuals is liable to change violently as the result of a sudden fluctuation of opinion due to factors which do not really make much difference. . . . (Keynes 1936, 154)

This is true of all flexible financial markets: for long-dated bonds, for short-dated money-market instruments, for equities, and also for foreign exchange.

This has the further consequence that any view about interest rates a long time ahead is very risky, so that operators do not take up long-term positions unless the prospective reward for doing so appears unusually great. On most occasions, financial markets tend to be dominated not by long-term investors making permanent investment decisions, but by operators with short horizons, who are concerned to make quick gains. Such operators need to forecast not the effect of fundamentals on the future price of bonds in the long term, but rather the evolution of the price in the short term, and in these circumstances what they need to assess is how others in the market will react to the arrival of items of news.

Financial markets are in this case likely to be not only erratic but unstable. In Keynes's parallel, the game becomes like a newspaper beauty contest, where prizes go to those who pick the most popular choice; to succeed, 'each competitor has to pick not those faces which he himself thinks prettiest, but those which he thinks likeliest to catch the fancy of other competitors, all of whom are looking at the problem from the same point of view'. Expectations are likely, for a time, to be extrapolative, and as others climb on to the bandwagon will, for a time, be self-fulfilling.

This account appears to leave interest rates operating in a vacuum and to suggest that they might be anywhere. We discuss in the next chapter the influence of the more stable administered rates set by the banks and the way in which the authorities may affect market sentiment. But even apart from this, there appear to be limits to the vagaries of market opinion. Erratic though interest rates have been, their fluctuations have been contained within a range. Thus, even the highest real interest rates in industrial countries (so far as one can judge them) have remained well below the high rates that are common in underdeveloped countries; and even though nominal interest rates have at times been below the rate of inflation, the occasions have been rare and relatively brief.

We suggest that the reasons why this should be the case are as follows. Our previous argument hinged on the relative speeds with which the classical and Keynesian mechanisms operate, and we argued that the former was relatively slow. But if interest rates ever got to extremely high (or extremely low) levels, it seems likely that the classical mechanism would begin to operate more quickly. There would begin to be some immediate effect on the desire to hold wealth or employ capital. Moreover, even if only incipiently operative, these effects could immediately be predicted ultimately to become significant, and operators concerned with long-run considerations would tend to become more dominant. Even without bringing into play large actual adjustments of flow supplies and demands, this would affect the behaviour of short-term operators, who, sensing the probabilities, would refrain from driving the rate to these heights in the first place.

We argued earlier that interest rates are not, within a 'normal' range, determined by the fundamentals governing the desire to hold wealth. But we now have to add that this is true only within a range, and that beyond this range the fundamentals would begin to exert a corrective force. They thus play a background role, putting limits on what the market expects and hence on the level that market rates reach. The bounds thus set to interest rate fluctuations are no doubt vaguely defined, and they may well be larger in periods such as the present, when rates of inflation and the attendant uncertainties have been high and variable. The limits to the 'range of indeterminacy' also restrict what the authorities can hope to achieve; for we argue in Chapter 4 that the widespread influence over rates that they are able to exert comes from their ability to influence market expectations.

4

The Behaviour of Interest Rates Continued

Our chief object in this and the preceding chapter is to explain and delimit the influence of central-bank rate on the structure of interest rates. Its influence is brought to bear most directly on the rates set by the banks and on short-term money market rates. In Section 1 below we turn to consider how short-term rates are determined, how administered bank rates can co-exist with market-determined rates, and how the central bank influences both. Here, the plane of argument is concerned with institutional questions more than with the questions of theory discussed in Chapter 3. (That appeared one reason to make a break and put this discussion in a separate chapter.) Section 2 attempts to relate the view about interest rates set out in these two chapters to existing discussion of the rate of interest. Section 3 ventures a possible explanation for the behaviour of interest rates since 1971.

1. THE DETERMINATION OF SHORT-TERM INTEREST RATES AND THE INFLUENCE OF THE CENTRAL BANK

The general discussion of interest rates in Chapter 3 did not get to the point of discussing what is for us the key question: how it is that the authorities can influence interest rates, as is in fact the case, without undertaking financial operations on any large scale. The answer we here give stems directly from the conclusion of Chapter 3. Because interest rate expectations are diffuse and weakly held and markets are footloose, markets are often willing (sometimes, one thinks, even glad) to follow an official lead. The authorities tend to be seen as having a clear view, and as potentially capable of large-scale action. Small-scale official action may then be seen as indicating a commitment to further action in future; that gives it an effect much greater than the actual scale of official operations by itself would be expected to have.

In principle, the central bank could seek directly to influence either bond rates or short-term rates. In practice, it operates chiefly on short rates. Perhaps a major reason is that it can, relatively easily, affect the banks' (administered) rates. Since the banks' operations are a major component of financial and capital markets, this provides the central bank with great leverage. In this country there are additional reasons for this predeliction, stemming from the facts that the public debt in earlier decades was relatively large, that it remains relatively long-term, and that it is the central bank that is responsible for managing it. Action undertaken by the central bank explicitly to vary long rates would make the price of bonds less predictable for market operators. That would make debt less attractive to hold, and thus more expensive as a source of finance for the government; and it might at times interrupt debt sales.

It is an important feature of the financial system that the banks tend to act in uniformity, so that, although banks are many and separate, collectively the banking system behaves in some respects as a bloc. In this country that might be thought to be because retail banking is dominated by the four large banks. Their base rates are usually identical, or, if temporarily divergent, close. But there is also a fringe of smaller and highly competitive banks that tend to follow the rates set by the large banks, while the building societies also follow (with some delay) these rates. The conformity in behaviour probably reflects not oligopoly but other reasons, deeply rooted in the nature of banking.

Individual banks have good reasons to conform to established norms of behaviour which they know other banks will follow. Banks are in the business of maturity transformation, i.e. of rolling over a sequence of short-term deposits to fund a longer-term loan. Short-term funding will become harder to obtain if doubt develops about the quality of a bank's loans; this may be particularly crucial if the bank needs money-market funding. Thus, it is essential to each bank to maintain market confidence in its management, and this in general will require following lending policies similar to those of other banks. It will also tend to mean maintaining the same rates as other banks for loans and deposits; for if it pays less it will not get funds, and if it pays more, that may be interpreted as a sign that it has to do so because of doubts about its viability. Another reason is that it is risky for a bank to embark on open price competition. If a bank unilaterally lowers its base rate, it will lose retail deposits and will have to borrow more on money markets, which is more expensive than taking retail deposits; and as an isolated heavy borrower it may have to pay above the odds. For a bank unilaterally to raise its base rates is also risky: it will lose market share of lending, which may prove difficult to recover, and it will end up with an increased net surplus to lend on money markets at an uncertain future rate. Major banks therefore tend to change base rates only when they have reason to suppose that other major banks will act similarly. They compete by less open means — by advertising, by trimming the margins between lending or deposit rates to major customers, and by improved financial services.

This means that, if the authorities can influence the rates set by banks, they can hope to have a large influence on the whole structure of short-term rates, and an important if more diffuse influence on interest rates generally. To investigate how this influence operates, and how far it extends, we need to analyse the nature of the structure of rates.

The interrelation between short-term interest rates

Fig. 4.1 illustrates the course of various short-term interest rates (showing rates at end-months) in the four years 1981–4, a period sufficient to illustrate the main facts to be explained. Each of the pairs of rates shown shows some degree of correlation, as might be expected in view of substitution by borrowers or lenders; and in each case there is a question as to the causality that produces this covariance.

- Money market rates and banks' base rates vary closely together. Is this because the banks fix their (administered) rates in line with money-market (market-determined) rates; or because banks' rates determine market rates?
- Central-bank rate tends to vary, though less closely, with the banks' rates (and thus also with money-market rates). Is central-bank rate fixed in line with other short rates, or are they determined by it?
- Interbank rates (and thus other short rates) in this country show some relation to Eurodollar rates (and thus to short-term rates in the United States). This, we will argue in Chapter 5, is not because (with floating exchange rates) US rates must influence UK market rates directly, but rather because, since international interest rate differentials affect the exchange rate, the Bank of England is influenced by US rates in setting its own lending rate. The Bank's action can be partly guessed, and thus US rates indirectly influence domestic short rates generally.
- Short bond rates show some relation to the banks' base rates (and thus other short rates); short and long bond rates (not here shown) also show some relation, though not an unvarying one.

Fig. 4.2 provides greater detail for individual money-market and related instruments, on which rates tend to move in parallel since they are relatively close substitutes for both borrowers and lenders. Thus, a lender will sell a certificate of deposit (CD) to buy a bill if bill rates rise relative to CD rates, and a bank will borrow through issuing a CD to repay a more expensive interbank loan when that is profitable. Such arbitrage should equate the yields of assets of comparable maturity after allowance for differences in riskiness and liquidity; thus, prime bank bills pay less than riskier trade bills, and banks expect a higher return on illiquid three-month deposits than on holdings of three-month prime bank bills.

The bottom part of the figure shows interbank rates on three-month and overnight money. Here there is less correspondence, since the difference in maturity of these assets makes them poor substitutes from the point of view of a surplus bank. A bank that borrows overnight to lend at three months is gambling that very short-term interest rates will be lower on average in the next three months than today's level of the

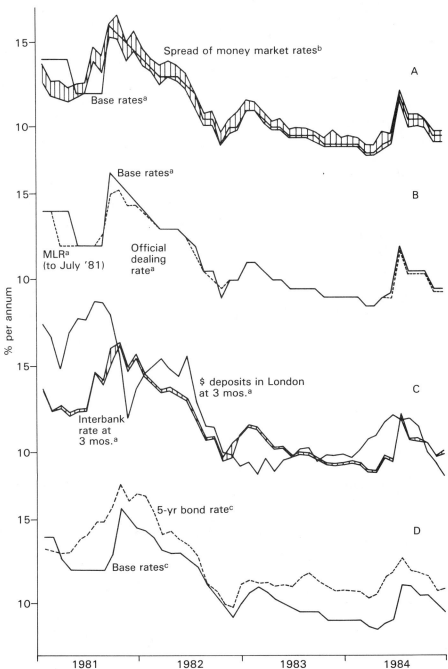

FIG. 4.1   *Short-term interest rates, 1981–1984*

[a] At end-month.   [b] For details see Fig. 4.2.   [c] Monthly averages.

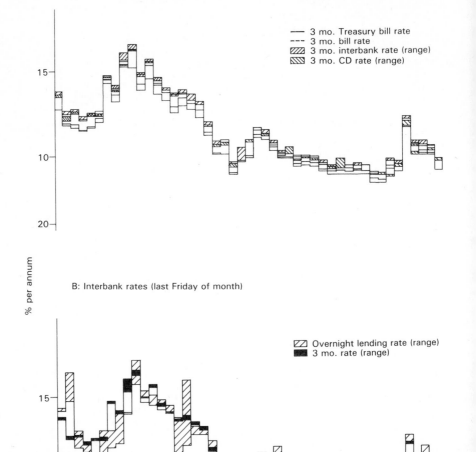

FIG. 4.2   *Money-market and interbank rates, 1981–1984*

three-month rate. The gap between these yields thus will reflect a whole sequence of expected future very short-term yields (and an allowance for the risks that expectations may prove false). The figure suggests that these expectations are volatile: there are similar rather volatile margins between rates at all pairs of differing maturities. The overnight rate reflects individual banks' needs to cover deficits expected to be of short duration (see Chapter 2), and is much affected by the distribution of liquidity among banks each day. It may therefore vary greatly in the course of a day. (To take an extreme example, on 31 August 1984 overnight rates varied from 3 per cent to over 11 per cent.)

The rates on different short-term assets are linked both because the assets are close substitutes and because rates on them are influenced by a common set of expectations. To disentangle the causality we need to look for key rates that anchor the system as a whole. As is evident from common observation (and from Fig. 4.1), central-bank rate is usually raised by sharp upward jumps. This provides a point of entry for analysis of its effects.

Central-bank rate is (in the usual phrase) 'made effective' by the central bank putting pressure on the reserve position of the banks, i.e. by forcing them to borrow from the central bank at its lending rate. This process will be examined in Chapter 8; here the important thing to note is that such pressure is not applied continuously, or not strongly. An account of the role of central-bank rate thus needs to look separately at periods when the banks are under reserve pressure, and periods when they are not. We will be led to conclude that, at times when the banks are not under pressure, the banking system as a whole has considerable freedom to determine the level of its rates, and that this in turn is a key element that serves to anchor the general structure of interest rates. That is possible because of what we have called the 'indeterminacy' of interest rates, and because of the importance of the banking system within the financial structure.

The possibilities of arbitrage provide a link between bank rates and money-market rates. If money-market rates are high relative to bank base rates (and expected to remain so), commercial borrowers will borrow on overdraft (at a small margin over base rate) to replace borrowing through bills; or they may borrow in order to purchase CDs or bills that are close to maturity ('round tripping'). That exposes borrowers to the risk of loss, if base rates move up before the bill matures; but when round-tripping offers a profit (as on occasions during the Corset), its scale can grow very substantially. Similarly, if money-market rates are low in relation to base rates, borrowers will replace bank loans by money-market borrowing (though there is in this case little counterpart to 'round-tripping', since banks' deposit rates are set well below base rate). Arbitrage will tend to lower money-market rates if they are initially high relative to base rates, and to raise them where they are initially low.

The banks, on their side, in order to limit such switches, will also be unwilling to allow base rates to remain out of line with money-market rates at short maturities for long, or by much of a margin. The effect of money-market rates on the cost to banks of their deposits (and hence the cost of lending) is another consideration that works in the same direction. For the large banks, not very dependent on money-market borrowing, this may be a minor matter. But those small banks that are relatively highly dependent on the money markets may base their lending rates on what they expect to have to pay for such marginal funds; their lending rates may in turn influence those of the large banks.

Money-market rates, however, are strongly influenced by expectations about the future level of bank base rates. To borrow an overdraft to purchase a money-market instrument is to take a risk of loss if base rates rise — small if the money-market instrument is of short residual maturity, but substantial for instance on one with three months to run. If base rates are expected to rise, the price of money-market instruments will therefore fall, bringing money-market yields to what base rates are expected to be. Money markets enable those with different short-term interest rate expectations to trade, and provide cover against the risk of interest changes; and there is an active secondary market in money-market instruments reflecting this activity. One may say then that, if the banks' base rates are influenced by money-market rates, they in turn reflect expectations about future base rates.

Moreover, as already indicated in Chapter 2 (Section 4), the greater part of activity on money markets represents the dealing not of non-bank participants, but of banks; and the expectations about future bank rates which determine money-market rates are predominantly those of the banks themselves. The argument has thus indeed become circular. We have therefore to go on to ask what determines the banks' expectations. In part, that will depend on what they think the authorities will force them to do to base rates, and we will turn next to the *modus operandi* of official intervention. Before coming to that, however, it is convenient to look at the question of how banks set base rates if the authorities leave things alone.

Bank base rates within the general structure of interest rates

We argued in Chapter 3 that, within a considerable range, the general level of interest rates is not rigidly determined by fundamental forces, but on the contrary is indeterminate. The banks rates are not erratic in the same way as flexible market-determined interest rates, but rather display considerable stability. Given the importance of bank intermediation within the structure of financial markets, an important question remains as to how base rates are determined. Our answer is that the nature of a banking system ensures both that banks apply conservative and conventional standards in determining their base rates, and that there are few competitive constraints on their so doing.

First (as we argued in Chapter 2), the banks ration the credit extended to their customers, and thus in most circumstances are confronted with an unsatisfied fringe of borrowers. Moreover, although they face potential competition from other forms of short-term finance, and less immediately from bond or equity finance, the cost of competing forms of finance is likely to follow their own lending rates (for reasons discussed further below). The banks therefore are free to fix base rates without a significant risk of losing business. (That might be thought to invest the banks with potential monopoly power; while in theory this may be so, we will argue that the banks are so placed as to be unwilling to exploit this.)

Second, though individual banks (and building societies) are in competition with each other both for deposits and in their lending, competition is muted by the dangers of open price competition and also by the need of each bank to follow common standards of banking prudence — factors that we have discussed above. To a considerable extent, therefore, the banking system and the building societies act as a single bloc whose behaviour is determined by accepted and traditional past norms.

Third, for the banks and building societies as a whole, it is largely the case that retail deposits are a captive supply. The yield on them is related to what the lending institutions charge for loans, and thus is governed by the same conventional norms that determine their lending rates. The forces of competition between financial institutions do work, and have raised the yield; but they work slowly. (In particular, the building societies in recent years have probably been more aggressive than the banks in expanding lending and attracting deposits, and the banks have responded by extending payment of interest on deposits: see Chapter 11, Section 2.)

Fourth, banks are politically exposed. High interest rates, and high bank profits, are unpopular and thus potentially liable to provoke government intervention of one kind or another. This reinforces the preference of banks for conforming to tradition, and their caution about fully exploiting opportunities for profit.

Our conclusion then is that, within the 'range of indeterminacy' of interest rates as a whole, bank base rates are determined by conventions that are largely historically determined, and thus subject to considerable inertia. Interest rates on different sorts of assets are interrelated both because of arbitrage and because all rates are influenced by a common set of interest rate expectations, which also determines the average level of rates; and expectations are strongly influenced by the rates set by the banks. Hence bank base rates play a pivotal role within the 'zone of indeterminacy' in pinning down the general structure of interest rates.

It might be argued that the increasingly competitive nature of financial markets, more particularly in the 1980s, has resulted in something approaching perfectly competitive financial markets, in which conventions can have little place in determining bank base rates. We have already argued in Chapter 2 (Section 2) that, given lenders' risk, it is still not the case, nor probably ever could be, that financial markets clear. Consequently, while many *relative* interest rates are competitively determined, administered interest rates still persist; and both continue to operate within a system in which the *general* level of interest rates is, within a range, indeterminate in terms of fundamental factors. That system continues to be influenced by the rates set by the banks — in part because the banks' rates are in effect determined by the authorities, whose intentions have disproportionate influence, a theme developed below.

The effect of central-bank rate

When the central bank raises the rate at which it lends to the banks, this raises the costs to the banks by only a very small amount (since they borrow only marginal amounts from the central bank). The banks however usually raise their base rates by the full extent of the rise in the central bank's rate. Banks do not usually price loans at the marginal cost of what they borrow, and quite why they do so in this case is to be considered in detail in Chapter 8 (Section 2). Perhaps the basic reason is that, interest rate expectations being (as we have argued in Chapter 3) fluid, a rise in central-bank rate affects interest rate expectations generally. It thus raises money-market rates, and the cost to banks of what they borrow in wholesale markets — much more important than the cost of what they borrow from the central bank. The central bank's general power over interest rates is reinforced by the fact that, in setting their administered rates, the banks follow central-bank rate. Such a convention, once established and expected, tends to be self-validating. Because all banks conform, each bank can count on others to do the same. Money-market rates (and hence the cost of wholesale deposits) rise too because, as we have seen, money-market rates are determined by what bank base rates are expected to be. The banks also raise rates on retail deposits, knowing that other banks will do likewise.

A rise in banks' base rates forces a similar move on the part of building societies. They have traditionally been reluctant to raise rates, and have acted only after an interval; but the effect on the flow of deposits to them has forced them fairly soon to raise their rates in line with the banks. In recent years building societies have been more competitive with each other, and with banks; and building societies have been quicker to move their rates, which have therefore come to follow banks' base rates more closely.

There is also communication between bank rates and the yields on bonds and equities. Long-term assets are for borrowers partial substitutes for bank loans, and for savers they are partial substitutes for deposits. To some extent, therefore, long rates will move in line with a rise in central-bank rate. Thus, while large companies have the alternatives of security-market issues or selling commercial paper, the cost of these sources of finance is likely to rise in some sympathy with the cost of bank finance. Neither small companies nor persons have such an alternative. For both of these reasons, banks can raise base rates in line with central-bank rate without provoking a significant contraction in the scale of bank intermediation. That, too, helps to explain the readiness of banks to follow central-bank rate.

When the authorities wish to encourage rates to fall, the means open to them are less clear-cut than in the upward direction. They cannot put 'reverse' reserve pressure on the banks (Chapter 8, Section 2). But they can make it clear that they will not resist a fall in rates; and a knowledge of their attitude will itself affect expectations. That will, over time, reduce base rates to what banks regard as a normal level. Thus, in contrast to an officially induced rise in rates, a downward move in bank rates tends to be gradual.

In practice, there is no sharp line between periods when the central bank is putting pressure on bank rates and when it is not. Even when the central bank is not active, it is still there and capable of being so. The market is thus constantly playing a guessing game as to what the authorities may do. If it is believed that the authorities will adjust central-bank rate in response to fast monetary growth, or to a fall in the exchange rate (or, more remotely, to a rise in US rates), then such developments will themselves create expectations of a rise — and hence a rise in fact — of interest rates. Even if it does not wish to put pressure on the system, the central bank is then likely — to avoid being a cheap source of finance to the banks — to raise its own lending rate in line with market rates, albeit passively and reluctantly. Thus, if official intentions are misunderstood, market expectations can on occasion frustrate, rather than reinforce, the authorities' wishes.

Although within a range the authorities have great power over interest rates, the argument of Chapter 3 implies that at a point they would come up against forces they could not override. Their power springs from their ability to influence expectations, and, beyond a point, official action would fail to take market opinion with it; in view of the fundamental considerations relating to the return on real assets and the desire to hold wealth, the policy would, beyond a point, cease to appear to markets to be sustainable. Nor can it ever be clear where the limits are, so that in practice the authorities must be cautious in using their power. Further important limitations to official interest rate policy will be discussed in Chapters 8 and 9.

2. THE RELATION BETWEEN OUR ACCOUNT AND PREVIOUS DISCUSSION OF THE RATE OF INTEREST

It may now be useful to relate our account of the determination of interest rates to previous theoretical discussion. Somewhere about 1960, the previous voluminous discussion of 'the rate of interest', as a subject on its own appears to have lapsed, and was subsumed in a more general discussion of the balance of the whole economy in which the rate of interest played a role as one element among others. In that discussion, some of the elements we have emphasized had small place; and to relate our account to the literature, we have first to go back to earlier discussion.

It is clear that our account is similar in some respects to that in Keynes's *General Theory*, but in other respects is not. Three elements are to be found in the *General Theory*.

First, our account emphasizes the inability of the rate of interest to reconcile saving and investment intentions. In a sense it can be said that 'the financial and capital markets are . . . highly imperfect coordinators of saving and investment' (Tobin 1981). But the defect is not in the capital markets as such, for they react quickly and sensitively to the data actually presented to them, but rather in the data that reach the capital markets. This results from the impossibility of making firm decisions a long time ahead in a world of great uncertainty, about either investment or consumption. Keynes wrote:

An act of individual saving means . . . a decision not to have dinner today. But it does *not* necessitate a decision to have dinner . . . a year hence or to consume any specified thing at any specified date . . . . If saving consisted not merely in abstaining from present consumption but in placing simultaneously a specific order for future consumption, the effect might indeed be different . . . the expectation of some future yield from investment would be improved, and the resources released from preparing for present consumption could be turned over to preparing for future consumption . . . . (Keynes 1936, 210–11).

Second, we have argued that the desire to hold wealth and to employ capital (or, in flow terms, saving and investment intentions) are reconciled by adjustments of income — given the inability of interest rests to perform this function quickly. This too mirrors Keynes: 'it is not the rate of interest but the level of incomes which ensures equality between saving and investment' — a proposition which he saw (1937, 250) as the 'initial novelty' of the *General Theory*.

Third, the dominant role given in our account to expectations in the determination of interest rates appears to correspond with what Keynes meant by calling the rate of interest a 'highly conventional' or 'highly psychological' phenomenon: 'its actual value is largely governed by the prevailing view as to what it is expected to be' (Keynes 1936, 203). Because interest rates have varied much more since the war than when Keynes wrote, we give greater emphasis than he to systematic swings in expectations as opposed to erratic movements.

Keynes might therefore have demurred at our formulation that interest rates are indeterminate. Nevertheless, other of his remarks not only point to this conclusion, but go too far in that direction. One may note for instance his unqualified statement that '*any* level of interest which is accepted with sufficient conviction as *likely* to be durable *will* be durable' (1936, 203), and also Joan Robinson's gloss that there is no escape from the implication that this 'leaves the rate of interest hanging by its own bootstraps' (Robinson 1952, 18). Our proposition that interest rates are indeterminate only within a range is in our view a necessary qualification. The fundamental 'forces of thrift and productivity' have (as Joan Robinson would have said) a final card of entry — not merely because it happens to be believed that they do, but because, beyond a point, there is good reason for this belief.

Most theorizing in this century about interest rates has been about the rate of interest on bonds, which may be taken as representative of rates that are flexible and market-determined. Wicksell (1898) by contrast, following the earlier English writers on whom he based himself, thought primarily in terms of the rate charged by banks. When he spoke of divergencies between the 'money rate' and the 'natural rate', the 'money rate' meant the banks' lending rates; and these were clearly administered rates. Our account incorporates such rates in a setting where flexible interest rates also exist. Our account of how the authorities influence interest rates differs from what Keynes (at times, at least: see Keynes 1936, 247) said, and what most later writers took from him — that the stock of money is an exogenous variable, and that it is by varying the stock of money (explicitly or implicitly by control of base money) that the authorities are able to vary the level of interest rates. Wicksell, on the other hand, has the authorities (in a way we regard as realistic) affect market rates by varying central-bank rate, which the banks then follow in their lending rates.

Our account in relation to Hick's IS/LM formulation

Keynes's account of the role of expectations appears, as we have noted, to leave interest rates indeterminate; and our insistence on the limitations to this indeterminacy may be regarded as a way of reconciling this aspect of Keynes with the classical view of the importance of the fundamentals. Hicks's 1937 article, and his apparatus of the *IS/LM* curves, were also an attempt to reconcile Keynes with the classics. But it was a different element of Keynes that he sought to reconcile from those we have emphasized, and it may be useful to make clear the ways in which our account is dissimilar.

Hicks's *IS/LM* curves illustrate in graphical terms the joint determination of the interest rate and of national income (assumed to be determined by the level of aggregate demand). The *LM* curve describes stock equilibrium in the money market: it shows those pairs of the value of the interest rate and of income at which the stock of (non-interest-bearing) money is willingly held by the public. By varying the stock of money, the authorities can vary the level of the nominal interest rate (and hence, assuming prices unchanged, the real interest rate). The *IS* curve describes flow equilibrium in the product market: it shows those pairs of the value of the real interest rate and of income at which saving is equal to investment. A rise in the interest rate will make some potential investment unprofitable and reduce investment: that will in turn reduce national income, and also saving, which is a function of income. The intersection of the two curves thus determines that pair of levels of income and interest rate that reconciles liquidity preference (in the money market) with the forces of productivity and thrift.

Our account of the determination of interest rates differs from this formulation both as regards the *LM* curve and as regards the *IS* curve. As already made clear, we do not see the stock of money as exogenous in the sense here implied, i.e. as something that is determined by mere decision of the authorities. We therefore do not see the authorities influencing nominal interest rates by varying the stock of money: rather, we see them influencing it by variations in central-bank rate. If that were all, we could abolish the *LM* curve, and feed in our mechanism for official influence over interest rates to the *IS* half of the construction. But our emphasis both on the importance of interest rate expectations and on the limited range to the indeterminacy of interest rates would lead us to apply some caution as to how far the authorities had it in their power to vary interest rates.

Our account, however, also diverges from what the *IS* side of the construction implies. In Chapter 3 (Section 2), we indicated the reasons for believing that neither capital nor the stock of saving are highly sensitive, in a short period of years, to moderate changes in interest rates of the sort the authorities can bring about. Furthermore, the multiplier takes time to work itself out: a fall in investment will set in motion a progressive fall in income, but it must take a period of years before intended saving is brought roughly into line by this route with intended investment. The idea that investment can be varied, and that saving can be adjusted to its new level, within any short period appears illusory: certainly not within 'a week' (as Hicks originally had in mind: but see Hicks 1981), or even within a year or two. Our account would imply that, for any such short period, the *IS* curve is practically vertical. If accepted, this makes the apparatus useless as a means of explaining the behaviour of interest rates over periods of two or three years.

Even more fundamental is the question of whether the construction is of great relevance for the analysis of the determination of income and employment. On our view of how the authorities influence interest rates, they can influence them only because, within a range, the fundamental forces affecting the desire to hold capital and saving do not bear strongly on the determination of interest rates. This insulation from the fundamentals implies the converse: that, within a range, saving and investment are barely influenced by interest rates. If on the other hand they were relatively sensitive to interest rates, fundamental forces would have a strong pull on interest rates; that would collapse the range of indeterminacy and make it impossible for the authorities to exert much influence. In other words, the authorities have influence over interest rates only because the influence that interest rates themselves exert is rather small. The conclusion appears to follow that the manipulation of interest rates cannot be a significant route to control effective demand (as is assumed in the *IS/LM* construction), or a policy instrument very relevant to the scale of unemployment that we in fact experience.

In recent decades the emphasis of economic discussion has shifted from a concern with the determination of interest rates as such to an analysis of the behaviour of the economy as a whole. The models of the economy devised for this purpose have built, with additions and refinements, on the *IS/LM* construction, and the general role played by interest rates within the model has been taken from that. Such models have been used to analyse for instance the responses of the economy to fiscal and monetary policy (e.g. Modigliani 1945; Mundell 1958; Fleming 1962; Dornbusch 1976; or more recently Tobin 1981). We discuss some aspects further in considering the determination of exchange rates in Chapter 5.

The debate on loanable funds versus liquidity preference

There has been a long-running dispute about whether it is stocks of assets or rates of change in the stocks (flows) that are relevant for the determination of the rate of interest; and it may finally be useful to indicate how our account relates to that issue.

The classical view of interest rates (as Keynes's summary of it, quoted earlier, indicates) was framed in terms of saving and investment, i.e. changes in stocks of wealth or capital. The rate of interest was seen as being determined by the supply of loanable funds made available by saving, and the demand for these for purposes of investment. Keynes's own analysis, on the other hand, had liquidity preference determining the public's choice as between holding a stock of money or a stock of interest-bearing financial assets, and to be consistent ought to have envisaged the relation between the yield on the stock of financial assets and on the stock of real assets as part-determinant of the stock of capital. One can perhaps then say that in principle his analysis was in terms of stocks of assets. The debate has been whether the loanable funds (the flow view) and the liquidity preference (the stock view) are equivalent, and if not which is correct (for instance Tsiang 1956, 1966; Kohn 1981).

Our own analysis is in terms of stocks. Analysis in these terms, however, tends to be stated in terms of long-term equilibrium; and that appears of questionable relevance to our emphasis on the short term.

On a neo-classical view, the level of interest rates in long-term equilibrium depends on the attitude of lenders and borrowers to the maintenance, depletion or extension of the capital stock. A reduced desire to hold claims on capital — to illustrate the argument — will raise interest rates. That in turn will reduce the capital stock, to the point where the return on capital is brought into equality with the rate of interest. (The return on a lower capital stock with the same stock of labour will be higher that it would be on a higher capital stock.) In the adjustment period, lower saving thus produces lower investment. An argument on these lines assumes that (despite lower saving in the interim) in the long term there are forces that ensure full employment.

Our analysis implies that in the short term any such adjustment process will fail to operate, for two reasons. First, we have argued that a change in the balance between *ex ante* saving and investment — in stock terms, but reflected in flows — will in most situations change the level of employment, not interest rates. This might not be true of a fall in the desire to save if the economy were already at full employment; but even here we have suggested that the effects of the resulting condition of excess demand might get 'suppressed'. We went on to argue that, under these conditions, fundamental forces relating to the productivity of capital and the desire to hold wealth fail to impinge on market interest rates, and do no more than set limits to their short-term fluctuations. A large and persistent change in the fundamentals could, in conditions of full employment, alter what market opinion saw as the limit to interest rate fluctuations. But the above two reasons in combination make actual effects on market interest rates doubly unlikely in most situations.

This appears to make neo-classical equilibrium considerations irrelevant to analysis of the short term — and if it is irrelevant in the short term, it is difficult to see how it could apply over a longer time horizon.

These questions have implications for the effects of fiscal policy, which we will discuss in Chapter 6. A change in the public-sector deficit (whatever its initial size) is analytically equivalent to a change in the community's propensity to save. On the neo-classical argument, that would in the long term affect interest rates; but this argument we have questioned. It is for these reasons — to take a particular application — that we do not see the growth in the deficit on the US federal budget in the mid-1980s (which in relation to GDP has been of only moderate size) as an explanation of the high level of interest rates in the United States, or in the world generally.

The central tradition in economic analysis is built on the idea of equilibrium, and is grounded on the presumption that market forces produce a movement towards an equilibrium and that the factors determining that equilibrium can, at least in principle, be clearly stated. Our argument — that the level of interest rates is within a range indeterminate in terms of fundamental factors, and within that range is tied down only by conventions that are historically determined, or by the exogenous action of the authorities — may appear to run counter to that tradition. Our qualification of a simple equilibrium analysis reflected an attempt to allow for the prevalence of uncertainty. Uncertainty appears to result in many situations where agents are driven, as second- or third-best, to follow rules of thumb. If that is correct, there is a need to find room within economic theory to analyse the circumstances in which conventions come to rule and the forces that help to keep conventions, once established, in place. Given the observed erratic behaviour of interest rates, it is not clear that there is room for a tidier explanation of their behaviour.

3. THE BEHAVIOUR OF INTEREST RATES SINCE 1971

We have tried to give an explanation that finds room both for the volatility of interest rates and for influence of the kind in fact exerted by the authorities; our aim has not gone beyond that point. To go further and offer explanations for the major fluctuations in interest rates that have occurred must clearly be hazardous and speculative. Even so, it may be useful to indicate the kind of explanations to which we ourselves are attracted, and which are at least consistent with our analysis. The main points to explain are why interest rates were for a time (1974–6) very low, and why more recently (after 1981) they have been so high.

In the late 1960s, bank base rates in the United Kingdom were consistently above the rate of inflation (by a margin of something like 2 percentage points). Accelerating inflation in the years 1972 and 1973 saw base rates rise more or less in line, keeping roughly level with inflation (see Fig. 11.8 below). Then, as inflation accelerated in the years 1974–6 (and again in 1977), base rates stayed well below the pace of inflation (by 5–10 percentage points, or at times even more). That does not mean that real interest rates were then negative, i.e. that nominal rates were below the expected rate of inflation. The inflation rate was above 12 per cent a year for a sustained period — for a time, indeed, above 20 per cent; but that was unprecedented in peacetime. A possible explanation is that continued inflation at these rates was not fully expected, and that (at this stage) it took several years for inflationary expectations to adjust. There is however the question of whose expectations it is that are crucial. We have given a pivotal role to banks' ideas of the norm for the base rates. We might better describe what happened by saying that banks were slow to adjust this conventional norm.

When inflation again accelerated in 1979 and 1980 (peaking briefly at 20 per cent), base rates rose much more nearly in line. Inflation then fell off steadily, getting down to under 5 per cent. But bank base rates, after 1981, stayed well above the rate of inflation (by a margin averaging 4 or 5 percentage points). Part of the reason why interest rates have been so high may be the action of the authorities: they, too, have got used to raising central-bank rate to levels earlier unthinkable, and they have varied it more greatly and more often than before. But even when the authorities were not putting pressure on the banks (and when, on the argument of Section 2, base rates ought to have gone down to what the banks regarded as a conventional norm), the gap between base rates and inflation remained large (3 or 4 percentage points, and at times more). We suggest the same sort of explanation, in reverse, as in the former case that inflation expectations did not immediately come down as inflation fell, so that the ideas of the market (and in particular the banks) about the 'normal' rate of interest remained high.

Explanation on these lines still leaves the question of why conventions should, even gradually, adjust to a change in the rate of inflation. If inflation accelerates and interest rates do not initially change, that will reduce the real cost of borrowing relative to the return on investment. We have argued that that kind of discrepancy, if relatively small, has no quick effect on the demand for loanable funds, and hence puts no significant upward pressure on interest rates. But changes in the rates of inflation in this period were considerable. It may perhaps be supposed that they were sufficiently large and persistent to make it seem probable that, without a change in nominal rates, the demand for funds would rise, and thus were large enough to cause a change in interest rate expectation. Perhaps, therefore, this experience tells us something both about where the bounds to the 'range of indeterminates' lie, and about the gradual nature of the reaction if these bounds are approached. The corollary may be that it will take several more years for markets to adjust to inflation rates of 5 per cent or less.

This chapter has considered what determines interest rates as a preliminary to considering interest rates as an instrument of policy. Chapter 5 will examine their effect on the exchange rate; and Chapter 8 their use as a means of controlling the pace of monetary growth. The questions discussed in this chapter are clearly as relevant to a monetary policy couched not in terms of the monetary aggregates, but in terms of interest rate objectives; and this will be discussed in Chapter 13.

5

The Behaviour of Exchange Rates

This chapter has two objects, and attempts to span two rather different areas of interest. Each has a necessary place in this study, though each is a step aside from its central line of argument.

First, the behaviour of the financial system was discussed in Chapters 2–4 in terms of a closed economy: one purpose here is to remedy this deficiency, and show how far, when external influences are taken into account, the previous analysis has to be modified. The way that external influences impinge on the domestic financial system depends, however, on the kind of exchange rate policy that the authorities pursue. This means that consideration of them is best left until exchange rate policy has been discussed, and accordingly comes at the end of the chapter.

The second purpose of this chapter, and more of a digression from the main line of argument, is to define the scope for official influence over exchange rates. To the extent that monetary policy is aimed at influencing the exchange rate, this would restrict its use for domestic purposes — and whether that would be desirable will be considered at the end of the study in Chapter 13. This chapter lays the basis for that later discussion, and covers a range of issues both as to how exchange rates are determined in general, and how far they can be influenced by exchange rate policy, of which interest rate policy is one constituent.

We are concerned especially with the short-term behaviour of exchange rates. Exchange rates under the floating-rate regime, which has been in force for most of the period covered by this study, have not adjusted smoothly, as had been hoped, so as to maintain balance-of-payments equilibrium. The theoretical literature is best at describing the equilibrium position of exchange rates. Its explanatory power does not extend to providing a detailed quantitative explanation of the erratic exchange rate behaviour that occurs in practice; and quantitative attempts to explain exchange rate movements, though extensive, have, like attempts to explain other financial asset prices, been singularly unsuccessful (see Hacche and Townend 1981). Empirical models turn out to be unstable when applied outside the data over which they were estimated; inside them, only a small proportion of the variation in the exchange rate is explained by the explanatory variables, even when these are statistically significant. On even the most favourable interpretation, then, most of the movement in exchange rates has proved to be inexplicable.

The starting point of the following discussion is to explain how it is that such erratic movements can occur, and what this implies for the theory of exchange rate behaviour. It will be argued that the long-term requirements of balance-of-payments equilibrium set limits to short-run exchange rate fluctuations, but that inside these limits exchange rates are 'indeterminate' and free to reflect expectational factors. This parallels the argument in Chapter 3 that interest rates in the short term are indeterminate in a similar sense. The general conclusion of this study is that the stock of broad money must in large part be regarded as endogenously determined. This entails an important departure (further discussed in Section 1) from much of the theoretical literature on exchange rates. The fact that many short-term interest rates are administered rates also has consequences for exchange rate behaviour not allowed for in the standard discussion.

The chapter has four parts. The determinants of exchange rates in the short run are discussed in Section 1. Section 2 analyses the scope for official action to influence exchange rates by means of interest rate policy and official intervention on exchange markets. Experience since the general adoption in 1973 of floating rates between major currencies is reviewed in Section 3 in order to provide a concrete illustration of the limits to the authorities' power over exchange rates. Some points are set out very briefly in Sections 1 and 2 so as not to break the thread of the argument; in Section 4 some of this ground has to be gone over in greater detail in order to answer the question of how far the description of financial markets in earlier chapters has to be modified to take account of external influences.

1. THE GENERAL DETERMINANTS OF EXCHANGE RATES

When floating rates between major currencies were adopted in 1973, many economists were in favour of that course and expected exchange rate adjustments to be smooth and moderate. This had been true of the Canadian dollar when it was floating in the 1950s, and was predicted by the theories then prevalent of exchange rate behaviour (in particular Mundell 1958; Fleming 1962). In fact, exchange rates have shown both great short-term volatility and large major swings lasting for periods of years (see further Section 3).

Before discussing the scope for exchange rate policy, we need to consider why exchange rates have been so volatile. In this section we consider the determinants of exchange rates in the absence of an active exchange rate policy, and we start with some of the elements that must figure in any account of exchange rate behaviour.

In the absence of official intervention, capital flows, period by period, must match any deficit or surplus in the current account. If the *ex ante* flows are deficient (or excessive) at the initial exchange rate, the excess supply of (demand for) the currency will cause the exchange rate to fall (or rise). At some point, provided that interest rates and future expected exchange rates remain unchanged, operators will think it profitable to buy or sell sterling in expectation of an exchange rate gain, restoring balance in the exchanges at a lower (or higher) exchange rate.

Because exchange rates fluctuate, inter-currency financial transactions involve exchange risk. In general, although such a preference may be overridden by other considerations, borrowers prefer to borrow, and lenders to lend, in terms of their own currency. The finance of a current account imbalance thus involves either borrowers or lenders accepting an exchange risk, which they will undertake only in expectation of a compensating gain (or premium). Over a run of years, therefore, it will most likely be difficult to sustain a continuous inflow or outflow of capital (or a flow of more than a certain size) into or out of the currency of a country in persistent deficit or surplus on current account. Exchange risk may nevertheless be willingly accepted if investment abroad appears sufficiently profitable (see Section 4). If that is the case fairly continuously, one may speak of a 'structural' inflow or outflow of capital, and may regard the current balance plus or minus the structural flow as the 'basic' balance. For the sake of exposition, we assume below that this is the case.

In the short term, imbalance in the basic balance is likely to change exchange rates; over a somewhat longer period, the latter are in turn, by affecting competitivity, likely to make the basic balance adjust. Over an extended period, then, there is reason to expect that the 'basic' balance will come close to balance. It is possible to envisage, perhaps, that exchange markets might be capable of foreseeing the results of this process of adjustment. If the determinants of the basic balance were stable or were changed only in a predictable fashion, and if operators in such markets had a correct view of them and also acted predominantly on long-term views, then exchange rate movements would keep the basic balance of payments in equilibrium (or, if fluctuating, on average in equilibrium), and exchange rate behaviour would be smooth and orderly.

Older theories of the exchange rate explained exchange rate behaviour in terms of factors affecting the current balance or, by extension, the basic balance. This was probably appropriate under the pre-1914 gold standard, and perhaps in the interwar period, but in recent decades it has become less adequate as the international mobility of capital has increased. This has made it necessary to see exchange rate behaviour as determined by operators' willingness to hold existing stocks of assets denominated in different currencies — an approach that has been the basis of more recent work on exchange rates since the mid-1970s. It would be out of place to try to give here a review of the course of the theoretical discussion (conveniently reviewed for instance in Williamson 1983), but it is useful to examine the kind of explanations for exchange rate volatility to be derived from it.

Exchange rates clearly continue to be affected by changes in factors affecting the current (or basic) balance, such as the rate of inflation or of productivity growth in one country as compared with others, or the discovery of new resources capable of profitable development (North Sea oil). If completely and confidently foreseen, such changes would not produce changes in the exchange rate. Unexpected developments, on the other hand, cause a reassessment of the level of the exchange rate that will keep a country's balance of payments in sustainable shape. There may also be reassessments of a country's future policy on matters likely to affect its current account, or assessments of the probable realizable value of investments abroad or in foreign currencies.

It is in the nature of a speculative market that the current level of prices reflects the evaluation of market operators, within some theoretical framework (often merely implicit) of what each knows of the likely future course of events affecting that market. Fluctuations in exchange rates can thus, in a sense, be explained in terms of the arrival of items of news, and the market's evaluation of news. Since either factor is difficult to measure quantitatively, such an explanation is somewhat empty; econometric analysis has been (and may continue to be) unable to explain the timing and extent of changes in exchange rates. From one angle, it is possible to regard exchange markets (like domestic capital markets) as highly perfect, in that they react sensitively to news. But in relation to the role that exchange markets play in the economy, their performance could nevertheless still be regarded as unsatisfactory. Changes in exchange rates provide signals that initiate adjustments in the rest of the economy, and if exchange rate changes are large and erratic, such adjustments will not be smoothly made. To the extent that such erratic behaviour is avoidable — a question to be considered in Sections 2 and 3 — this is an important failure.

It is a reasonable starting point for analysis to assume that there is in principle an exchange rate path which, if established now, would produce a sustainable balance-of-payments position in the period ahead. For exchange rates to be fairly stable, exchange rate expectations need to be based on a good assessment of what that equilibrium path is. Such an assessment however is difficult, both for economists and for market operators, for it needs to forecast developments stretching a long way ahead. Thus, adjustments to exports and imports in response to changes in exchange rates require decisions about where to sell output already available (decisions that can be acted upon quickly), or about the scale of output of exportable goods or import substitutes (decisions that may take months to implement), or about investment to produce such goods (decisions that may take years to implement). Moreover, the more important decisions will not be undertaken in response to apparently transitory phenomena, but only if a change in exchange rates has been maintained for some time and seems likely to last. When exchange rates are volatile, lasting changes will take time to be detected. Adjustment to exchange rate changes may also take a long time to carry out, at least in cases where major changes in the capital stock are involved. It must therefore take many years before adjustment to any considerable change in the exchange rate is complete.

Assessment of the exchange rate required to produce balance-of-payments equilibrium in the long term is inevitably subject to several sorts of uncertainty.

- The equilibrium payments position is not necessarily a balance on current account, but a current account that will match sustained capital flows. The size of the latter depends on the desire of foreigners to increase (or run down) their holdings of financial assets denominated in terms of the country's currency or of real assets in the country, and on the similar desire of residents to add to (or run down) their holdings of foreign currency or assets abroad. This is difficult to forecast many years ahead, particularly if the present payments position is abnormally good or bad.
- The current account balance may be affected by factors other than exchange rates, e.g. developments in technology or resource discoveries, both in the country concerned and in competitor countries.
- The current account will be affected by changes not in the nominal but in the real exchange rate. The rate of inflation may change as a result of changes in the exchange rate, or for other reasons, to an extent difficult to foresee.
- The extent to which exports and imports respond to changes in the real exchange rate is itself (as just indicated) difficult to estimate.

These uncertainties are so great that market participants can scarcely have a well determined expectation of the future exchange rate, in the way required for speculators to absorb any shocks that fall upon the external account. Expectations about future exchange rates are weakly held. A very large risk premium must surely be required to induce anyone to assume exchange risks on a long-term (i.e. quasi-irreversible) basis. Thus, shifts in the 'fundamentals' affecting the relative supplies of assets in different currencies, or the returns on them, can be neither accurately assessed, nor expected to result in a rapid, predictable, adjustment of spot exchange rates.

Nevertheless, some decisions involving exchange risk are constantly made that are intended to be long-term. Financial institutions hold investments in foreign securities on a fairly continuous basis, and firms acquire plants operating in other countries — such decisions being indeed different only in degree from investment in capacity to produce goods largely for export. These decisions must be based on a hunch or a hope about exchange rates many years ahead, and presumably will be undertaken if the investment is likely to show very substantial profit apart from exchange rate considerations. Investment decisions of this sort will affect the relative current demand for different currencies, and their influence must put some brake on extreme sustained fluctuations in exchange rates (except, perhaps, in cases of extreme inflation or political turmoil).

In most circumstances, however, foreign exchange markets (like security markets) are not dominated by operators who themselves take long-term views about exchange rates. The timing of sales and purchases is influenced by shorter-term expectations about exchange rates, and hence in effect by expectations as to what other operators will expect (as in Keynes's beauty contest). The exchange rate must then simply be where it is expected to be (a bootstrap phenomenon), and if operators expect exchange rates to change in the future as they have in the recent past, such expectations will for a time (until the bubble bursts) be self-fulfilling. There is little doubt that the latter mechanism is important, though since it is erratic and inherently unstable its importance is difficult to demonstrate. Some tests of the mechanisms have been attempted; but these are difficult to make because they require as a standard of comparison an account of what would happen without the bubble mechanism, for which there is no satisfactory basis. (For discussion at the theoretical level see Flood and Garber 1982, Blanchard and Watson 1982, and Farmer 1984; for empirical studies see Okina 1985, and Wadhwani 1984.)

Nevertheless, exchange rates do respond to news that bears on the long-run equilibrium, and the reaction can be rationalized only by supposing that operators are sensitive in some degree to where they suppose the long-run equilibrium to be. For instance, exchange rates react to changes in the rate of inflation, or to discoveries of oil reserves, even though these will not affect the current account, and thus the availability of different currencies on exchange markets, for many years to come. It seems reasonable, then, to suppose that very high or very low levels of the exchange rate will appear unlikely to be maintained. This, together with the possibly more stable views of those, discussed earlier, who have to take decisions involving a long-term view of exchange rates, must impose limits to the fluctuations of exchange rates.

Exchange rates of major currencies have moved 10 or 20 per cent in a single year, and more over consecutive pairs of years (see Fig. 5.1 and the discussion in Section 3 below). The long-run equilibrium position of a country's exchange rate cannot be estimated with any precision, for reasons already indicated. That means that no one can surely say, in any particular case, whether the peaks or troughs were nearer to it. But it seems unlikely, as a rule, that the equilibrium point will change violently in the course of a year or so — or, if it does, that it will shortly afterwards change back equally violently. Thus, it seems reasonable to believe that the limits set to possible fluctuations of exchange rates by fundamental long-run forces are indicated by the range of some actual fluctuations, and are rather wide, e.g. 10 or 20 per cent on either side of a hypothetical equilibrium point.

This view of exchange markets has important consequences for the possibility of official action on the exchange rate. If fundamental long-term forces rigidly determined exchange rates, monetary authorities could influence exchange rates only by massive purchases or sales of foreign currencies. (It will be argued in the following section that officially determined changes in relative interest rates provide a relatively weak means of influence.) But if it is true, as here argued, that exchange rates within a range are indeterminate in these terms, then relatively small official actions will be capable of having a large influence on exchange rates; for, since exchange rate expectations are weakly held and markets have no good basis for forming them, markets appear ready to follow a clear lead from the authorities. The use of intervention and interest rates as instruments to affect exchange rates will be examined in detail in the next section. But if effective, their influence will come chiefly through affecting exchange rate expectations. By the same token, the power of governments to influence exchange rates must be seen as circumscribed, for such expectational effects are to be obtained only so long as official exchange rate aims appear to markets to be credible.

Our divergence from Dornbusch-type models

Our account of the effects of policy on exchange rates will depart in some respects from the major strand of thinking, which stems from Dornbusch (1976) and from the extension of his model by Buiter and Miller (1981a). This is essentially because we assume that the stock of money is endogenously determined. Dornbusch-type models, by contrast, assume that the money 'supply' is exogenous and is what the authorities decide, and that the domestic price level is determined by the money 'supply'. If the future money 'supply' were known (a large assumption), that would provide an 'anchor' to the price level at the terminal date when equilibrium is attained — at which point it is assumed that there is full employment and payments balance. In equilibrium, the nominal exchange rate is determined by purchasing power parity; the real exchange rate is assumed to depend (in a predictable way) on real factors. Thus, operators in foreign exchange markets can predict, from their knowledge of monetary policy at home and abroad, the likely price level at home and abroad at some future 'terminal' date at which equilibrium can be expected to rule — and thus can predict the future nominal exchange rate. Early 'monetary' models of the exchange rate made only these assumptions (Frankel and Johnson, 1976), but after some early success (see articles in the *Scandinavian Journal of Economics*, 1976, vol. 2) they failed to capture the later volatility of exchange rates.

In this kind of model, the future expected nominal rate is one element in determining today's exchange rate, but interest rates also matter. The expected exchange rate change in each future period has to be offset by an expected interest rate differential in that period. (For agents to be willing holders of both currencies, expected capital gains have to be exactly offset by expected running losses of interest.) The spot exchange rate thus also depends on actual and expected future interest rates. In the model, these depend in a complex way on the interplay between the exogenous money 'supply' and the demand for money. The demand depends on interest rates and on nominal incomes, with the latter determined by wages (a function of unemployment and past prices), import prices, and activity (a function of incomes, real balances, and competitiveness).

The result of a model constructed on these lines is that the fundamentals of balance-of-payments equilibrium (in a predictable though complex fashion) bear on the spot exchange rate. For example, a tightening of monetary policy — interpreted as a credible commitment to lower future monetary growth — raises the expected future nominal exchange rate at the terminal date — and thus today's spot rate. Since nominal wages are initially unaffected, a higher level of interest rates will be required to reconcile a lower rate of monetary growth with initially unchanged nominal incomes, which will raise the spot exchange rate further. A process of adjustment follows; the high real exchange rate reduces domestic output and, by raising unemployment, reduces the growth of wages, allowing interest rates to fall. In this process, the real exchange rate falls along with inflation until the new growth equilibrium is reached.

'Overshooting' of some such sort appears a feature of much recent experience, and is preserved in our account, which however pictures a less mechanical and less closely knit process. Given our position as to the endogeneity of the stock of money, we have no comparable 'anchor' to expectations about the future price level at some future terminal date. Thus, even if changes in the real exchange rate can be regarded as predictable, we see expectations about the future nominal exchange rate as especially diffuse. In the short run, we see interest rates as determined directly by the authorities. Interest rate expectations and exchange rate expectations, however, remain as important as they are in the Dornbusch model. A tightening of policy may act both to raise the expected future exchange rate and to raise actual and expected future interest rates; if so, there will be overshooting. But such effects are, in our account, far from mechanical; they are rooted in market participants' expectations, which (for reasons set out more fully in Section 4) are intrinsically volatile.

2. POLICY EFFECTS ON EXCHANGE RATES

It was argued in the previous section that exchange rate expectations, being weakly held, may be influenced by the monetary authorities. The authorities, however, are unlikely to exert a lasting effect on expectations unless they undertake a credible commitment to the use of interest rates or exchange market intervention. This section will examine the direct effects of these instruments, and for this purpose will ignore for most of the way the indirect effects, powerful though they may be, obtained through influencing expectations. These, however, remain in the background. The analysis is primarily in terms of floating rates, with fixed rates as a possible state to be achieved by use of these instruments.

We will first consider the effects on the exchange rate of a rise in domestic interest rates, and then consider the additional effects of official intervention on the exchange markets. The manner in which the authorities influence domestic interest rates has already been indicated in Chapters 3 and 4 and will be examined in greater detail in Chapter 8. For reasons there given, the authorities' control over domestic interest rates is itself not unlimited. Strictly speaking, exchange rates will be affected by a change in interest rates only if that change is unexpected. But this subtlety gets one into difficulties. If official action on interest rates had been fully expected by markets, interest rates would already have changed. In fact, such action is never fully expected; even when half-expected, action that confirms it will remove a doubt, and thus will be a new element that affects both domestic interest rates and the exchange rate. These qualifications being borne in mind, we will therefore talk simply in terms of changes in interest rates.

For similar reasons, we will assume that, before the rise in interest rates, the exchange rate is expected to remain unchanged. Now consider the effect of a rise in central-bank rate, which raises domestic interest rates in general so that they are now higher than in other centres. This will raise the spot exchange rate and create an expectation that it will subsequently fall — and will raise it to the point where the expected fall in the rate over the period for which the interest differential is expected to remain compensates for the expected interest differential. (Complications to this simple statement are considered in Section 4.)

Markets have thus to guess for how long interest rates in this country will remain high relative to those abroad, and the effect on the exchange rate will depend on how long they expect this period to be. Suppose that short-term interest rates are raised by 4 percentage points, and that markets are certain that the differential thus created relative to interest rates abroad will remain for three months (one quarter of a year) and will then fall back to its original level. If one ignores questions of exchange risk, one can then suppose that the exchange rate will rise immediately by 1 per cent (one quarter of 4 per cent), and will be expected to fall uniformly over the following three months. If the interest differential were firmly expected to remain for ever (and assuming the risk premium unchanged), one must suppose that the immediate rise in the exchange rate would be infinite. In practice, markets are highly uncertain about the course of the exchange rate, and are equally uncertain about the future course of interest differentials; for the policy of the authorities in this country and the future course of interest rates abroad are both highly uncertain. These uncertainties must greatly diminish the effect of an interest differential on the exchange rate, and, since interest expectations will shift, the effect of a rise in interest rates is likely to be erratic.

Some of these uncertainties are removed if the authorities accompany the use of interest rates with an announced policy to intervene on exchange markets to keep the rate within a certain range. If the policy is fully credible, this will eliminate the likelihood of exchange loss, and must in some sense increase the 'pull' of a given interest rate differential although, since the effect will now be on the reserves rather than on the exchange rate, the effects are difficult to compare).

A policy of intervention accompanied by the use of interest rates is, similarly, likely to be more effective than one without it; for, if the underlying situation is one of payments deficit, intervention alone would result in a loss of reserves — which could be sustained only for a period. Higher interest rates may then prevent the loss of reserves or at least may increase the period during which intervention can be sustained, and thus increase the credibility of the policy. In these ways, the use of interest rates together with intervention will increase the effectiveness of each instrument as compared with its use singly and without the support of the other.

Limitation to the effectiveness of policy steps

The assistance that the use of interest rates can provide to intervention policy is, however, essentially limited. Assume, for simplicity, that the underlying situation is one of payments balance, and suppose that there is then a move to a higher level of interest rates. The main effect will be to produce a *finite* increase in reserves. The increase in the interest differential in favour of sterling will make it more attractive to hold financial assets denominated in sterling, and will induce a reallocation world-wide of the currency composition of the existing stock of financial debts and assets. But even with a declared policy of holding the exchange rate, exchange risk will remain. In response to the interest rate advantage, asset-holders will therefore be averse to increasing their exposure to the risk of holding sterling beyond a certain point. Holders world-wide of foreign currency assets or sterling debt will therefore find it worthwhile to move only a certain way into sterling assets, or out of sterling debt. In practice, this portfolio shift will not be instantaneous but will take some time. But it is essentially a stock adjustment: once made, the main flow will cease. (It is true that the world stock of financial assets grows over time, and that a larger portion of the growth will be diverted in favour of sterling by the changed pattern of interest rates; but additions to the stock are small relative to the existing stock, and may for present purposes be ignored.) If — to vary the assumptions — there is a continuing payments deficit, a step move to a higher level of interest rates will prevent the loss of reserves only for a time.

The finite nature of the response to any given interest differential is thus a major limitation to the use of interest rate policy. To provoke a continuing portfolio shift would require a progressive rise in domestic interest rates. But (for reasons set out in Chapter 3) the authorities are not able to force up interest rates indefinitely, for their power to raise them depends on their ability to influence market expectations about interest rates, and that is limited. At some point — even if the authorities were able to keep interest rates high — the credibility in domestic markets of their interest rate policy, and thus also the credibility in exchange markets of the use of interest rate policy to support exchange rate policy, would start to erode.

There are limits also to the possible scale of official intervention on exchange markets. Intervention to support the rate is limited not only by the initial size of the foreign exchange reserves, but also by limits to how much the authorities can borrow. Extremely large borrowing will raise questions of sovereign risk, i.e. doubts as to the political will of the borrowing country to continue servicing and to repay debt, and beyond a point additional borrowing will become impossible on any terms. Short of that point, there is an increasing exchange risk: the borrowing government will borrow either in terms of its own currency, on increasingly unfavourable terms, or in foreign currency, and then assume an increasingly onerous risk itself. The limits on intervention in the reverse direction to keep down the rate are less narrow. But there must be a point where the acquisition of foreign currency would similarly present the authorities of the country acquiring it with an unacceptably large exchange risk, and that must put some limit on how much intervention they will be willing to undertake.

It is sometimes also argued that the domestic financial corollaries of intervening to hold the exchange rate against upward pressure further limit the feasibility of an exchange rate policy. This argument, though it has had some official support in the United Kingdom, seems largely invalid. During the course of 1977 — in the aftermath of the exchange rate crisis of 1976, discussed in Chapter 7 — the exchange rate was so held, and the reserves grew largely. But at the end of the year the policy of 'capping' the rate was discontinued, on the grounds that it was undermining control of broad money. We later question the possibility and desirability of such control. But even accepting that aim, this argument against an active exchange rate policy appears less than absolute.

Official intervention in the exchange markets provides foreigners with sterling which they may be presumed to wish to hold partly in fixed-interest sterling assets and partly in variable-rate assets such as bank deposits. The authorities have to make additional borrowing in sterling to finance the acquisition of the foreign exchange they have bought; and it would be a possible and reasonable aim for them to seek to provide foreigners with the sorts of assets they want, in proportions that would meet their preferences and produce no change in the yield curve, for the authorities are in a position either to issue fixed-interest debt or to provide additional bank deposits by themselves borrowing from the banks. To the extent that such a policy involved additional borrowing from the banks, it would have meant a partial 'non-sterilization' of the domestic monetary effects of the gain in reserves. Bank deposits held by non-residents were not, however, included in £M3, the target variable. It is true that some residents, too, would switch from foreign currency into sterling, and might wish to hold part as bank deposits — which, if accommodated, would have raised £M3. That could have been offset by greater debt sales, although at the cost of higher long interest rates. The difficulties foreseen by the authorities thus stemmed essentially from a rigid adherence to a broad money target combined with an unwillingness to accept the interest rate implications of achieving it.

So far, constraints on policy have been discussed in terms of the limits to the use of interest rates and intervention. But the important constraint on exchange rate policy is more intangible. The ability of the authorities to control the exchange rate comes mainly from their power to influence exchange rate expectations. Policy action has a direct effect, but also an indirect one, since the market takes a message from it about likely future action. The scale of this indirect effect depends on the reputation of the authorities and the credibility of their policy, and these are essentially fragile. Reputation and credibility take time to establish, and can be lost overnight.

Where do the limits lie? As argued in Section 1, long-run factors (relating to the current balance and the 'structural' capital flow) impose general limits to how far floating exchange rates can fluctuate. The same factors put limits to the authorities' power over exchange rate expectations. Although operators in exchange markets are not able to form clear and definite views as to the way that long-run forces will work out over a period of years, they have views of a less clear-cut sort; and these set limits to the credibility of exchange rate policy. A level of the exchange rate too far from the vague centre of market opinion will cease to appear sustainable, and at some point, the increasing precariousness of attempts to maintain it will become evident to markets and will constitute a strong and proximate market factor.

3. POSTWAR EXPERIENCE WITH EXCHANGE RATES

In previous sections we have argued that the authorities have considerable power to influence exchange rates, and we have indicated in general terms some of the limits to their influence. It may now be useful to look briefly at postwar experience with exchange rates, in order to get a clearer idea of where the limits lie, and of the difficulties that would arise in any return to managed exchange rates. Since the general adoption by major countries of floating rates in March 1973, which marked the demise of the Bretton Woods system, it has been a common view that anything approaching a fixed-rate regime is no longer a possibility. But opinion is shifting. The following discussion suggests that, though experience with floating rates underlines the limitations to official influence over exchange rates, it does not rule out the possibility of a policy of cautious management.

The first questions are how serious were the difficulties encountered in operating the Bretton Woods system, and why the system was abandoned. Neither in intention nor in practice was it a regime of absolutely fixed rates. Provision was made for adjustments in official rates when required to correct a 'fundamental disequilibrium'. Although member countries were expected to defend their rate against downward pressure by restrictive monetary and fiscal policies, they were not required to do so to the point where this created serious unemployment. If policies to defend the official rate promised this result, that was an indication that depreciation was required. The crucial difficulties were in respect of the exchange rates between major currencies. Adjustments to exchange rates tended to be made too late, and consequently had to be relatively large — though not larger than have subsequently occurred over short periods with floating rates. In periods when it became clear to markets that an adjustment of rates was inevitable, fixed rates prompted large changes in reserves, for holding the parity in these circumstances appeared to promise speculators the option of a safe one-way bet. Efforts to defend an old rate, or establish a new one, therefore, frequently assumed the dimensions of a political crisis.

The persistence of different rates of inflation as between one country and another was the most common cause of payments difficulties which eventually necessitated exchange rate adjustments. Governments tended to be reluctant to admit the necessity of adjusting exchange rates; with fixed rates being seen as a defence against inflation, it became almost a moral presumption that adjustments should be resisted. Since the 1970s, current account imbalances (whether arising from differential rates of inflation or in other ways) have continued to occur, but under the floating-rate regime (and perhaps because of it), shifts in asset preferences affecting the capital account have become more important as a source of pressure on exchange rates. Nevertheless, differential rates of inflation remain a potential source of imbalance; and one lesson to be learned from the failure of Bretton Woods is that tardy acceptance of the inevitability of correction means that corrections, when eventually made, have to be unnecessarily large and disruptive.

There were other reasons, some general and one specific, for the over-rigid way in which the Bretton Woods system was operated. First, exchange rate changes, since they affect other countries, had to be approved by the International Monetary Fund, and in principle required prior informal discussion between major governments. This took time, and hardly seemed worthwhile for small changes.

Second, a change in a fixed rate, unlike changes in floating rates, is an overt decision by the government. Many groups are affected by it, some favourably and some unfavourably, so that change in either direction is likely to be politically unpopular one way or another. Thus, a depreciation usually followed a period of trying to avoid it and appeared a demonstration of failure. The British devaluation of 1967 was resisted for three years because the government (given that a Labour government had acceded to the 1949 devaluation) was loath to incur the stigma of Labour 'devaluing the currency' a second time. Other countries resisted appreciation because that would hurt exporting industries which are usually a powerful lobby.

Third was the difficulty of changing the exchange rate of the US dollar. Exchange rates under the Bretton Woods system, nominally declared in terms of gold, were in effect pegged to the US dollar, and other countries' reserves were held largely in dollars. The dollar thus was central to the system, and for long appeared impossible to revalue. The growing weakness of the US balance of payments in the 1960s undermined confidence in the dollar, and made other countries increasingly reluctant to continue to add dollars to their reserves. The rigidity of the dollar exchange rate was therefore the worst rigidity in the system. Most adjustments in official rates had been downwards, tending to raise the effective rate of the dollar. To devalue the dollar itself required a multilateral negotiation, eventually achieved in the Smithsonian agreement of December 1971. The process was inevitably protracted and public, and was inevitably a compromise: it gave the United States less than it felt it needed, but left other countries also dissatisfied.

The United Kingdom contracted out six months later by opting to float, originally as a temporary measure. That course was adopted because the depreciation that was expected to follow (and did) would not then appear to be a decision of the government, as a formal devaluation would have been. The subsequent decision by other major countries to adopt floating rates, in March 1973, in effect doubled the depreciation of the dollar (and the appreciation of the Deutschemark and the yen) that had been agreed under the Smithsonian agreement. Since then, the exchange rates of industrialized countries have been more or less freely floating. (This does not apply to the cross-rates of members of the European Monetary System (EMS) exchange rate mechanism, or before that of the Snake; but it has remained true of their exchange rates *vis-à-vis* non-members.)

One general influence in the conversion of governments to floating rates was the fervour of academic argumentation in its favour, which acquired almost the force of a lobby. Premised on an optimistic view of exchange markets, these arguments offered the hope that market forces, given their head, would smoothly produce the adjustments that governments had so long failed to achieve — a hope that subsequent experience had not seen fulfilled. Other considerations were the practical difficulties, in a world that had got far from equilibrium, of re-establishing by negotiation a viable pattern of rates, and, in its absence, of operating a system of fixed rates in a world of increasing capital mobility. This difficulty in the way of a return to managed rates may, at least in part, remain.

The internationalization of financial markets

Since the early 1970s, international markets in bonds and short-term financial assets have grown very rapidly. (The growth of direct investment has been retarded both by economic nationalism and by the increased currency risks resulting from the volatility of exchange rates.) The foreign currency lending of London banks, which was only $2.3 billion twenty years ago and $90–100 billion in 1974, stood at end-1985 at about $500 billion — larger than the United Kingdom's GDP. According to the statistics of the Bank of International Settlements (BIS), banks in the BIS reporting area (Western Europe, Japan, Canada, and the United States) had international loans amounting to $1,800 billion (almost as much as a quarter of OECD GDP). Most was interbank business: non-bank customers' borrowing was little over $300 billion, much of it in dollars by the richer non-oil developing countries.

Though international bank lending had started to grow rapidly before then, its growth was stimulated by the escalation of oil prices in 1973/4 and 1979/80. These gave the OPEC countries larger revenues than they could quickly spend — or, indeed, have even now spent completely. For many years they ran large current account surpluses, and initially chose to hold the resulting balances as bank deposits, largely denominated in dollars. Given this behaviour by OPEC countries, it was inevitable that the current balances of other countries should be less favourable, and, for lack of any other mechanism, current balances were financed largely by bank loans.

Residents of industrial countries also have increased their holdings of bank deposits and other financial assets denominated in foreign currencies. Although statistics are lacking, these must have increased considerably in real terms since the early 1970s. By the 1980s UK residents held a fifth of their financial wealth externally — as foreign currency deposits with UK banks, as deposits with foreign banks, or as foreign portfolio assets. Foreigners' holdings of sterling financial assets are of comparable size.

There is thus a very large volume of liquid funds able to move quickly between currencies. There are, too, channels other than direct purchase or sale of liquid financial assets: agents can postpone or accelerate the payment of commercial debts, borrow one currency to purchase another, and transact in forward and futures markets. Managers of the very large volumes of funds now held in various liquid forms world-wide stand ready to switch them between instruments and currencies in response to small variations in interest differentials or in exchange rate expectations. What is at least as important as the larger holdings of liquid funds is the spirit in which they are managed. The fact that exchange rates have been volatile means that managers' responses have had to become quicker. This in turn has increased the volatility of exchange rates against which managers are seeking to protect themselves or from which they are seeking to profit.

Fluctuations in exchange rates since 1973

Since 1973, exchange rates have not only shown great short-term volatility, but have also exhibited large swings over periods of one or two years. Although it is possible to hedge against short-term exchange risk, this by no means eliminates risk completely. How far this short-term volatility has impeded trade is not clear. (There is some evidence that it has not done so in the case of the United Kingdom: see *Bank of England Quarterly Bulletin* (henceforth *BEQB*) 1984, 346–9). Longer-term swings in exchange rates, however, clearly have important effects. They act powerfully to brake or accelerate inflation in the countries concerned, and significantly alter the distribution of world demand between industrial nations. By increasing the risk in producing goods that incorporate imported materials or are for sale abroad, they may well have significantly reduced investment to produce such goods, and thus may be having serious long-term effects on the extent of trade.

The major medium-term swings in exchange rates are illustrated in Fig. 5.1, which shows indices of real effective exchange rates. Since relative prices generally change only slowly, large movements in real rates mostly reflect swings in nominal rates. What we are interested in is changes in competitiveness, which are probably best measured by changes in unit labour costs in one country as compared with changes in unit labour costs in a weighted average of its main competitors, and it is indices of relative labour costs that are shown in the figure. (Indices of relative export prices might be thought to be a more direct measure of what is wanted. But export prices tend to be shaded down if for instance competitiveness has weakened, and the resulting loss of profits (not shown in such a measure) will also in the longer term discourage exports. Broader measures sometimes used, such as relative retail prices, also seem inappropriate.) Different methods of calculation produce significantly different estimates of real effective rises at any one point of time and, over time, divergent though rather similar movements (see for instance alternative estimates in Williamson 1985). Given the imperfect nature of the measures, the summary below is in broad terms; even so, it is clear that the swings in real exchange rates have been very large.

The swings since 1973 have been particularly great in the case of the United States, Japan, and the United Kingdom. After several smaller fluctuations, the real effective rate of the United States rose at least 50 per cent — perhaps even doubled — between 1979 and the early months of 1986. By the end of the following year, most of that rise had been reversed. The Japanese rate rose by at least a fifth, and perhaps by as much as a third, from the end of 1976 to the autumn of 1978; this rise was then much more than reversed in the next eighteen months. The UK's real effective rate rose 50–60 per cent from the middle of 1978 to early 1981, then fell progressively, reversing (say) half of that rise up to early 1985, and then rebounded. The swings in Germany's real effective rate, although still considerable, have been on a somewhat smaller scale.

These fluctuations were not predicted, and the explanations proferred

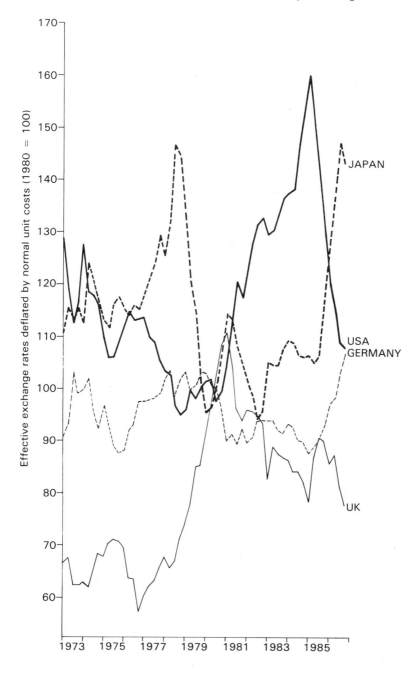

FIG. 5.1 *Real effective exchange rates for four major countries, deflated by unit labour costs, 1973–1986*

after the event remain matters of opinion. One explanation offered for the rise in the UK exchange rate after 1978 is the election in 1979 of a Conservative government pledged to a strict monetary policy. It has been ascribed also to the rise in the world price of oil, coupled with the growing output of North Sea oil which made the United Kingdom self-sufficient in oil by 1981. (Large estimates of the latters' effect on sterling were published by Forsyth and Kay in 1980.) Since then, the exchange rate has tended to fluctuate with the price of oil — more widely, indeed, than can easily be explained on these grounds, perhaps reflecting the fact that such a connection was widely believed.

What now is the sustainable pattern of rates?

With a more managed exchange rate regime, private-sector behaviour could be expected to change. Even without promise or any clear expectation of an active policy, markets have on occasion paid considerable attention to what they infer is the official attitude to the exchange rate. The potential mobility of international capital is not in itself a fatal obstacle to attempts at management; if the policy of the authorities appeared credible to markets, private capital flows would powerfully support official intervention. But after a long period when markets have been left without official guidance, the credibility of an official policy of managing the rate would be weak until there had been a period of successful management. Even when credibility had been established, the power of the authorities over exchange rates would not be unlimited. Moreover, the consequences of ill-judged attempts at management are likely to be more rapidly apparent, since the stock of potentially mobile capital is larger and quicker to move. After the long period of floating, recent experience provides no guide to where the limits to the power of the authorities lie. There are three reasons to be cautious.

In the first place, fundamental forces limit what official policy could achieve (in the same way that they impose broad limits on the fluctuations of floating rates). The long-term equilibrium level of the exchange rate depends in large part on forces bearing on the current account, and (as already emphasized) these are difficult to predict.

In the second place, the equilibrium rate is not simply the rate that in due course would produce a zero current balance, but rather, the rate that would produce a surplus or deficit that will be financed by sustained private capital flows. Even if it can be supposed that the size of the 'structural' capital flow is relatively constant, it is particularly difficult in present circumstances to gauge how large it will be. Since 1982, for instance, the growing US current account deficit has been financed by an equally massive capital inflow. No one can be sure how far that will continue; if it proved permanent, it would have to be accepted as the equilibrium pattern of the US balance of payments.

Third, capital flows may now be inherently less stable than previously (which would imply that there is now little meaning in the idea of a 'structural' flow). The medium-term swings in major exchange rates have reflected swings in investors' asset preferences. These could in some way be a product of the floating-rate regime, and would be likely to be much moderated if control over exchange rates were reasserted — indeed, if this were not so, a managed regime would probably prove impossible. But swings in asset preferences on some scale are likely to continue. There could therefore be a major question for policy as to how far such swings should be resisted, or alternatively accepted.

Section 2 presented general arguments for believing that the authorities have considerable power to influence exchange rates, but that the power is not unlimited, and the limits to it are shadowy and difficult to determine. This section emphasizes the latter conclusion. The present time, after a long period when rates have been left to unguided market forces, is not a good time to form a view as to what is possible. This suggests that a renewed attempt at exchange rate management should be unambitious and flexible. Rather than aiming at the maintenance of fixed rates, the appropriate aim might be the more modest one of preventing large erratic fluctuations and as far as possible keeping rates adjusting smoothly to what fundamental forces require (see further Chapter 13).

There seem two other conclusions. The first is that the authorities cannot use interest rates to put the exchange rate where they like (as commonly assumed in much neo-Keynesian discussion of macro-economic policy). Used on their own, the effects of interest rates on the exchange rate are likely to be erratic; and even when used in conjunction with intervention, their power is limited. Second, given the fragility of the authorities' control over it, the exchange rate can hardly serve as a firm 'anchor' against inflation — a hope that underlies a great deal of theoretical and political discussion (a question to be discussed further in Chapters 12 and 13).

4. EXTERNAL INFLUENCES ON THE DOMESTIC FINANCIAL SYSTEM

We must now come back to the question raised at the start of this chapter, namely, how the account given in earlier chapters of the behaviour of the financial system needs to be modified to take account of influences from abroad. We will first consider how far the account of interest rates in Chapters 3 and 4 stands in need of modification, and will then look at the way influences from abroad affect the process of money creation as analysed in Chapter 2. The conclusion will be that, despite the increasing internationalization of financial markets, the simplified account given earlier remains essentially intact.

It will be argued that the importance of external factors depends entirely on the nature of official exchange rate policy. In a fixed exchange rate regime, interest rates in a non-dominant country such as the United Kingdom must follow interest rates abroad; at the other extreme of completely free-floating, interest rates abroad would have no influence on domestic rates. In order to establish these propositions, this section recapitulates and amplifies the argument of previous sections from a somewhat different point of view. For simplicity, we will consider only private transactions. This is less arbitrary than might appear, for government transactions consist either of intervention (which has been discussed earlier), or transactions which are very like commercial transactions.

Before examining relations between areas with separate currencies, it is useful to consider relations between the different regions of a single country with a single currency, that being the extreme case of a fixed exchange rate regime. The private sector of what for the moment we assume is a closed economy is made up of individuals and firms, any one of which may spend more than its income provided it is able to borrow, or sell new or existing financial assets to other agents. As argued in Chapter 2, each agent's access to finance in any period is limited by the risk felt by the lender that the borrower may not be able to repay, or that the borrower's debt will be unattractive to other lenders. Each agent's financial deficit is therefore subject to some limit, with consequences for his expenditure.

Within any region, there will be some agents in financial deficit (i.e. agents who spend on consumption or investment in excess of their income) and others in financial surplus. The region as a whole may thus be in financial deficit or surplus, but the financing of regional deficits gives rise to no problem additional to that of financing the deficits of the individuals who compose the region. For, in the first place, the size of the deficit for the region is constrained by the credit rationing arising from lenders' risk to which individual agents within it are subject; and in the second place, within a single currency area, the credit extended and debts incurred are denominated in the common currency, so that there are no complications arising from currency preferences.

Since there is no exchange risk, interest rates on similar financial instruments will be the same throughout the country; if there are influences raising (or lowering) rates in one region, they will raise (or lower) interest rates throughout the country. One such influence is the policy of the central bank. It has been argued in Chapter 4 that the central bank's rate both determines the lending and deposit rates of the banks and, by influencing interest rate expectations, influences also the flexible, market-determined interest rates, most strongly in the case of short-term rates and less strongly for long rates.

Contrast now what happens with separate currency areas. There is now the possibility of borrowing and lending in foreign currency (whether in marketable form or via banks) or by direct physical investment across borders. Agents are not indifferent as to the currency composition of their assets and liabilities: even in a supposedly fixed-rate regime, there is a risk that the exchange rate may change. Other things equal, borrowers and lenders will prefer that their debt and their assets be denominated (like their income and planned future spending) in their own currency. If there is a current surplus or deficit, it has to be financed by the (net) import or export of financial assets; other things equal, some agents at home and abroad will have to be persuaded to accept extra exchange risk; i.e., they will hold the other currency only if they earn more interest on it than on their own, or expect its exchange value to rise.

There is however a variety of considerations other than interest differentials or exchange rate expectations which make agents willingly incur exchange risks, and which the above argument implicitly assumes are unchanged. Thus they undertake direct investment abroad because of its expected profitability, or hold some foreign currency assets for reasons of trading convenience if they trade abroad, or hold a foreign currency because political risks make it appear a safer vehicle in which to hold funds. Holding of foreign currency assets is frequently reciprocal: investors in pairs of countries have each built up large holdings of such assets in the other country, so that stocks have been built up by exchange of assets between holders, rather than as a result of current deficits. The dismantling of barriers to international diversification has allowed the stock of foreign assets to grow rapidly as a result of this process in recent years, as the facts cited in Section 3 make clear, and stocks are now not all closely related to the cumulation of past current account imbalances. Since they are often large in relation to any likely flow from that cause, fluctuations in the attitudes of those who hold such stocks will predominate in exchange markets. Such attitudes are likely to vary (and changes in attitudes seem more likely to complicate than facilitate the financing of current imbalances).

Even aside from such fluctuations, the risk premium is unlikely to be a stable magnitude. Thus, if a country experiences an increase in its current account deficit, this is likely to generate an excess supply of assets denominated in its currency, and an (expected) positive premium is likely to be required in order that the assets should be willingly held. A surplus is similarly likely to generate an excess demand for such assets, and thus the need for a negative premium on holding assets in its currency. A continued deficit (or surplus) will add cumulatively to the excess supply (or demand), and since increasing exposure is increasingly onerous, the size of the premium is likely to be a function of the cumulative current account imbalance. The required premium will also rise because continued imbalance is likely to increase the market's assessment of exchange risk. Both the sign and the size of the risk premium are thus likely to vary with circumstances. (Since changes in exchange rates are essentially unexpected, the size of the *ex ante* premium cannot be deduced from observation of *ex post* data. Because the premium is unobservable and cannot be taken to be a constant, explanations of the short-run behaviour of exchange rates in terms of relative interest rates and exchange rate expectations are impossible to test econometrically at all directly; see Hacche and Townend 1981.)

Even though differentiated by exchange risk, assets denominated in different currencies remain partial substitutes. This does not necessarily entail that interest rates on similar assets denominated in different currencies must move in parallel, for the exchange rate may change. A rise in interest rates abroad must (in the absence of change in the risk premium) have one of two effects, or a combination of the two: either a rise in domestic interest rates, or a rise in the expected appreciation of the domestic currency over the horizon for which the higher rates abroad are expected to persist. Which form the adjustment will take may be clear only in extreme (and thus largely theoretical) cases. Thus, if a large rise in interest rates abroad was firmly expected to be permanent, it would be bound to lead to a rise in domestic interest rates, since the alternative adjustment by exchange rates would require an expectation of continuous, eventually infinite, appreciation. In fact, interest rate expectations never are firm. Nor would an exchange rate adjustment so large as to take the rate beyond what in Section 1 was denoted as the range of indeterminacy be credible — partly because interest differentials sufficiently large to produce it are themselves hardly feasible.

Under normal circumstances, it would seem that the form of response to a rise in interest rates abroad depends primarily on what kind of exchange rate policy the authorities are following. At one extreme, if the authorities were truly indifferent to the movement of the exchange rate, and directed interest rate policy purely on domestic considerations, domestic interest rates would be insulated from fluctuations in interest rates abroad. The latter would cause fluctuations in the exchange rate: these the authorities would accept, and leave interest rates unchanged, and that reaction would be expected. For a year or two after 1979, policy in the United Kingdom came close to such a posture of indifference. After that there was a half-way state. Policy stopped short of specific exchange rate aims, but the exchange rate became a more important consideration in determining interest rate policy, and changes in central-bank rate were occasioned largely but not exclusively by the behaviour of the exchange rate (Chapter 7). Since the market was aware of this, interest rate expectations were determined by how the authorities were expected to respond to movements in interest rates abroad or to movements in the exchange rate, and flexible interest rates often moved in advance of changes in central-bank rate (Chapter 8, Section 3). Nevertheless, there was room for doubt as to the authorities' probable response. That would be much reduced if the authorities declared clear targets for the exchange rate (i.e. a range within which they would seek to hold it); dependence on interest rates abroad would then be further strengthened.

The extreme case would be where there was near-certainty that the exchange rate would remain fixed. Exchange risk would then become negligible, assests denominated in any of the currencies within the fixed-rate area would become more or less perfect substitutes, and one pattern of interest rates would rule throughout the area. There would then hardly be room for more than one central bank with effective control of interest rates. The possibility of a central bank having some control over interest rates within its currency area depends on the existence of exchange risk, which acts as a partial barrier to the pull of interest rates elsewhere; central banks other than the dominant one would lose control over their domestic interest rates. The situation would in fact approximate to the single-country case which we started out discussing. For many years after the republic of Ireland became independent, the Irish pound continued in that relation to sterling. Such a relation once broken is difficult to reconstitute, and members of the EMS, for instance, might need years of unbroken exchange rate stability to establish it.

The process of money creation in an open economy

Chapter 2 described the process of money creation in a closed economy, and we must now consider how far that account needs to be amended to allow for the openness of the economy. In the closed world of Chapter 2 it could be assumed that all bank lending and bank deposits were in sterling; that, assuming banks' lending criteria remained unchanged, the stock of bank lending and bank deposits grew with UK GDP; and that, if banks relaxed their lending criteria, this initiated a multiplier expansion of UK GDP.

We may relax the assumptions of a closed economy in two stages, and consider first the case where there is cross-border trade but all transactions remain in sterling. This is the case of a single region within a national currency area. Given extensive interregional trade, variations in activity within separate regions are likely to be correlated, though not perfectly. Assuming banks' lending criteria remained unchanged, the borrowing of individual agents within the region would be related to their income, so that bank lending to them (we may assume) would be related to regional GDP. Agents' interregional trading would, however, make it convenient for them to some extent to borrow from and hold deposits with banks located outside the region, and for agents outside the region to borrow from and hold deposits with banks operating within the region. Lending by banks in the region to agents within the region, therefore, would not necessarily be equal to bank deposits placed with them by agents residing in the region. Banks in the region might take more (or fewer) deposits from outside then they lent inside; and banks outside the region might make larger (or smaller) loans to agents in it than they took deposits from them. (Net discrepancies — bank borrowing less increase in deposits — might be one way in which a regional current account imbalance of payments got financed.) The effect on expenditure of a relaxation of lending criteria by banks operating within the region would in part spill over into other regions, such leakages reducing the multiplier effect within the region.

Much of this continues to apply to a single country trading in a multi-currency world. The fact that some agents trade across national borders would, as before, make it convenient for them to borrow in part from banks abroad, and for non-residents to borrow in part from UK banks. But considerations relating to the risks of lending make banks prefer to lend to customers they know, and customers to borrow from banks they know, so that in this case cross-border lending to any but the largest firms and organizations is likely to be only marginal. The same considerations of convenience would lead residents to borrow in part, and hold deposits in part, in foreign currency (whether with UK banks or banks abroad), and for non-residents to borrow in part, and hold deposits in part, in sterling. But prudential considerations (self-imposed or enforced) forbid significant exposure by banks to exchange risks; foreign currency loans therefore match foreign currency deposits, and sterling loans match sterling deposits.

To fit this kind of world, the analysis of Chapter 2 must now be taken to apply to total lending by banks (at home or abroad, in domestic or foreign currency) to residents; and, if banks' lending criteria remain unchanged, this, it may be assumed, will grow with national GDP. If residents' cross-border or cross-currency bank borrowing and holding of deposits became more important than it now is, it might in principle be appropriate to place prime emphasis on the presentation of monetary statistics on these two aggregates — residents' total bank borrowing and total bank deposits — rather than on £M3, which consists of residents' sterling deposits with UK banks. (In Chapter 11, though we take £M3 to represent broad money, we give most attention to the asset side of banks' balance sheets, and in doing so look at UK banks' lending to residents in both sterling and foreign currency.)

Despite the increasing importance of international trade, and the growing internationalization of capital markets, the qualifications required at the present stage of development to allow for external influences thus appear surprisingly small. Geographical propinquity for the most part still makes banks and their customers deal locally, the process of monetary growth in different national currency areas appears to remain largely separate and self-contained, and the amendments required in the definition of the monetary aggregates to take account of cross-border banking appear, as yet, marginal.

The ability of national monetary authorities to control interest rates within their own national currency areas stands (as we have indicated) to be more profoundly affected. Except for 'dominant' currency areas, central banks are able to influence interest rates in their area (it was argued above) only while exchange risk remains considerable, and their power to do so would necessarily diminish the more successfully exchange rate flexibility was limited. We would not, however, see that as entailing, in these circumstances, a diminution of national authorities' power to control the rate of monetary growth; for we do not in any case (for reasons indicated in earlier chapters and discussed further in Chapter 8) regard the manipulation of interest rates as an effective method of monetary control.

6

Government Transactions, Money, and Interest Rates

Chapters 2–4 discussed the behaviour of the financial system in terms of its response to the private sector of a closed economy. Chapter 5 extended the analysis to take account of transactions with other countries. The aim of this chapter is to take account of the impact of public-sector transactions on the financial system.

The wider question of the impact of public-sector financing on activity and prices has been the subject of extensive discussion. We are concerned with these issues only indirectly. But the narrower question of the financial impact of government operations cannot be discussed without reference to them; and in Section 1 we review some main issues in that debate. Section 2 then turns to consider the impact of government operations on the stock of money and on interest rates. That will involve the same methods of analysis developed in Chapters 2 and 3 — without however requiring major revision of previous conclusions. Since the points can most easily be made in terms of a closed economy, we simplify the argument by ignoring the complexities of relations with other countries. In Section 3 we relate our conclusions more particularly to the policy debate in the United Kingdom. The most important question here is whether the scale of public borrowing of itself affects the rate of monetary growth, and thus whether a curtailment of public borrowing is, as recent government policy has assumed, a means of monetary control.

1. THE GENERAL IMPACT OF PUBLIC-SECTOR DEBT AND DEFICITS

In 1948 Lerner could declare, in the conclusion to his discussion of the burden of national debt,

We see then that the kinds of evil most popularly ascribed to national debt are wholly imaginary . . . and that the direct application of the basic principles of Functional Finance are an adequate general guide to fiscal policy. If the short-run equilibrium is taken care of so that there is . . . neither inflation or depression, and a normal amount of reasonableness is applied in choosing between the different ways of achieving this short-run equilibrium, the long-run equilibrium of the size of the national debt will look after itself. (Lerner 1948, 275).

This simple approach has been subject to attack from various directions. Much of the discussion relates to long-term equilibrium, assumes full employment, and in some cases rests on extreme assumptions about the expectations of economic agents. Our concern is for its relevance to the determination of the money stock and for interest rates in the short run. For that purpose we confine ourselves to stating our own provisional stand on issues in a debate that will no doubt continue to expand, and indicate briefly our reasons. References will be selective: fuller references are in (for instance) Buiter (1985).

There have been three main lines of attack on the Keynesian proposition that action that raises the public-sector deficit increases total demand.

- It is argued, first, that an increase in government spending (or a decrease in tax rates) 'crowds out' private spending, so that the 'direct' effect of a government deficit is offset at least partially.
- A second argument is that a public-sector demand stimulus can be only temporary, and must later be reversed. A government deficit increases public debt and the future level of interest payments on the debt; this process, it is argued, cannot continue indefinitely since there is a limit to the possible scale of debt. On a long view, it is therefore argued that an increase in government spending or decrease in taxation now (which increases total demand now) entails a decrease in spending or increase in taxation later (which will decrease total demand then).
- A third argument is that private agents are aware of these intertemporal implications, and adjust their current behaviour in consequence. If tax rates are reduced, taxpayers save more to pay for higher taxes later, so that the initial reduction of taxes does not increase total spending in the first place. Thus a government deficit has no effect on total demand.

We will consider these arguments in turn, taking first the crowding-out argument. If there are constraints on the expansion of real output, the expansionary effect of fiscal policy is prevented ('physical crowding out'). So much is common ground.

The argument for 'financial crowding out' is frequently couched in terms of the static *IS/LM* model. If the stock of money is fixed, a fiscal stimulus that raises output will increase the demand for money. On the assumption of an unchanged stock of money, that will raise the rate of interest on financial assets, and so (it is argued) reduce private investment. Since this argument achieved prominence (for example Spencer and Yohe 1970, quoted as representative by Blinder and Solow 1974), there has been much argument about the size of the monetary effects accompanying fiscal action, and whether they offset partially or completely the effects of a fiscal stimulus, or possibly even reverse it.

In a sense, however, this discussion would appear to have been unnecessary. The monetary counter-effects, as is clear, depend entirely on the assumption that the money stock is fixed. Even if the authorities could ensure this (which we question), it would surely be perverse; for they would be deliberately offsetting with their monetary left hand what they aimed at with their fiscal right hand. As Buiter (1977) and Currie (1981) suggest, it is more appropriate to regard such crowding out not as a necessary part of an expansive fiscal policy, but as due rather to an inappropriate choice of monetary policy. To quote Currie, 'if fiscal and monetary policy work suitably in tandem, this form of crowding out need not occur'.

The assumption of a non-accommodating monetary policy could be justified on the argument that the use of monetary policy was predicated to the control of prices, and that non-accommodation was needed to counter inflation. We later query this proposition (partly on the grounds that the authorities' power is insufficient, and that the assumption of a non-accommodating policy is thus unrealistic).

A different starting point for the crowding-out argument is the notion that there is a fixed pool of saving or finance; if the government takes more, there is less for others:

Fiscal policy provides additional spending in a world of sparse spending opportunities. But it does not provide a new source of finance in a world where spending is constrained by sources of finance. The government expenditures are financed in debt markets in competition with private expenditures. The case least favourable to fiscal policy is that in which the additional government borrowing simply crowds out of the market an equal (or conceivably even greater) volume of borrowing that would have financed private expenditures. (Culbertson 1968, quoted in Meyer 1980).

The fallacy lies in supposing that there is a fixed 'pool of finance'. If allowance is made for the effects of a debt-financed fiscal stimulus on financial stocks, it can be shown (as in Chapter 2, Section 3) that, in the course of the expansion of activity in response to the stimulus, additional saving will arise which will result in additions to the stock of financial assets which the private sector desires to hold. Moreover, the effects on interest rates that can be deduced from analysis of this process depend on what assets are included in the model. If it includes only one non-monetary asset (representing both government bonds and privately issued debt or equities), the deduction is that interest rates must rise. If bonds and equities are both included, the deduction is that it is the bond rate in particular that must rise: the cost of finance of private investment may not, and 'crowding out' may be zero. (We develop this argument in Section 2 below.)

The second line of attack on the proposition that public borrowing increases total demand is that it can do so only temporarily. This starts from the consideration that the size of the public debt cannot be allowed to rise indefinitely as a result of continued deficits: beyond a point, the credit of the government would be damaged and the cost of borrowing would rise, and at some further point additional borrowing would become impossible at any rate of interest. It can then be argued that in the long run there is a ceiling to the size of the debt, so that any additions to the stock of public-sector debt can be only temporary. From this it would seem to follow that in long-term perspective 'a decision to borrow should be seen not as a way of reducing taxation (or increasing spending) for ever, but as a way of postponing taxation (or bringing forward spending)' (Britton 1983, following a line of argument going back at least to Domar 1944). A version of this view assumes that there is a fixed ceiling to the ratio of debt interest to the tax base, taken to grow with national income. On the further assumption that the rate of interest equals the rate of growth of national income, it follows that no increase in the debt/income ratio is feasible.

This argument draws attention to important considerations, but it cannot be applied literally to interpretation of the short term. It could hardly be true, for instance, that the debt/income ratio could never be permanently raised above its *present* level; for in this country the ratio is now less than a quarter of its peak in 1947 (or its peak after the Napoleonic wars: see Fig. 6.1 below).

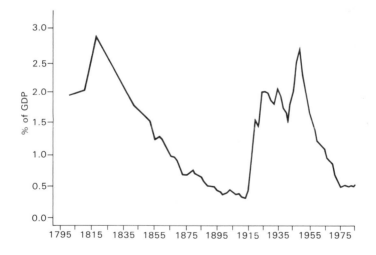

FIG. 6.1 *National debt as a proportion of GDP, 1801–1985*
Source: Reproduced by permission from Buiter (1985), who gives detailed sources.

To believe that some increase in debt is possible is not to deny that too large or too rapid an increase could damage the government's credit standing. Creditworthiness however is complex. For a government to have good credit standing, not only must everyone believe that it will continue to pay interest on debt and repay particular debt instruments on maturity, but also, everyone must believe that others will continue to have such confidence. If the latter condition fails, the market value of debt instruments will fall and interest rates on new debt will rise. In most countries the danger of debt repudiation may seem too remote to count as a market factor, but there must always be a possibility that this second-degree confidence will erode, and it is difficult to predict at what point that might occur. Confidence, moreover, may be eroded not simply by the scale on which a government borrows, but by its poor performance in general — e.g. by inept handling of exchange rate or other matters, by events such as a crop failure or inflationary trend that disturbs financial markets, or even by the hostility of important groups and an insecure political base. These multitudinous uncertainties are plainly difficult to incorporate in a formal analysis.

Our account (in Section 2 below) of the effect of public-sector operations on the financial system is intended to be an account of what happens in 'normal' times, and it assumes that public borrowing is not undertaken on such a scale as seriously to damage the government's credit standing. (We try to allow for the possibility that, even within these confines, there may be times when the government temporarily finds it difficult to raise new debt, or to do so on terms that would not appear likely to damage its future credit standing.)

The third attack on the proposition that public deficits increase total demand is that restated by Barro (1974), reviving an argument that goes back to (though was not endorsed by) Ricardo. This starts from the argument that a reduction of taxation (or an increase in government spending) must later be matched by an increase of taxation (or a reduction of spending); but it adds the argument that economic agents will foresee this inevitability, will perceive no change in their permanent income, and thus will make no change in their current spending. It further assumes that agents are perfectly 'altruistic', and treat as equivalent to their own welfare that of their heirs — and (their heirs also being held to be altruistic) by implication the welfare of the heirs of their heirs. Thus, even though the subsequent increase in taxation may be deferred until after the death of taxpayers now alive, debt-financed expenditure is shown to be equivalent to tax-financed expenditure, and government borrowing to be innocuous.

Arguments and evidence against this thesis are given by Buiter and Tobin (1979), Tobin (1980), and Buiter (1985). For us, three points seem compelling. First, people must in practice doubt whether public debt will be repaid (it often has not been) and even more doubt when. Second, it seems clear that people typically are not altruistic in the sense required (perhaps particularly nowadays — since, with economic growth, they can normally expect their children to be better off than they themselves have been). The possibility of higher taxation at a much later date thus counts for little. Third, governments change, and political parties have very different social priorities, so that what taxes any individual will have to pay in future is in any case very uncertain. Even if a taxpayer expected public borrowing later to lead to higher taxes, and even if that would affect his actions if he knew that he (or his heirs) would have to pay them, he would be highly uncertain whether the future tax increase would bear on him (or them) individually. This question is not relevant to much of the argument in Section 2. In what follows we assume that debt-financed public expenditure affects the level of activity (although much of the argument of Section 2 stands without this assumption).

We have already discussed in Chapter 4 (Section 2) the neo-classical argument that public-sector saving or dissaving will affect the long-term equilibrium size of the capital stock, and thus the equilibrium level of interest rates; and we need not further discuss that question here.

2. THE EFFECT OF PUBLIC-SECTOR TRANSACTIONS ON THE FINANCIAL SYSTEM

Government decisions on expenditure or on rates of tax may result in a deficit (or surplus) entailing extension (repayment) of public-sector debt. It is convenient to regard government financial decisions as made up of two components:

- a decision about what size of deficit (or surplus) to plan for;
- a decision as to the form of debt to increase (or retire).

Following a common convention (Tobin 1963a, Blinder and Solow 1974), the former may be called the *fiscal policy* component and the latter, the *debt-management* component.

If a deficit or surplus is planned for, decisions have also to be made on what kind of debt is to be increased or decreased; but the two sorts of decisions are conceptually separate. Thus, even if there is no deficit or surplus, so that total debt is unchanged, the composition of the debt may still be varied. Debt-management decisions relate to the composition not just of increases or reductions in public debt, but of the whole stock. (Tobin, who attaches more importance — see below — to debt management than we do, alternatively calls debt-management policy 'monetary policy'. We confine the term 'monetary policy' to the use of central-bank rate and various instruments of direct control.)

In this chapter we are not directly concerned with the impact of fiscal policy on the level of total output and expenditure (already discussed in Section 1) but with the effects of fiscal policy and debt management on the stock of money and interest rates. We discuss these financial effects in two stages, corresponding to the distinction just drawn. We first discuss the effect of changes in the *composition* of public-sector debt, assuming its total is unchanged. We then go on to discuss the financial impact of public-sector financial deficits or surpluses (and of changes in deficits or surpluses), i.e. increases (decreases) in total debt (or changes in the rate of increase or decrease). The first question (concerning the composition of public debt) can best be discussed on the assumptions that the total stock of financial assets and the level of income is · unchanged. These assumptions cannot be retained in discussing fiscal policy decisions since (we assume) these themselves may produce changes in income, asset accumulation, and the stock of assets. The process is thus more complex and for this reason is discussed second.

The central government in this country handles most of the financing required both by itself and by local government and publicly owned enterprises. The bulk of public-sector borrowing is done by the central government; and it is the composition of central government debt that is most directly within the control of the monetary authorities. Central government borrowing in any period is equal to the financial deficit of the central government (its expenditure less its revenue), plus lending to other sectors (or less borrowing from them),* plus compensation for any enterprises nationalized (less the value of any denationalized). If there were no lending to other sectors and no asset sales of purchases, the outstanding stock of central government debt would be the cumulation of past central government deficits.

Given a rising trend in national income, there is usually each year an increase in the notes and coin in circulation. This has provided part of the central government's financial needs, and should be included as part of its borrowing along with the issue of what are more usually thought of as debt instruments and included in what is called the 'national debt'. In this country the value of the national debt in real terms (and as proportion of GDP — see Fig. 6.1) has since the 1950s been heavily eroded by inflation. Perhaps about a tenth of it is held by foreigners. National debt held domestically, together with notes and coin in circulation, amounted in the mid-1980s to something under half the value of annual national output (Table 6.1).

---

* This includes public-sector lending or borrowing from abroad. Other large items under this head are exchange market intervention, public-sector mortgage lending, and in some recent years the lending to the private sector which (Chapter 10, Section 2) must accompany 'overfunding' by the public sector.

TABLE 6.1. The composition of central government debt: private domestic holdings, end-March 1983[a]

	Non-banks	Banks	Total	
	(£b)	(£b)	(£b)	(% of GDP)
Notes and coin[b]	11.1	0.8	11.9	(4.7)
Banks' deposits at Bank of England[b]	—	0.6	0.6	(0.2)
National debt[c]	94.0	6.6	100.6	(41.8)
Total	105.1	8.0	113.1	(44.7)
of which:				
Debt corresponding to money[d]			19.1	(7.6)
Non-marketable debt held by non-banks			20.8	(8.2)
Marketable debt held by non-banks			73.2	(28.9)

[a] Figures for national debt are at issue prices. At this date these were fairly close to market value, and thus with rough accuracy can be combined with figures for notes and coin and the banking figures.

[b] At 16 March 1983.

[c] At end-March 1983.

[d] Banks' holdings of central government debt (£8.0 b) plus notes and coins held by non-banks (£11.1 b).

Deficits can be financed in various ways. In the United Kingdom these include sales to the non-bank public of interest-bearing assets, either in marketable form or as non-marketable instruments such as National Savings; borrowing from (or sales of financial assets to) the banks; and on a small scale by issues of notes and coin to the public and the banks. Table 6.1 illustrates the recent composition of UK national debt (the year 1983 is taken for convenience). Since bank lending is matched by deposits from the public, public sector borrowing from the banks and notes and coin are grouped together in the table as 'debt corresponding to money', constituting one fifth of domestically held public-sector debt.

The effects of changes in the composition of public debt

One way in which the composition of government debt may be varied is by changing the maturity of marketable debt held by non-banks (two-thirds of the total: Table 6.1). Another possibility is to vary the composition of the debt as between debt that corresponds to money and other types of debt. The latter consists not only of marketable debt, but also of non-marketable National Savings instruments — which, it may be noted, are fairly close substitutes for bank deposits. Any kind of compositional change will have effects on the relative interest rates borne by different debt instruments, which we discuss further below. The second sort of compositional change — a shift between debt corresponding to money and other debt — has (it will be argued) effects on the money stock.

Notes and coin are issued to the public on demand, and since demand is barely if at all sensitive to interest rates (Trundle 1982b), the authorities have no means of influencing the stock held. The authorities are able to alter bankers' balances at the central bank (Chapter 8). But these are too small to matter in the context of debt management, and, since they constitute banks' reserves, they cannot be varied merely as a minor part of debt management.

The authorities can vary how much they borrow from the banks. In the static situation now being considered, the government could buy back some of its debt now held by non-banks (or sell more debt to them) and to offset this sell more Treasury bills to the banks (or place fewer with them). What effect does this have on the monetary aggregates?

Discussion in Chapter 2 of the determinants of bank lending was entirely in terms of lending to the private sector. The impossibility of making a precise assessment of the risks incurred in such lending (it was argued) impelled banks to impose limitations on the scale on which they lend to a private customer. The same risks do not arise in lending to (or acquiring the liabilities of) the government. In normal circumstances, banks do not regard such lending as becoming increasingly risky as the scale of such lending increases. This means that what banks lend to the public sector is in addition to, not in substitution for, what they lend to the private sector, and in the first instance at least will produce an equivalent increase in the money stock. (It is true that banks for prudential reasons need to maintain minimum capital/deposit ratios, and if they had great difficulty in obtaining new capital this might limit their total lending. That might make lending to the government an alternative to lending to the private sector. In practice, however, this requirement appears not to have imposed much brake on the growth of bank lending.)

As with lending to the private sector, an increase in bank lending to the public sector will have a sequence of further effects of the sort already analysed in Chapter 2. Assuming that the banking system was initially in some sort of equilibrium, the additional deposits created would be greater than the public would wish to hold at the existing pattern of interest rates; and it would accordingly attempt to move out of deposits into alternative assets. By so doing it would bid up the price of those assets and reduce their yield relative to that on bank deposits, to the point where the extra deposits would be willingly held. As in the case of additional lending to the private sector, this would create an incentive to private borrowers from the banks to issue securities and fund bank loans — thus tending to reverse the initial increase in the money stock. But, as in Chapter 2, there would be many hindrances to this corrective process, which would therefore be slow and incomplete. The conclusion is thus that bank lending to the public sector in the first instance increases the money stock on an equivalent scale, just as does bank lending to the private sector; and that, although (again as in that case) there will later be some offset, this is likely to take a considerable time to appear, and even in the longer term may not be considerable.

It is for these reasons that government borrowing from the banks is treated in this study as making an independent contribution — along with private-sector borrowing from the banks — to the growth of money, and variation in such borrowing is treated as a potential method of monetary control. There are, however, practical limitations (Chapter 8, Section 2) to how far the stock of broad money can be reduced by reducing public-sector borrowing from the banks — limits largely set by how large public-sector borrowing from the banks is in the first place. Since the stock of public debt held by the non-bank public is large, the limits to an increase in public-sector borrowing from the banks are less narrow.

Changes in the composition of debt entail changes in relative interest rates on the sorts of debt where interest rates are flexible. Consider first the effects of a switch from short to long marketable debt. It may be assumed (on general portfolio grounds, as for instance in Tobin 1969) that the public has preferences, at any existing structure of relative interest rates, as to the quantity of short and long debt it wishes to hold, and that it is willing to hold more long debt and less short only if the yield curve shifts in favour of long debt.

In Chapter 2 we suggested that the banks' administered rate acts as a pivot to the general structure of interest rates. This view implies that a change in the maturity composition of public debt is likely to involve not only a shift in relative interest rates, but also a change in the general level of rates. Banks' base rates are administered rates and relatively inflexible in the short term. They will change if central-bank rate changes; and for the rest are determined (so it is argued in Chapter 2) by conventional ideas of what banks' base rates normally are. Since short-term marketable public-debt instruments are closer substitutes for bank deposits/bank loans than are long-term instruments, rates on them are more closely tied to the banks' rates than are long rates. A shift in the composition of public debt from short to long debt is thus likely to raise long rates without significantly reducing short rates, implying a rise in the average; and a switch in the composition of public debt from borrowing from the banks to long marketable debt will similarly raise yields on long debt relative to banks' rates.

The contention that the banks' administered rates can, for purposes of the present analysis, be taken as a fixed point has a further consequence. Short- and long-term public debt are relatively close substitutes for private financing instruments of similar maturity. A shift in the yield curve on public debt in favour of long debt must then be supposed to be accompanied by a rise in yields on long corporate debt and equities, but little change in rates on short corporate debt (and none on rates for bank loans to the private sector). We will digress to consider the implications of this for private investment.

Tobin has championed the theory that the flattening or steepening of the yield curve associated with changes in the composition of public debt can have powerful effects on the profitability of borrowing to invest, and that debt management should therefore be directed with this aim — that indeed in his view being the essence of what monetary policy is about (Tobin 1963a; and Tobin and Brainard 1977). The mechanism envisaged is that a fall in interest rates on long-term public debt produced by the authorities switching the composition of their debt away from long-term debt will also entail (as above) a fall in the yields on long-term private financial instruments such as equities. The yield on equity finance will therefore fall relative to the return earned on physical investment. (Equivalently, the stock market valuation of firms will rise relative to the replacement cost of the capital that firms employ.) Private investment will therefore be stimulated.

Though this argument has attractions (formerly partially persuasive with one of the present authors — Dow 1964, ch. XII), there are several reasons to doubt its practical importance. These have for the most part been set out earlier, and may be stated briefly.

- First, there are limitations to how much the composition of public debt can be varied, and how quickly. It is only if public debt is large that variations in its composition give the authorities much leverage over the yield curve of financial assets as a whole. In practice, the composition of a large stock of debt cannot be varied very quickly, so that over a period of a few years long-term interest rates could not be varied greatly by this means, and in any case this could not provide the authorities with a means of influencing investment much in the short term. (If pressed very energetically, shifts in debt composition could have expectational effects and cause large and erratic changes in interest rates. That is something different — and also is not likely to be useful as a way of managing investment.) Policy might have to look ahead many years; if it was desired to encourage private investment, the policy rule might be, 'shift as fast as possible over the next decade into short-term debt.'
- Second, investment decisions, at least in the short term, are not highly sensitive to changes in the rate of interest.

- Third (and perhaps most important), the argument assumes that investment is financed predominantly by issues of equity on long-term debt. But bank loans have now become the predominant source of finance for companies, and (as already argued) rates of interest on bank loans are likely to be little affected by a rise, or fall, in rates on long-term public debt.

It is probably the case that no country has made any consistent attempt to apply a Tobinesque debt-management strategy. The above reasons may help to explain why.

The financial impact of public-sector deficits

So far we have been looking at the effects of debt-management operations, that is the effects of changes in the composition of public-sector debt, assuming that the total size of the debt is unchanged. We now consider the effect of a change in total debt, i.e. of the effect of a public-sector deficit (or surplus). In doing so we have to bring in the effects of a deficit on private income, and hence on saving and expenditure — but we still have to look as well at the consequences of different ways of financing the deficit. That is, the effects of 'fiscal policy' and 'debt management' have both to be brought in.

We can suppose that there is a way of financing the deficit without changing the pattern of relative interest rates, and we first assume that the authorities choose to finance it this way. This requires that the authorities accommodate the preferences of the public as to the composition of an increment in its holdings of financial assets; what that involves will become clearer in the course of the analysis. We also argue that financing a deficit in this way involves no change in the *general level* of interest rates.

The effect of a move by the public sector into deficit is often discussed as if there were a fixed flow of new saving, and as if the position of the public sector were the only change to have occurred (and we have given a quotation that illustrates that view). The public sector, however, cannot move into financial deficit without affecting the financial balance of other sectors of the economy. An example of the kind of change we need to consider here is a move into financial deficit by the public sector from a position of balance, as a result of either a fall in tax rates or a rise in public spending: either will make the financial position of other sectors taken together more favourable.

One way to illustrate the interconnection between the financial position of different sectors is by deduction from the basic national income identity:

national income ≡ national output ≡ national expenditure.

Income earned (counting profits as income) is equal to the value of what is produced; and what is produced is sold, and is equal to expenditure (goods put into stock counting as expenditure). It follows that, if a single sector spends more than its income (is in financial deficit), then other sectors taken together spend less than their income (are in financial surplus). This must be true for each point in time, and for any period (as recorded in flows-of-funds accounts).

An *ex post* identity, however, tells what *has* happened, but nothing of the forces at work, or of the way in which, *ex ante*, one sector influences another. Because of the interconnection between sectors, the income of one sector may differ from what was expected, and/or its expenditure may differ from what was planned. Such divergencies between a sector's *ex ante* and *ex post* income or expenditure subsequently lead to adjustments of its expenditure — with further repercussions on other sectors. In developing the argument, we first assume that there are unemployed resources, and that a move by the public sector into deficit (as on the Keynesian view) raises economic activity.

A move to a larger public deficit will, then, result in a cumulative expansionary process as in the standard 'multiplier' analysis. The larger deficit raises (post-tax) private incomes. Assuming that the rise in incomes is unexpected, the first result will be a higher rate of accumulation by the private sector of financial assets. The public's preference at this stage will presumably be for liquid assets, and on the assumption of an accommodating debt-management policy, this preference will be met, leaving relative interest rates unchanged. Later, the rise in incomes will lead to higher spending, which at first may be met out of stocks, but later will lead to higher output — and hence to a further round of income increases, with similar effects. When the expansionary process has been completed, the private sector will continue in larger financial surplus, adding to its holding of financial assets at a higher rate equivalent to the public-sector deficit. At this stage, the public's preference is likely to be less largely than before for liquid assets. These preferences, too, will (by assumption) be met, and relative interest rates again will remain unchanged. (The process is analogous to the expansionary repercussions, described in Chapter 2, of an increase in spending resulting from greater lending by banks.)

If, on the other hand, debt policy failed to meet a preference by the public for short-term assets, long rates (and probably interest rates on average) would indeed be raised. The conclusion thus is that a change in the size of the public-sector deficit has no necessary effect on interest rates.

It appears to be a fact of observation that the announcement of an increase in the scale of public-sector borrowing (even when it turns out to be a false forecast) may raise interest rates. We suggest that the explanation is that what markets are then expecting is not larger public-sector borrowing as such, but larger offers of government bonds, i.e. a larger public deficit together with a non-accommodating policy of financing it. On our analysis that would be expected to raise yields on government bonds. The public sector is not unique in this respect. It also appears to be a fact of observation that an expectation of large equity issues by companies — for instance in the course of a recovery — may also put upward pressure on long-term rates. For this, too, we offer an analagous explanation. We conclude generally that the pattern of intersectoral balance is irrelevent to the level of interest rates, provided sectoral deficits are financed in a manner to accommodate the preferences of sectors in surplus.

There is an additional argument, which we note for completeness. Even if in principle a large budget deficit did raise interest rates, the effect would be inconsiderable for a single fairly small country (like the United Kingdom) with access to world capital markets — or even, perhaps, given the size of the world markets, for a single large country (like the United States). Our contention is however general, and does not rest on this argument.

This chapter set out to consider how the account in earlier chapters of the behaviour of the financial system has to be modified to take account of public-sector transactions. Chapter 2 saw the growth of broad money as largely determined by the growth of bank lending to the private sector; to that we have added, as a determinant on equal terms, bank lending to the public sector. Chapters 3 and 4 considered how the general level of interest rates was determined; we have here built on that account to argue that, although the size of the public deficit has no effect on interest rates, they can be affected by how it is financed.

3. THE RELATION BETWEEN FISCAL AND MONETARY POLICY IN THE UK POLICY DEBATE

The policy debate in the United Kingdom has followed lines not found elsewhere, and some of the propositions that have come to be accepted appear in part erroneous and call for comment.

In the decade since 1976, the objective of monetary policy was to control the growth of broad money, and it has been usual to hold that that aim has a close connection with fiscal policy:

- either it has been held that the scale of public-sector borrowing is part-determinant of the growth of broad money;
- or the contention has been that the scale of public-sector borrowing is also part-determinant of the level of interest rates, and that there

is thus a 'triangular relationship' between the size of the deficit, the growth of broad money, and the level of interest rates. Control of public borrowing is then needed to control the growth of broad money without provoking a rise in interest rates, and thus to avoid 'crowding out' private investment.

This second view after 1979 became official government doctrine (see for instance the summary in the Treasury Select Committee's (1981) *Report on Monetary Policy)*, and from 1981 to 1986 underlay the government's 'medium-term financial strategy' which envisaged a progressive reduction of public-sector borrowing (the PSBR) as a proportion of GDP. Presentation of the strategy made no reference to the direct effect on the level of activity of such a decline in the public-sector deficit. Given the emphasis on control of broad money, either view entailed a subordination of fiscal to monetary policy.

The first proposition, that the growth of broad money depends *inter alia* on the scale of total public-sector borrowing, has usually been justified by appeal to the identity that shows the stock of money as the sum of its so-called credit counterparts. This identity is derived as follows. The balance sheet of the banking system shows on the one hand bank deposits, the main constituent of broad money, and on the other hand the banks' lending to the private sector and its lending to the public sector. Public-sector borrowing, in turn, consists (if borrowing abroad is ignored) of borrowing either from the banks or from non-banks. Manipulation of these two prior identities thus allows public-sector borrowing to be included among the 'credit counterparts' of broad money; i.e., the growth of broad money can be written as public-sector borrowing *less* debt sales to non-banks *plus* bank lending to the private sector (together with various other items, usually small but quite variable). An identity, properly interpreted, cannot be misleading: it is true by definition. But when used, without additional supporting evidence, to insinuate causality in the course of interpreting events, it is bound to be misleading. In the usual statistical presentation (for instance in the *Bank of England Quarterly Bulletin*), public borrowing is shown as the first item, and readers inevitably derive the impression that it is a main reason for the growth of the money stock shown below it, in relation to which it is usually large. Whatever disclaimers are made as to the dangers of incautious interpretation, that is close to *suggestio falsi*.

The question turns on whether the authorities have the ability to choose how to finance a deficit. If they can sell more debt to non-banks when the deficit increases, it is not inevitable that they should borrow more from the banks; and in that case an increase in the deficit cannot be regarded as the 'cause' of an increase in the money stock, even if the authorities choose to finance it in that way.

As a general rule, the authorities have fairly complete freedom as to the type of debt they sell; but there are exceptions which need to be noted. Sales of non-negotiable debt (e.g. National Savings instruments) may be increased by making the terms more attractive; and indeed, steps have been taken in recent years to enable the authorities to rely somewhat more heavily on this source of finance. But since it is sold at numerous retail outlets, the terms cannot be varied frequently to keep in step with rates available on competing assets, or improved rapidly to meet an unforeseen need for finance.

Sales of negotiable debt (e.g. government bonds) may also be increased by offering better terms. But an increase in the bond rate means that those who had bought earlier will suffer a capital loss, and would have got a higher yield if they had delayed their purchase. Therefore if market operators think that a rise in bond rates may be followed by a further rise, they will hold back until they see that the process is completed — although they will not hold off indefinitely, since in general they lose earnings by staying liquid. The converse is also true: the authorities find it easy to sell debt on a rising market. This makes it difficult for the authorities, however well-intentioned, altogether to avoid resorting to the 'Duke of York' tactic: and that tactic makes selling debt an imperfectly controllable and jerky process. As already noted, news (right or wrong) that the public-sector deficit is set to increase may also lead markets to expect a rise in interest rates on public debt, and this may cause potential purchasers of public debt to postpone purchases. These difficulties are magnified at times where there is general distrust of government policies — on which, it is to be noted, the scale of government borrowing may be only one ingredient. A pause in debt sales may then give rise to expectations that interest rates will have to be raised, thus prolonging the pause.

In this country, unlike most others, the central bank rather than the ministry of finance is responsible for managing the public debt. Its day-to-day business makes the Bank of England constantly aware of the problematic nature of debt sales. Since it has had responsibility also for controlling the rate of monetary growth, it is understandable if — despite the complex relationships discussed in Section 2, to which theorists may point — it sees having to sell more debt as increasing its problem. Nevertheless, the fact that there can be difficulties does not justify a general attribution of causality. Interruptions to debt sales are short-lived, and it is only over a period of months that the authorities may be forced to borrow from the banks. In the reverse direction, in the case of a reduction of the public-sector deficit, the authorities remain free as to how they adjust their financing. By and large it proves possible, after the event, fully to fund the public-sector deficit if that is the policy — or, indeed, even to overfund it (Chapter 10, Section 2). There appears, then, no general justification for treating the size of the public-sector deficit as a factor determining the rate of growth of the money stock.

The so-called 'triangular relationship' may be regarded as a second line of defence to the argument that the size of the public deficit is nevertheless important from the point of view of monetary control. This argument is that, although more public debt could be sold, that would raise interest rates, which would harm private investment. This is a complex argument with several components.

It is true that, assuming a monetary target, the size of the public-sector deficit will affect rates of interest on public debt. For any given monetary target (and any given rate of bank lending to the private sector), there is some size of deficit that will be compatible with stable interest rates *on public debt*. A deficit larger than otherwise will entail interest rates on public debt higher than otherwise, and vice versa. Alternatively, given the size of the deficit, slower monetary growth (perhaps however involving overfunding the deficit) can be had at the cost of higher interest rates on the debt. The government may thus make it more expensive for itself to borrow, or may avoid doing so.

But 'crowding out' arguments too readily assume that the cost of financing private investment will be affected in the same way. Industrial debentures may be close substitutes for government bonds, and equities fairly close, so that yields on them may rise in sympathy with yields on government debt. But a rise in bond rates may have little if any effect on the cost of financing private investment when, as is now the case, bank lending is more important in its finance than equity issues.

There is one further consideration. A policy of reducing the public-sector deficit is likely, on the arguments deployed earlier, to depress the level of activity: that itself is likely to depress investment. This effect, in our view, is likely to outweigh any indirect effect stemming from a lower cost of finance. Considerations relating to the impact on private investment are probably the reverse of those justifying the 'triangular relationship'.

It is for these reasons that we do not treat the scale of public borrowing as a means of monetary control. Discussion of the options is obstructed by treating the stance of fiscal policy as a matter to be decided merely as a corollary of monetary policy.

PART II

Monetary Control and the Course of the Aggregates

7

UK Monetary Policy Since 1971

Chapter 2 sought to describe how the banking system is likely to evolve, and how the stock of money is likely to grow, in the absence of intervention by the authorities to influence its growth. The authorities have been concerned chiefly to control the growth of broad money, and a number of different methods have been used to influence its growth, which will be analysed in turn in the following chapters. To set these in context, this chapter provides a brief outline of the course of monetary policy since 1971.

The publication of the Bank of England discussion document *Competition and Credit Control* in 1971 marked a considerable divide in the course of monetary policy. Before then, primary reliance had been placed on credit ceilings (or direct control of the growth of bank lending). The new arrangements were 'intended to replace such controls with a market mechanism whereby the total, and the allocation, of credit would be determined by cost'; as the Bank explained, when it wished to influence the total 'the Bank would vary interest rates' (Bank of England 1984, 31). Despite evidence of its ineffectiveness, the authorities have continued to use central-bank rate as a means of influencing the monetary aggregates; and although in more recent years it was varied also with a view to the exchange rate, central-bank rate has remained the main instrument the authorities used in trying to control monetary growth, and will be discussed in Chaper 8.

Monetarist critics have argued (more particularly in the late 1970s) that the reason for the ineffectiveness of monetary control was that the authorities were insufficiently rigorous in controlling the reserves of the banking system (monetary base). Monetary base control was never adopted as official policy, and in Chapter 9 we argue that it could provide no solution. Chapter 10 discusses two other methods of monetary control, used at different times: the 'Corset' — in effect, a return to direct control of lending — which was intermittently in force for much of the last two-thirds of the 1970s, and the policy of 'overfunding' the public-sector borrowing requirement, which was operative for some years in the 1980s. Both were to a degree effective in reducing monetary growth, both involved 'distortions' of the financial system that were regarded as unacceptable, and both have been abandoned. Chapter 10 also discusses official banking supervision.

Fuller accounts of the evolution of monetary policy are to be found elsewhere (for references see Chapter 1). Here we have tried to stick to the bare outline.

The guiding ideas behind Competition and Credit Control

Among the body of people who had most part in the redirection of policy in 1971, three groups of ideas were probably important, relating respectively to the aims of monetary policy, and to old and new ways of achieving them. These find some reflection in the official documents of the time. (Those marked † below are reprinted in Bank of England 1984.)

It is important to recall that at that stage monetary policy was seen not in monetarist terms but rather as part of demand management. In 1970, for instance, the then Governor of the Bank remarked, without disapproval: 'the authorities have not operated in a strictly monetarist way over the past twenty years, but have broadly accommodated the rising demand for money as incomes rose'; and he went on to say: 'the proper questions for discussion in a situation such as the present are first how much reduction in real activity is appropriate, and second how much weight should be placed on monetary policy in achieving it?' (Jane Hodge Memorial Lecture: *BEQB* 1971, 93–5†). In judging the 'thrust' of monetary policy in that context, it had come to be recognized that at a time of inflation interest rates alone were not a reliable guide, and that high interest rates did not for instance necessarily indicate 'tight' policy; for this reason it was right to look also at the growth of the monetary aggregates. In a general sense, this had long been done; for policy had long focused on the rate of growth of bank lending. For a while after 1967 a precise target — for domestic credit expansion (DCE) — had indeed been accepted at the instance of the International Monetary Fund as a condition for providing financial assistance; when the need for it passed, this lapsed.

Thus, although the aim of policy was seen as being the control of the growth of money, in 1971 this aim was loose and imprecise, and a good way off from monetary targets which came only five years later. From the beginning, emphasis was on a broad aggregate (M3 or later £M3). This was partly because of the long concern with bank lending, partly because of the brief experience with DCE (a broad aggregate), and partly because advantage was seen in relating monetary to fiscal policy, which a broad aggregate appeared to allow (Chapter 6, Section 3). When monetary expansion became rapid in 1973, it was the growth of broad money that occasioned alarm (narrow money, indeed, did not grow especially fast — see Fig. 11.1 below); and it was to arrest the growth of broad money that the Corset was imposed at the end of that year.

The second important element was the desire to end direct controls on bank lending. There had earlier been pointed criticism (by the Prices and

Incomes Board in 1957 and the Monopolies Commission in 1958) of the cartel arrangements of the London clearing banks, and this was followed by wide public debate which evidently much influenced the Bank (see Governor's Mansion House Speech, October 1971: *BEQB* 1971, 506†). Controls on bank lending were seen as preventing competition between banks and driving business away from the clearing banks, and to some extent therefore as ineffective; also, it was felt that, by preventing allocation by price, they were causing a misallocation of resources. These charges may have been overstated, but lending controls were seen as having had their day. As one architect of the 1971 changes has said, 'there was a lively disposition to move sharply away' from such methods 'because of their diminishing effectiveness, and in the interest of competitive efficiency in banking' (Fforde, 1982, 202). When lending controls were abolished, the banks agreed to abandon the cartel arrangements which tied their deposit rates to Bank rate; it was similarly intended that the banks' lending rates would cease to be rigidly tied to Bank rate. Neither was really achieved (Chapter 4, Section 1); nor perhaps, given the nature of banking behaviour, was that to have been expected.

The third element in the new policy was that monetary control, formerly obtained by direct controls, should now be obtained via interest rates. This was more of a jump into the unknown than may appear. Bank rate was certainly the well tried and traditional instrument of the central bank. But the fluctuations it could induce in short-term interest rates had traditionally been used to influence short-term capital flows, and hence the reserves or the exchange rate. Now they were to be used to alter the rate of growth of broad money. Belief that this would be possible derived from recent research, for econometric evidence at the time suggested that broad money could be controlled by changes in interest rates (Fforde, 1982, 202; Goodhart 1984, 95). The apparent relation between broad money growth and interest rates, however, 'broke down entirely after 1971, and has not reappeared' (Bank of England 1984, 44).

Certain other new arrangements made in 1971 also need to be mentioned; for, although they have not lasted, importance was attached to them at the time (and the Corset scheme later rested on them). A minimum reserve assets ratio was laid down for the banks: all banks were required to hold a proportion ($12\frac{1}{2}$ per cent) of their sterling deposit liabilities in specified assets, of a sort that the Bank was normally prepared to convert into cash, either through open-market operations or by lending. Arrangements already existed under which the Bank could call on the banks to make 'Special Deposits' with it — which in effect allowed the reserve assets ratio to be varied — and until 1976 a major increase in central-bank rate was usually accompanied by a call for Special Deposits. These arrangements were intended as an additional means by which Bank rate could be made to bite, by obliging the banking system to borrow from the central bank to rebuild its depleted reserves. Though there were several ways in which the banks, given time to adjust, could 'manufacture' reserve assets,* Special Deposits were on occasion probably helpful in making central-bank rate effective. But clearly, they proved much less useful than originally intended and, together with the reserve ratio, were later abandoned — leaving the banks (apart from any prudential requirements) free of constraint as to the size of reserves they held.

Background to policy developments after 1971

The Conservative government under Mr Heath, elected in June 1970, generally favoured removal of controls; the new monetary arrangements of 1971 were introduced fairly early in its term. Growing unemployment led the government, contrary to earlier intentions, to adopt expansionary budgets in 1972 and 1973. Faster expansion in the United Kingdom was accompanied by a world boom and rising world commodity prices; the huge oil price rises came in the autumn of 1973.

Given the general expansion, a more rapid expansion of broad money would anyhow have been expected. But what occurred was more than a purely passive response, and, though far from the only cause, must have added to demand and inflation. In the two years to September 1973, M3 grew at an annual rate of about 25 per cent but M1 more slowly, by 10 per cent. By mid-1973 the authorities were seriously alarmed, and in the second half of the year central-bank rate (MLR) was raised steeply from 7 per cent to an unprecedented 13 per cent (where it stayed for over a year). But since there seemed no certainty of that quickly slowing monetary growth, the newly devised Corset control was applied in December — in effect, this constituted a return to direct lending control. On this occasion demand for credit quickly slackened, and the Corset was lifted after fifteen months.

The United Kingdom's effective exchange rate was little changed by the general readjustment of currencies under the Smithsonian agreement of December 1971. Though the United Kingdom did not join the European Economic Community till January 1973, it joined the 'Snake'

---

* Banks could surrender reserve assets, such as Treasury bills, to the Bank to meet a call for Special Deposits, maintaining their reserve ratios by re-designating lending to discount houses as lending at call; this added equally to eligible liabilities and to reserve assets. Another method was to persuade companies to borrow via bills accepted and held by banks, rather than through a non-negotiable instrument (the scope for this was, however, limited by a stipulation that such bills would not count as reserve assets beyond 2 per cent of the bank's eligible liabilities). On occasions, too, banks borrowed at long term from discount houses (who obtained deposits from non-banks) and redeposited at call; this also added equally to eligible liabilities and to reserve assets, and could be carried on extensively without coming up against any early limit.

(the precursor of the European Monetary System) as a 'candidate' country in April 1972. A month later it left it to float 'temporarily' — which has continued to date. In March 1973 most other industrial countries also adopted floating rates. Thus, for almost the whole period of this study, exchange rates have been unpegged, and since the mid-1970s have turned out to be highly unstable. The effective rate of sterling, for instance, depreciated almost 25 per cent between early 1972 and early 1974.

Though incomes policies continued for another five years, the period of the Heath government was perhaps their high-water mark. At the end of 1973, when the coal miners (in opposition to the incomes policy in force) banned overtime, industry had to be put on a three-day week. When they voted to go on strike, the government called a general election, and lost.

The Labour government that took office under Mr Wilson in February 1974 was re-elected in October 1974, and (with Mr Callaghan as prime minister after April 1976) continued until May 1979. It ruled over a sea of troubles, and had little room for manœuvre. With the North Sea oil fields still under development, the current balance of payments was in deficit, at first in large deficit. The exchange rate tended continuously to fall; and in part as a result, inflation was very rapid until 1978, with a peak of nearly 25 per cent in 1975. Output fell in both 1974 and 1975, in this country and abroad, and unemployment doubled (to around 5 per cent, which then seemed a high level).

The situation in effect forced the government to cut its own spending (and thus, despite recession, to deepen recession further) in order to control inflation. Although this was not so apparent at the time, fiscal policy now appears to have been extremely severe, which put strains on the cohesion of the government. Monetary policy caused less anxiety until 1976. As if in reaction to the boom of 1973, the pace of bank lending declined, and in the three years 1974–6 the growth of £M3 was about 10 per cent a year. Though that still seemed fairly rapid at the time, it was much less than the rate of inflation, or the growth of nominal GDP. Interest rates were reduced fairly steadily up to early 1976.

The year 1976, however, saw a major exchange crisis. Between March and early December the effective exchange rate fell about 20 per cent, and that necessarily had repercussions on domestic policy. The crises started because the authorities appeared to be following a policy of edging the exchange rate down; the fall then passed out of control. Reasons cited at the time (see *BEQB* 1976, 419) were the rise in prices, which continued to be more rapid than elsewhere, the continuing large payments deficit (with North Sea oil output still inconsiderable), and unease about the scale of public borrowing. None of these seems very impressive in retrospect, and none might have been decisive, but for the evident discord within the government about the control of public spending. As it was, loss of confidence impeded debt sales, which accelerated the growth of broad money, which further increased unease. Confidence returned rapidly from November, when the promise of moderate cuts in public spending secured a loan from the International Monetary Fund. In the event, the loan was not then needed: the exchange rate rose rapidly, reversing half its previous fall. It may be judged that this was essentially a confidence crisis which was not firmly handled.

Increased importance had by now come to be placed on the monetary aggregates. In October 1976, a 'target' figure for the growth of £M3 was announced for the first time. It was against this background, with broad money then appearing to rise more rapidly, that the Corset was reimposed in November, for what proved a short while.

The first monetary target was comfortably met. But in the next two years monetary growth tended to be faster than officially desired (see Table 7.1), and central-bank rate (MLR) was raised almost continuously, from 5 per cent in October 1977 to 17 per cent in November 1979. The major motive prompting increases in interest rates (as official commentaries make clear) was still at this stage the control of broad money, and the need to sell debt with that object (rather than concern with the exchange rate). The pressure behind bank lending, however, was now starting to strengthen. Given its apparent unresponsiveness to interest rates, the Corset was reimposed for the third and last time in June 1978.

The Conservative government formed by Mrs Thatcher in May 1979 put monetary policy as the centrepiece of economic strategy; and having been re-elected in June 1983, this government was in power during the rest of the period covered by our study. In some respects its inheritance paralleled that of the Wilson government that had take office five years before. As then, there had just been another boom in world commodity prices and, right at the start, another massive rise in the world price of oil. As earlier, output in this and other countries again fell off (in both 1980 and 1981), and unemployment rose (to over 11 per cent by 1982 and over 13 per cent by 1985). And as before, inflation, initially rather low (some 8 per cent a year in 1978), accelerated steeply in the first years. (It took until 1983 to get back to 5 per cent.) Now, however, the balance of payments, with North Sea oil on full stream, was very strong and consistently in current surplus; and the exchange rate rose steeply (in 1979 and 1980) and stayed strong throughout. That made for an altogether smoother ride.

Control of monetary growth was now seen not merely as of assistance in controlling inflation, but as the sufficient and necessary route to achieve it. In the hope of reducing inflationary expectations, a 'medium-term strategy' was announced of a progressively declining pace of monetary growth for a number of years ahead. The scale of public borrowing was regarded as a means to monetary control (Chapter 6, Section 3), and its intended size was also pre-announced, on a similarly progressively declining scale. The government generally favoured removal of controls: exchange controls were abolished in October 1979, and the Corset in June 1980.

It was now, however, that bank lending began to accelerate markedly — as rapidly indeed as in 1971–3. Ironically, this may have owed much to the authorities' endorsement of financial competition (see Chapter 11, Section 4). The growth of broad money thus stayed high; it exceeded the target range in the first two years, and stayed only just within it in the next two years, and far exceeded it in the fifth. Under the 'medium-term strategy', indications were given of the desired rate of monetary growth not just for one year ahead, but for three or four. In the event, the outcome was always well above these longer-term hopes (see Fig. 7.1 and Table 7.1). By the end of 1986, the authorities were evidently preparing to abandon monetary targets (Governor's Loughborough Lecture: *BEQB*, 1986, 507).

The apparent failures with monetary control brought into question the methods used by the Bank of England, and led to a continued discussion of monetary base control as a method allegedly more effective. Failure to control bank lending by high interest rates also led the authorities in later years to resort to overfunding; if bank lending could not itself be restrained, its effect on the broad aggregates could, in this way, at least be offset.

In principle, the exchange rate was supposed to be left to 'market forces'. In fact, interest rate policy was increasingly dictated not only by hope of controlling broad money but also by exchange rate considerations; and, though motives were always mixed, it seems clear that increases in central-bank rate after 1981 were chiefly occasioned by the behaviour of the exchange rate. Considerations relating to monetary growth have nevertheless remained important. It is probably in part because of such considerations that, despite their apparent ineffectiveness, interest rates were kept relatively high.

TABLE 7.1. Monetary targets, 1976–1986
(% rise over financial year)

Date when target set	1976/7	1977/8	1978/9	1979/80	1980/81	1981/2	1982/3	1983/4	1984/5	1985/6	1986/7
Targets[a] for broad money (£M3)											
July 1976	12[b]										
March 1977		9–13[c]									
April 1978			8–12[c]								
June 1979				7–11[d]							
March 1980					7–11[e]	(6–10)	(5–9)	(4–8)			
March 1981						6–10[e]	(5–9)	(4–8)			
March 1982							8–12[e]	(7–11)	(6–10)		
March 1983								7–11[e]	(6–10)	(5–9)	
March 1984									6–10[e]	(5–9)	(4–8)[f]
March 1985										5–9[g]	(4–8)[f]
March 1986											11–15[g]
Outturn[h]	*10*	*16*	*11*	*10*	*18½*	*13*	*11½*	*10*	*12*	*15*	*20*

Targets for narrow money (M1) and very broad money (PSL2)

March 1982	8–12[e]	(7–11)	(6–10)	
March 1983		7–10[e]	(6–10)	(5–9)
Outturn[h] for M1	*11*	*11*	*14½*	*22½*
Outturn[h] for PSL2	*9*	*12¼*	*15½*	*14½*

Targets for monetary base (M0)

March 1984	4–8[e]	(3–7)	(2–6)
March 1985		3–7	(2–6)
March 1986			(2–6)[g]
Outturn[h]	*5½*	*3½*	*2*

[a] Targets were set for forthcoming year; from 1980, 'indicative ranges' were given for subsequent years.
[b] Target for M3 for financial year.
[c] Target for 12 months to mid-April.
[d] Target for 10 months to mid-April at annual rate.
[e] Target for 14 months to mid-April at annual rate.
[f] Indicative ranges for later years were 1987/8 (3–7), and 1988/9 (2–6).
[g] Target for 12 months to mid-February.
[h] Outturn in period covered by target set in preceding year.

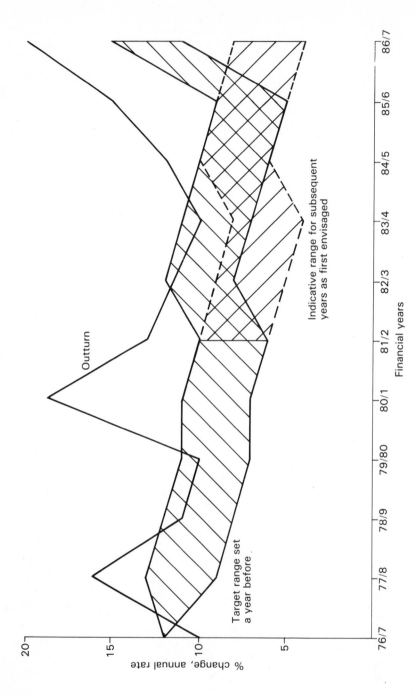

FIG. 7.1   *Targets and outturns for £M3*

Source: Table 7.1

8

Central Bank Rate as an Instrument of Monetary Control

When the new policies were introduced in 1971, it was intended that the 'traditional instrument' of central-bank rate would be used to influence short-term market rates, and that this would be the way monetary growth was controlled. Despite growing evidence that this route was far from completely effective, the use of central-bank rate has retained its favoured place among the instruments of policy. This chapter builds on the conclusions of Chapter 3 about the role of central-bank rate in the determination of interest rates, and looks at some more detailed questions about how central-bank rate impinges on the banking system. Section 1 discusses the *modus operandi* of central-bank rate, Section 2, the limitations to its use, and Section 3, its effect on the aggregates.

Central-bank rate may be regarded as the price at which the banks can obtain additional reserves. There has been a long discussion (starting with Poole 1970) as to the relative merits of the central bank operating to control the price, or alternatively the quantity, of money — in many expositions this is regarded as equivalent to the choice between operating on the price or quantity of bank reserves. This question is considered in connection with monetary base control in Chapter 9.

1. THE *MODUS OPERANDI* OF CENTRAL-BANK RATE

Twenty years ago, this chapter would have been about the use of Bank rate. The Bank of England's method of operation has since undergone succesive changes, though without changing the essentials of the matter, and this conventionally simple nomenclature has disappeared. In 1972 Bank rate was replaced by Minimum Lending Rate (MLR). At first, MLR was a rate linked by formula to the market rate on three-month Treasury bills — not, as Bank rate was, an administered rate. It was hoped thus to take it out of the area of political decision. That hope proved illusory; for Treasury bill rates are themselves influenced by the central bank, as became obvious. By 1978 the pretence that MLR was dependent on market forces had become transparent, and was abandoned, and MLR again became an administered rate — a return in fact, though not in name, to Bank rate.

Bank rate or MLR is the rate at which the Bank of England stands ready to let the banking system replenish its reserves by borrowing from it. In the United Kingdom, the central bank has chosen to deal not directly with the banks but through the discount houses, and has preferred to keep them in existence as an intermediary between itself and the banks. In relieving a shortage in the money market, the Bank of England thus makes advances only to (or buys assets only from) the discount houses. (The banks deposit funds with the discount houses, and when short of cash recall such loans and deposit them with the Bank and thus rebuild their balances at the Bank; the discount houses are then short of borrowed funds and come to the Bank for advances.) Since the discount houses are merely an intermediary, we treat them as part of the banking system.

In 1980 changes were made in the way the Bank of England operated in short-term markets. Assistance to the banks through the discount houses ceased normally to take the form of lending by the Bank to the banking system, but became a matter of the Bank buying bills from it. The instrument thus became not the Bank's lending rate but the Bank's dealing rate. (The discount houses offer bills at a rate of their choosing, which the Bank may reject or not: technically therefore the Bank's dealing rate is not set by the Bank, but is the rate that it accepts.) The Bank's dealing rate was not now known in advance. (It remained within an 'unpublished band' not disclosed to the market.) Although the publication of a minimum lending rate was thus abolished as a normal way of operating, a 'posted' MLR could be (and has been) reinstated on occasion. The reason for these changes was, again, in part the hope of making official interest rate objectives 'less obtrusive' and less political. (Official operations have been normally concentrated on very short-term rates. Even though market forces were not truly independent, the official argument was that this gave market forces 'greater influence' over longer money-market rates.) The essentials of what could formerly be said of Bank rate or MLR can now be described in terms of the Bank's dealing rate; and in this study the term 'central-bank rate' is used to describe all three.

Although the banks were previously required to hold minimum amounts of some wider classes of liquid assets (see Chapter 7), they have always been free to decide for themselves their holdings of reserves in the narrow sense, i.e. their balances at the Bank of England. It is true that since 1980 the banks (and before that the clearing banks) have agreed to hold a fixed proportion (in 1980 0.5 per cent, since reduced to 0.45 per cent) of their liabilities as a (non-interest-bearing) deposit with the Bank of England. However, its purpose is not operational but to provide the Bank with an income (the Bank lends the funds to the government at market rates): it is in effect a small proportional tax on bank intermediation. For operational purposes, the banks hold balances at the Bank of England over and above this amount.

The *modus operandi* of central-bank rate is familiar from older textbooks about Bank rate. The central bank is always ready to lend to the banking system, but at a rate of its choosing, and is able to put pressure on the banks' reserves and thus force them to borrow from the central bank (through the discount houses) at this rate. A typical account runs as follows:

By forcing the discount houses to borrow at Bank rate, the Bank do not only raise the cost for the houses of some part of their funds; they also indicate to all who operate in financial markets that they are unwilling to see interest rates, particularly short-term rates, fall significantly . . . . In contrast, by lending at market rates, or ensuring that there is sufficient cash to make borrowing unnecessary, the Bank indicate that they would not wish to oppose any trend in interest rates which is taking place. This signalling system is important in the market for Treasury bills and short-dated gilt-edged stock, in which demand is strongly influenced in the short run by expectations of changes in interest rates. It helps the authorities to bring about changes in short-term interest rates without extensive dealings in the market. (Bain 1970, 44–5)

(Bain had worked for a period in the Bank of England and follows what was at that time the Bank's odd practice of referring to itself as a plural entity.)

Although this account is in our view perfectly correct, there are two questions more particularly that deserve fuller explanation.

- The scale of a bank's reserves is a matter of its choosing. How is it then, that the central bank is able to put pressure on the banks' reserve positions, and make them feel short of reserves so that they are impelled to borrow from the central bank at a penal rate?
- When central-bank rate is raised (for example) by a percentage point, the banks typically raise their administered rates by a percentage point also — thus immediately greatly widening the impact of the central bank's move. Yet the banks, when they borrow at central-bank rate, borrow very small sums, so that the increase in the cost of funds to them is quite small. Why do they raise their rates so much?

These questions are discussed in Section 2 below.

The ability of the central bank to put pressure on banks' reserve positions

Since the banks are free to choose what size of reserves to hold, the question is: how is the central bank able to make them short of reserves? The exact answer depends in part on institutional arrangements, which differ from country to country.

In the United Kingdom the largest banks are party to the interbank clearing system, under which each bank settles daily only its net position with other members. Banks who are members of the clearing system find it convenient to keep an operational balance at the Bank of England to settle any deficit in the daily clearing. Other banks who are not members of the clearing, and also building societies, hold an account with one of the clearing banks, and settle deficits in their interbank position by drawing on that account.

Each clearer must decide how large a balance to hold at the Bank of England. Its net position in the clearing can be expected on average over a run of days to be zero but will vary widely day by day, and on any particular day cannot be forecast with any certainty. How large a balance a bank decides to hold against this contingency is influenced by the knowledge that it can, if short, recover its position by borrowing on the interbank market (which is in effect borrowing reserves from other banks) or by borrowing from the Bank itself. Thus a bank may bid for deposits from other banks through the interbank market or bid for money-market deposits from non-banks (which amounts to indirect interbank borrowing); and on occasions this results in abnormally high overnight interbank rates. The effect in either case is to redistribute the existing total of bankers' balances at the Bank, but not change it in total. A bank short of reserves may also sell assets to the central bank, or borrow from it against assets: this increases its balances at the central bank, and the total balances of the banking system as a whole. Central-bank lending to the banks increases the total of banks' deposits with the central bank — just as lending by the banks to the non-bank public increases the bank deposits of the public in total.

The authorities may take action to make the banking system short of reserves, and thus to drive it to seek relief from the central bank by borrowing from it. Perhaps the most direct way of doing so, adopted in many other countries, is for the authorities to specify the minimum level of reserves that the banks must hold, and to increase that level when such an effect is desired. In the United Kingdom that method has not been used, although the power to call on the banks to make Special Deposits at the Bank of England had the same effect. The Special Deposits arrangement was, however, used only occasionally, and by the 1980s had fallen into desuetude.

The normal way by which the authorities in the United Kingdom have influenced the banks' reserves was different, and depended on two special features of the institutional arrangements in this country. First, whereas in many countries the government banks with the commercial banks, in the United Kingdom the central government (but not other public-sector bodies) banks with the central bank. Consequently, the banks' reserves are affected by the government's debt operations. Any deficit incurred by the central government may on occasion be financed, or financed in part, by borrowing abroad or by depletion of foreign exchange reserves. Apart from that, sales of debt by the central government in excess of its own financial deficit (or any lending to other bodies) result in transfers from the banks' accounts at the Bank of England to the government's account — and thus in a reduction of the banks' balances at the Bank (and vice versa if its debt sales fall short of its deficit).

Traditionally, the residual source of finance for the government has been the issue of Treasury bills. The second special feature of UK institutional arrangements is that the discount houses undertake always to buy the full amount of the Treasury bills on offer each week. By selling more Treasury bills than were needed to cover the government's deficit, the Bank was thus able to make the banking system short of reserves.

Since the banks would not wish to see their balances with the Bank reduced beyond a certain point, they could be driven to seek assistance from the Bank, i.e. to borrow from the Bank, or sell acceptable short-term assets to it, in order to replenish their balances. Such requests are never refused, but the rate that the Bank charges on such loans (or the price it pays for assets bought) is at is discretion: normally it is close to money-market rates, but on occasion it may be a higher, somewhat penal, rate.

To be in a position readily to put pressure on the banks, the Bank normally aims to keep the banks slightly short of reserves; but there have been changes in the technique employed by the Bank to do so. As a result of the policy of reducing public-sector borrowing from the banks (see Chapter 10, Section 2), the stock of Treasury bills outstanding had by the early 1980s been reduced to minimal proportions; and the weekly Treasury bill tender has thus ceased to be so important. But (for reasons to be explained in Chapter 10) the policy of overfunding the public-sector deficit resulted in the Bank acquiring a large holding of commercial bills. It has thus been able to put pressure on the banks by letting maturing bills run off without replacing them; and in practice it has kept markets persistently short of liquidity, relieved by substantial and discretionary purchases of commercial bills. Despite a considerable change in technique, the purpose and results are the same.

The arrangement that the government banks with the Bank of England creates practical difficulties in day-by-day money-market operations. The Bank has to try to estimate daily the government's net borrowing requirement. But neither on a daily basis, nor over a longer term, is government borrowing accurately predictable. Mistakes are reflected both in the large fluctuations in overnight interbank rates (Chapter 4, Section 1) and in large fluctuations in banks' operational balances with the Bank of England. (To give an example, on different reporting dates during 1984 these varied from £50 million to £278 million.) This area of uncertainty probably strengthens the Bank's hand over the banks. For it entails a daily flow of business, and thus continuous contact between the Bank and the banks; it creates great uncertainties for the banks; and it makes them potentially dependent at any time on the Bank for assistance.

The central bank's power over the commercial banks is however elastic and based on uncertainties, not rigid and tight. It is able to control the banks' reserves in total, although not those of individual banks which may always act to redistribute reserves among themselves. Except in the extreme case of a run on the banks, the banking system as a whole has no ultimate need of reserves: what an individual bank has to insure against is the risk that banks will not be able to redistribute reserves quickly enough among themselves to avoid individual imbalances each day. Large banks can therefore reduce their needs for reserves by careful planning and pooling of information. They could go further, as non-clearers now in effect do, and by mutual credit arrangements eliminate their dependence on balances at the central bank. The authorities on their side, wishing to be in a position to put banks to a degree of discomfort, would not wish to drive them to the point of contracting out of a system that gives the central bank this power. If they tried to, the outcome would be an uneasy truce in a continuing game. (The implications for the limits to the authorities' power will be further considered in Chapter 9 in relation to monetary base control.)

The ability of the central bank to force banks' rates up

When the banks are made short of reserves, the effect is not to force them to curtail the scale of their operations: that would in any case not be possible instantaneously (nor, for reasons to be spelled out further below, does it work out that way in the longer run). The immediate effect is rather to oblige banks to borrow reserves from the central bank at what may be a higher rate of interest. That is the trigger from which all other effects must follow. In fact, it typically triggers a rise in banks' administered rates of similar size. The question now to be examined is why the effect is anything like as great.

The financial penalties imposed on the banks by an increase in the central bank rate are in fact trivial. That was especially true of the arrangements in force up to 1980. Thus, at the end of 1985 the stock of broad money was about £125 billion. M0 (total notes and coin in circulation plus banks' balances at the Bank of England) was about £12.5 billion, of which about £1.5 billion was held by banks; of this, under £0.5 billion represented banks' operational deposits. Official lending at above market rates, when undertaken, is only a small margin of that, and the penal element in the rate charged is only a few percentage points. Thus the financial penalty spread over the total of banks' balance sheets can at times amount at most to some thousandths of a per cent.

The policy of overfunding altered this somewhat. It has resulted in not only the Bank but also the banks themselves acquiring a large stock of commercial bills (much of which they may in due course expect to sell on to the Bank when of appropriate maturity). If the Bank raises its dealing rate, it pays less for bills; if the banks fail to follow, they pay more for bills than (at present prices) they can expect to get if they later sell them to the Bank. Since the banks' holdings of commercial bills may typically be a few per cent of net sterling assets, the risk of loss in not following a rise in the Bank's dealing rate is more significant than earlier. Though difficult to estimate because of the uncertainties, it could, when spread over the total of banks' balance sheets, be put at up to some tenths of a per cent though probably less. Although larger than previously, this is still small.

Why is it, then, when central bank rate rises by a percentage point, that banks do not increase their rates merely by a fraction of a percentage point? Official operations to allow the banks to replenish their liquidity are on a very small scale, and the cost of paying a somewhat penal rate to obtain it represents a quite small increase in the costs of bank intermediation. The question is thrown into relief by comparing the reaction of manufacturing industry to an increase in the cost of a minor component of its input — for instance the cost of printing ink or lubricating oil. If that rose 1 per cent, the price of manufactured goods would not rise 1 per cent, but (if at all) by a small fraction of that. The banks do not in other cases price according to the cost of marginal finance: why do they behave differently in this case? The question is not much discussed and appears more puzzling than the absence of discussion would seem to allow.

The explanation cannot be simply in terms of arbitrage, as is sometimes suggested. Arbitrage transactions by members of the non-bank public keep the price of and yield on assets held by the public in line with each other, but only the banking system has access to borrowing from the central bank. The elements of an explanation perhaps start with the fact that, in the United Kingdom, the discount houses are the intermediary between the central bank and the banks. When the discount houses are charged more for borrowing from the central bank, they reduce the price of (and raise the interest rates on) all bills they trade in, and all short-term rates adjust to that. What is remarkable is that market interest rates in general respond to a signal from the central bank — the phenomenon we set out to explain in Chapters 3 and 4. Given that that happens, the banks are faced not merely with an increase in the cost of assistance from the central bank, but with an increase in the cost of their wholesale deposits — which are considerably more important. But these are still only a fraction of their total deposits, so that there remains a question as to why the banks put up all lending and deposit rates as much as they do. We suggest three groups of reasons, which together may explain this feature of banks' behaviour.

First, banks have to take definite decisions in conditions of indefinite sorts of uncertainty. We have argued (in Chapter 2) that the difficulty of evaluating the risks of lending forces banks to fix quantitative limits to the scale of loans (rather than allocate loans by price). For similar reasons, they apply rules of thumb in setting their lending rates. They will want to charge what the going rate is going to be; without obvious signals this would be difficult to determine, and central-bank rate provides a pointer that is in fact self-validating. It appears to have been usual practice for banks to follow central-bank rate at least since the beginning of the twentieth century (Sayers 1957, 61; 1976, 44). Since all banks can be expected to follow it, and deposit rates to rise with lending rates, the expected cost of providing loans in fact varies with central-bank rate. Moreover, all interest rate expectations move together, so that the cost of stock exchange finance, which over time could be a substitute for bank finance, rises along with the cost of bank loans. The banking system thus does not have to fear that it will lose business to competitors by putting up lending and deposit rates.

Second, there are a number of forces that, once the convention is established and commonly followed, keep the convention in being and protect it from erosion. Banks have a strong incentive to act in conformity with accepted standards (Chapters 2, Section 2, and 4, Section 1), and the large banks, as oligopolists, have an incentive to avoid open price competition. To an individual bank considering non-conformist action there must appear also some risk of financial loss. Lending is less sensitive to a change in interest rates than are most deposits, so that a bank that failed to raise its rates would have to rely more on interbank borrowing to fund its lending. Although the surpluses and deficiencies of liquidity of different banks must balance and be offsetting, banks have a greater fear of being short of deposits than long of them; shortages of individual banks thus lead to sharp rises in interbank rates. A bank that failed to follow an upward move would thus risk having to pay high rates to get marginal deposits.

Third, there are a number of semi-political factors that encourage banks to follow central-bank rate. The profits of the large retail banks gain from higher interest rates (since a portion of their deposits are non-interest-bearing). In all countries banks are potentially unpopular; and if, as in the United Kingdom, there is a near-oligopoly of four big banks, they tend to be especially careful to behave in an acceptable way. When they raise rates in line with central-bank rate, they have good official sanction for what they do. The Bank of England, furthermore, undoubtedly expects the banks to follow its lead; and it retains a degree of extra-constitutional authority* which (though this must be decreasing) entails that its wishes tend to be obeyed.

2. LIMITATIONS TO THE USE OF THE CENTRAL BANK'S POWERS

Although the central bank has great power over interest rates, there are overriding limitations to how far it can utilize such power. These limitations are in part technical; in part they reflect the limits set by circumscribing economic forces; and in part they reflect the realities of the political process and the place of governments, central banks, and banks themselves within it.

First, the central bank's power over interest rates is in a sense uni-directional. While it can put pressure on banks' reserve position and force an upward movement of rates, there is no parallel power to embarrass the banks with an excess of reserves and force a downward movement of rates. All the central bank can do is to refrain from putting pressure: market rates then gradually return to whatever is the ruling conventional idea of the normal level of short-term rates (Chapter 4, Section 1). Since the signals it then makes are less dramatic than 'forcing the banks into the Bank', the effect on expectations generally is likely to be more diffuse. This is perhaps the basic reason for the fact already noted (Chapter 4, Section 1), that upward moves in interest rates tend to be abrupt, and downward moves more gradual and extended.

In this country the central bank is responsible not only for managing short-term interest rates but also for managing public-sector debt operations, which may complicate the former task. Under the current tap system, a rising trend in short-term rates appears to be liable to interrupt official sales of new debt (though it does not prevent piecemeal private sales of old debt on the secondary market). For when short rates appear to be on a rising trend, long rates also tend to rise; bond prices tend to fall, and institutional investors tend to delay purchases till prices appear to have reached bottom. The public deficit then has to be financed in other ways — by selling new Treasury bills, or (as is now more likely) by allowing commercial bills held by the Bank to mature; and it is likely that as part of this process the government for a while borrows more from

---

* Conventions are influenced by history. Sayers (1976, 282–3), for instance, relates how in the late 1920s Montagu Norman 'besides operating in the market . . . used the Thursday meetings [with the discount houses] as an aid in influencing market rates of discount', and thus came 'to give the firms in the market guidance, and at last virtually orders, on the level of market rates'. Later this 'regimentation' was eased, but 'the Governor was now too powerful a figure for the market ever to revert to any semblance of independence'.

banks — which will be reflected in temporarily more rapid growth of broad money.

Under a regime where the aim of monetary policy is to control the aggregates and where interest rates are used to this end, these potential repercussions on the gilts market can never be absent from the minds of those who conduct money-market operations. Such considerations are likely to reinforce the central bank's tendency to raise rates in large infrequent steps, and to lower them (or allow them to fall) more gradually during extended periods of continued debt sales. This is the tactic commonly called — and commonly with disapproval — 'The Grand Old Duke of York' (who led his troops up the hill, and down again). Whether the tactic is effective or not on a long view is difficult to tell. But if interest rates are moved at all, it is difficult for the authorities not to fall in with it; they are thus constrained to steer interest rate policy, as it were, with a jerky steering wheel.

There are more fundamental reasons that set limits to how far the authorities can push their power over interest rates, of which the most basic stems from the general considerations set out in Chapter 3. The authorities' power to influence interest rates (it was there argued) depends on their power to affect interest rate expectations. These are malleable within a range, because within a range interest rates are indeterminate in terms of the desire to employ capital and the desire to hold wealth; but beyond a point these fundamental factors would become dominant. Since market operators have a sense of this, a policy that sought to push interest rates beyond a certain limit would not appear credible; and were that the case, the policy would not be enforceable. The limit must depend on what the starting point is, and thus on the current perception of the underlying rate of inflation. It is clearly impossible to put any precise figure on it; but a rise of central-bank rate by, for instance, 5 percentage points, or a level of 25 per cent, might perhaps (even nowadays) be stretching the limits of credibility.

The authorities' power, moreover, must depend to some extent on political credibility. An interest rate policy that appeared rather extreme might be credible to markets if it was evident that it was a policy that the government had support for and could see through, and one that seemed likely to be effective in achieving its purpose — but perhaps not otherwise. The monetary authorities' power thus is analagous not to the mechanical power of a lever, but rather to the more elusive concept of political power.

This may be particularly the case in a country like the United Kingdom, where many things are done informally. None of the regulations imposed on the banks has rested on any statutory basis. Under the Bank of England Act the Treasury may instruct the Bank to issue orders to the banks, but the power has never been used. It is instructive to note that this informality extends even to the rudimentary question of providing the central bank with a source of income. Before 1980, as already noted, it had been an agreed practice for the clearing banks to leaves balances on deposit, interest-free, at the Bank of England. The arrangement was informal and private and was intended to provide the Bank with an income. By 1980 the clearers had come to think it unfair that they should bear the whole burden; and the arrangement was extended to all banks, and continues to depend on their consent. But the alternative of a statutory deduction, it must be supposed, was less attractive to the banks, the Bank, and the Treasury.

It has been argued in Section 1 above that the authorities' power to put pressure on banks' reserves and force increases in the banks' rates depends on working arrangements as to how balances are settled under the clearing, and on the rules of thumb that banks use in fixing their base rates. How much pressure the authorities can put on such working conventions depends ultimately on the public acceptability of the policy being followed; but each would begin to be modified if the authorities put too much strain on them. When central banks say that they 'operate in a market environment', they mean not that they operate like other market operators, but that in exercising their power to influence markets they are in touch with market opinion, and know that there are limits beyond which they cannot take markets with them.

3. THE EFFECT OF INTEREST RATES ON THE MONETARY AGGREGATES

It is clear that, within limits, the authorities have considerable power over interest rates. We must now come to the question of how useful this power is as a means of controlling the rate of growth of the monetary aggregates — which is how the authorities in the last decade and a half have hoped to use it. We have to consider, first, the effect of interest rates on the level of activity, and second, their effect on how a given level of activity is 'financed'. Both could in principle be relevant to the pace of monetary expansion.

On the first question we will argue that, although interest rates may affect the level of activity, they do not do so on a scale that has great effect on the rate of growth of the monetary aggregates. This argument does not require us to take an extreme position on interest rate elasticities. We have argued that there are limits to how far the authorities can affect interest rates. We have also argued (Chapter 3, Section 2) that in the short term the interest sensitivity of most sorts of expenditure is so small as to be negligible. But if a relatively low or a relatively high rate of interest could be maintained by policy means for a period of years, it must be supposed that this might begin to have a significant impact. There may also be effects of another sort. We have argued that lenders typically impose quantitative restrictions on how much they lend. The spending of many borrowers is thus limited not merely by their incomes or prospects of income, but by their ability to borrow against their prospective incomes. If interest rates rise, the spending of many of these borrowers is likely to be more severely contracted than the spending of those whom higher interest rates benefit is expanded (see further Chapter 13, Section 1).

Suppose then that the effects of interest-rate changes on economic activity may at times be significant. The effect that that would have on monetary growth is still likely to be inconsiderable in relation to the scale on which fluctuations in the rate of monetary growth are judged. Suppose, for instance, that higher interest rates could slow economic growth by as much as 1 per cent in the course of a year — which seems unlikely; and suppose (in line with the argument of Chapter 2) that that, in turn, slowed monetary growth by 1 per cent over twelve months. The effect on economic growth would be regarded as significant and as a matter of concern. But, given the erratic course of monetary growth and the kind of deviations that take place from a steady course, an effect on monetary growth on that scale would be too small for policy to attend to.

Over the last decade and a half, it is probably true to say that monetary policy has in fact aimed to control monetary growth without affecting economic growth. Speaking of the aims of policy in 1971, Fforde for instance remarked (Fforde 1982, 202) that experience at that date suggested that sufficient control of monetary growth could be obtained 'without movements in interest rates so large as to set up intolerable economic side effects'.

To achieve this aim, bank lending would have had to be affected; and to reduce bank lending without reducing expenditure requires a diversion of the flow of finance from the banks to other sources of finance, in particular the stock exchange. To induce that, bank finance would have to be made dearer than other sources of finance. That, however (for reasons set out in Chapter 2), is unlikely to happen as a result of a rise in central-bank rate.

- Though a rise in central-bank rate will raise the banks' lending rates, it will (as we argued earlier) also raise interest rate expectations generally, and thus will also raise the cost of alternative finance: the authorities have little or no control over relative interest rates.
- Even if there were some inducement to switch from bank finance, this would not nececssarily provoke a switch, given that the banks ration credit and thus usually act in a way to maintain an unsatisfied fringe of borrowers. Small borrowers, moreover, have in practice no ready alternative source of finance.

• Even if a switch away from bank finance occurred, it would be likely to require considerable time to be accomplished.

The conclusion would seem to be that central bank rate is likely to be more or less completely ineffective as an instrument for controlling the rate of growth of broad money (and the same arguments imply that it is equally ineffective as an instrument for controlling very broad money). There was mounting evidence through the decade when monetary targets were in force to suggest that this was the case. The attempt to use the central bank's 'traditional instrument' for this purpose appears, then, to have been misguided, and to have rested on inadequate analysis.

Whereas policy-induced interest rate changes appear generally ineffective as a means on controlling the broad aggregates, the position is somewhat different for some of the narrower monetary totals. A rise in interest rates, supposing it leaves bank lending unaffected, results in a switch from non-interest-bearing sight deposits to interest-bearing deposits. Studies of narrow money (M1) — the major part of which during most of the period earned no interest — have generally found significant interest sensitivity (Trundle 1982a, Hendry 1985). There is little evidence (at least in the United Kingdom) that the holding of notes and coin (and hence M0, of which they constitute the greater part) is sensitive to interest rates (Trundle 1982b).

The non-interest-bearing component of narrow money seems likely to remain interest-sensitive. Even so, there are limits to what could be accomplished by use of central-bank rate. The effect of a rise in interest rates to a new higher level is to induce a once-for-all portfolio shift away from non-interest-bearing deposits. The public's holdings of such deposits will tend to grow over time as nominal incomes increase. If the target growth for M1 were fixed below that rate of growth, there would be growing discrepancy. To correct that, not a one-step increase in the central-bank rate, but a continually rising rate, would be required. But we have argued that, beyond a point, a rise in central-bank rate would cease to be effective in raising the general level of interest rates. In any case, the sensitivity of M1 to interest rates must probably be diminishing. In the past, it has reflected the facts that the greater part of M1 consisted of non-interest-bearing deposits, the return of which was services provided by the banks without charge, and that the scale of service provided (like a sticky price) was not adjusted frequently. If the proportion of interest-bearing sight deposits in M1 continues to increase, M1 is likely (like M3) to become sensitive only to relative interest rates, and not to their general level.

Considerable importance has been attached to financial innovation in general as a development that has undermined official control over the monetary aggregates (see for instance Goodhart 1986). The relevance of this development can, however, be exaggerated. The process of innovation, which has been particularly rapid in the 1980s, has tended to create new substitutes for bank deposits and bank loans. The difference between bank assets and liabilities and other assets and liabilities was always a matter of degree. The greater ease of substitution between them resulting from financial innovation should make the monetary aggregates more sensitive than before to changes in relative interest rates. They would therefore be *more* amenable to official control, if the authorities had any effective means of influencing relative rates. That, however, they have never had; and it is for this reason that, ever since 1971, control over the aggregates by means of interest rates has failed to work. The spread of financial innovations has been highlighted as a reason for abandoning monetary targets (see for instance the Governor's Loughborough Lecture: *BEQB* 1986). But even without that, monetary control by variation of interest rates was ineffective.

9

Monetary Base Control

In Chapter 8 we argued that central-bank rate is ineffective as a control over the growth of broad money. Many advocates of monetary targets would agree, but would argue that the wrong instrument of control was being used: the Bank of England should instead have been trying to control the growth of the 'monetary base'. Monetary base control might take various forms, and in Section 1, in order to isolate the main propositions to be discussed, we describe the range of possibilities.

The idea underlying all types of monetary base control is that banks need a minimum of base (or high-powered) money as the reserve base for their operations. The money stock is thus related, even if loosely, by a 'money multiplier' to base money, and control of the base provides control of the stock. This idea is very widely accepted, and to those accustomed to thinking in these terms our having until now ignored monetary base must inevitably appear an omission of a vital element.

Our contention will be that adoption of a different operating procedure by the central bank would not bypass the essential difficulties in controlling the process of monetary growth. These spring both from the nature of monetary growth and from the authorities' limited power over interest rates. While deployment of our argument has required that these general points be discussed first (Chapters 2, 3, 4, and 8), the present chapter clearly remains a crucial link in our argument.

1. THE IDEA OF MONETARY BASE CONTROL

The monetary base is usually defined as the liabilities of the monetary authorities. There are (1) notes and coin held by the public, (2) notes and coin held by the banks as till money, and (3) deposits with the central bank by the banking system; and it is these that are included in the 'wide' monetary base (MO) as defined in UK monetary statistics.

Notes and coin held by the public preponderate in the total so defined. For most purposes, however, they are an unnecessary complication, and it considerably simplifies the argument to state it in terms of bankers' balances at the central bank. It is reasonable to think of the banks relating the size of balances they feel they need to the size of their deposits; that is less true of their holdings of notes and coin, and does not apply to the public's holdings. Moreover, neither the banks nor the authorities have means to influence the stock of notes and coin. For the banks must leave bank deposits freely convertible into notes and coin, which the authorities issue to the banks on demand; nor does the stock of cash held by either the public or the banks appear sensitive to the level of interest rates within the normal range of variation, and thus it is not controllable by that route.

Although it is for each bank to decide what balance it holds at the central bank, the total held by the banking system in the United Kingdom (as explained in Chapter 8, Section 1) may be increased (or decreased) by the authorities selling debt on a scale greater (or less) than the central government needs to borrow domestically, or by the central bank lending to the banks (or running down lending to them). It should be noted that many smaller banks do not hold balances directly with the central bank, but only indirectly, by holding a balance with a larger bank that holds a balance there. Such arrangements could change — a point to be developed later.

Monetary base control has been advocated chiefly by monetarist economists (for instance in the United Kingdom by Griffiths 1979, and Greenwell Associates 1980). The debate about it was most lively in the year or two before and after the Conservative government took office in 1979. Important contributions were Foot, Goodhart, and Hotson (1979); the official Green Paper, *Monetary Control* (Treasury/Bank 1980); a number of reactions to that, mainly in financial publications, both for and against base control (for references see Artis and Lewis 1981); and hearings before the Treasury and Civil Service Committee in its 1979–80 session (Treasury and Civil Service Committee 1980).

Many proponents of base control see it as differing radically from the attempt to control monetary growth by use of central-bank rate. Milton Friedman, in his Memoranda to the Treasury and Civil Service Committee, is particularly vivid and worth quoting at some length:

I could hardly believe my eyes, when I read [in the Green Paper]: 'The principal means of controlling the growth of the money supply must be fiscal policy . . . and interest rates'. . . . Direct control of the monetary base is an alternative to fiscal policy and interest rates as a means of controlling monetary growth . . . and a very different thing. . . . Trying to control the money supply through 'fiscal policy . . . and interest rates' is trying to control the output of one item (money) through altering the demand for it by manipulating the income of its users (that is the role of fiscal policy) or the prices of substitutes for it (that is the role of interest rates). A precise analogy is like trying to control the output of motor cars by altering the incomes of potential purchasers and manipulating rail and air fares. In principle, possible in both cases, but in practice highly inefficient. Far easier to control the output of motor cars by controlling the availability of a basic raw material, say steel, to the manufacturers — a precise analogy to controlling the money supply by controlling the availability of base money to banks and others. (Friedman 1980)

While the comparison with a direct control is suggestive (and will be taken up later), it over-dramatizes the contrast with the present system. Under one possible form of base control, the authorities would lay down mandatory ratios for each bank's holding of balances at the central bank in relation to its deposits. The authorities would then indeed have something close to a direct control over bank lending. Many advocates of base control (including Friedman in his evidence) do not envisage this. The ratio could then (and in practice would) vary, and control over the money stock would be altogether looser. The principal difference as compared with the present use of central-bank rate would be one of attitude and of operating procedure. To quote Friedman again, 'the authorities . . . currently . . . have surrendered control of the base by standing ready passively to provide reserves to the banking system at the option of the banks'. They should, by contrast, decide on the quantity to be provided, exercising control (roughly as now) by open-market operations. 'The key point . . . is that the Bank should decide in advance each week how much to buy or sell, not the price at which it will buy or sell. It should permit interest rates to be determined entirely by the market.' Interest rates would thus be a by-product of the quantity decision — not, as now, the reverse.

The advantages that can be claimed for a base control of this sort, in comparison with the present discretionary use of central-bank rate, are that action by the central bank (once the decision as to the scale on which the banks would be provided with reserves had been taken) would be 'automatic', and thus not subject to the delay now likely as the authorities deliberate, and that the effect on interest rates could, depending on circumstances, be larger — in principle, whatever was required to keep the growth of base money on the course set in the first instance. It would not remove the need for judgement in deciding on the course of base money, nor would it instantaneously ensure that the target monetary aggregate followed the desired course (since the ratio of base to deposits could vary). These differences from the present system can be regarded as differences of speed and scale; it would still be changes in interest rates that provided the incentive to the banks to modify their behaviour. The analysis in Chapter 8 of how the banks respond to the use of central-bank rate thus provides a starting point for considering how the banking system would be likely to respond to this potentially stricter control mechanism.

A further variant (though perhaps not amounting to base control, but discussed in the Green Paper) would be for the authorities to continue to operate by discretionary use of central-bank rate, and to use the course of base money as an 'indicator' by which they would judge the need for changes in interest rates. While this would not give all that advocates of base control are seeking, it is mentioned here to show that there is continuous gradation between the present system and forms of base control of increasing strictness, ranging at the far end to a base control with prescribed ratios.

In Section 2 we will consider more closely the effects of a base control without prescribed ratios, because that is the form that its advocates usually envisage; and we will consider it as a means of controlling broad money, discussing more briefly its use for controlling narrow money. In most discussions of monetary base control it is assumed that the power of the authorities over the banks comes from the fact that the banks keep balances at the central bank. We will later query how much power over the banks this in fact provides, and whether, in the final analysis, the authorities' influence is not more political in nature.

2. THE EFFECTS OF MONETARY BASE CONTROL

The Green Paper was even-handed in its presentation of base control, and left it somewhat unclear as to whether it was a possible system. This was perhaps partly because the government had been influenced by the case made for it by monetarist economists, and because the Green Paper was intended as a discussion document to test opinion. This attitude may also have owed something to the fact that the alternative method of operation by central-bank rate could at that date still be held to offer an effective means of controlling monetary growth. The official authors of the Green Paper could therefore point to difficulties and disadvantages that base control was likely to have as compared with the existing system, and to significant costs in making the transition to a new and untried method of control. Since then the argument has lapsed, and has remained inconclusive by default. For the purpose of this study we need a more radical answer. In Chapter 8 we sought to establish the reasons why it is not possible to control monetary growth by use of central-bank rate; the basic question is whether base control would work.

Let us consider then how a base control without mandatory reserve ratios would operate. Suppose that banks' balances at the central bank (the base) are allowed to grow only at a certain rate, and that banks' deposits and liabilities (and hence broad money) when uncontrolled tend to grow at a faster rate. The first result is likely to be that banks will make do with smaller balances in relation to deposits, and this process could go a long way. Banks would become progressively shorter of reserves, would compete for base assets that are limited in supply, and would drive up short-term interest rates. Markets (in the words of the Green Paper) 'generate the interest rates necessary to bring the rate of growth of the money supply back to the desired path'.

Advocates of base control tend to some ambiguity as to how far interest rates would rise. It is usually admitted that in the course of the adjustment short-term rates would rise, but only (it is usually implied) in a short transitional stage. That assumption may reflect a view, which it is important to make explicit, about the ease with which the pace of inflation can be slowed down. If prices are rising rapidly, the stock of money is likely to be rising rapidly also, because (as we have argued) the amount that the banks' clients wish to borrow in nominal terms and the amount that banks feel it safe to lend will both be rising. If the adoption of base control itself quickly moderated the pace of inflation, then the pressure behind the control, and the banks' shortage of reserves, would be quickly eased, and interest rates would not be driven high.

Take however the contrary view — that the iterative nature of the wage/price spiral is deeply entrenched, and that inflation is at best to be slowed only gradually, perhaps via a fall in the level of demand and employment. The stock of money may then be supposed to continue to rise over-rapidly despite restriction of the growth of monetary base. The banks' shortage of reserves would then continue to grow, and short-term interest rates would mount progressively, as the banks competed ever more strongly for reserves. This second case is in our view the more realistic. It thus appears useful to consider how base control would stand up to the strong pressures then put on it, and how the banking system would respond.

If base money is to control the growth of broad money, it must somehow control bank lending. We have argued (Chapter 8, Section 2) that under the present system the use of central-bank rate is ineffective in controlling bank lending for essentially two reasons.

1. Given the way in which the general level of interest rates is determined, all interest rates rise when central-bank rate is raised; there is therefore no diversion of borrowing away from banks to alternative cheaper sources of finance.
2. There are limits to how high the central bank can raise interest rates. But expenditure is not greatly or quickly sensitive to interest rates, so that expenditure financed by borrowing (of all sorts) is not significantly curtailed by a rise in central-bank rate.

The same arguments would appear to apply to the reaction to the imposition of a monetary base control of any significant severity. It would be as if an irresistible force — continued excess growth of bank lending — met an immovable object — the prescribed path of base money; and something would have to give. In the process interest rates might, it seems, inevitably be driven to unprecedented levels. To try to trace out how the banks and the financial system would respond would be largely surmise, and an attempt to do so would have a distinct air of unreality. For advocates of base control have never extended their analysis into these realms of possibility, or envisaged base control causing major perturbations to the financial system. Nevertheless, the logical exercise of sketching possible repercussions seems worth persisting with. It is unlikely that the process would be orderly, and one possibility is that the banks, faced with unaccustomed uncertainties, would simply resort to rationing credit. We will leave that possibility for a moment, and come back to it later.

There would be many new elements confronting banks and financial markets. To keep base money on its prescribed path, central-bank lending to the banks would have to cease to be on demand, and would become at best rare. At present, the authorities provide signals to financial institutions not so much by declaring a central-bank rate (a practice that has already ceased), but by indicating their wishes through the way they lend. Though that too would now disappear, the banks would probably continue to set their base rates with some regard to short market rates — for if they did not, they would appear to be lending rather cheaply. Lending rates might thus rise steeply.

What result that would have would depend on the behaviour of long-term rates, which is even more difficult to gauge. If short-term rates reached a new stable plateau, and it appeared that the authorities were prepared to leave them there, market expectations might adjust to that and put long-term rates at a comparable level. But the situation seems unlikely to stabilize and the probable outcome unlikely to become clear to markets. Some of the conflicting forces may be indicated as follows:

- High interest rates might induce recession, slow down the growth of bank lending by this route, and remove the pressure for progressively rising interest rates. Alternatively, and perhaps more probably, this process might not work quickly enough.
- Markets might fail to be convinced that the authorities would persist with strict base control. For extremely high interest rates are unpopular and not what governments usually want, and high rates would tend to bring a high or very high exchange rate, which might also appear to make continuance of the policy unlikely. In that case, long rates would probably remain below short rates.
- If the disparity between long and short rates continued, there might be disintermediation out of bank finance into finance by stock exchange issues. That would moderate the banks' demand for reserves and might thus provide, at least temporarily, a stable response to the tight grip of base control. But it could hardly be truly stable since, if it looked like continuing, market expectations would bring long rates up to match short rates, so removing the incentive to fund bank loans.

Enough has perhaps been said to indicate that financial markets might be considerably confused. In that situation, however, it is possible that the banks might simply impose direct restrictions on their lending, and adjust their balance sheets in this way to the restricted growth of their reserves imposed on them by the authorities. Although the parallel is not exact, the banks' reaction to the Corset is perhaps suggestive. The Corset imposed penalties on the banks in the event that their liabilities grew at more than a specified rate. In principle, the penalties applied were activated by the behaviour not of individual banks, but (as with base control) by that of the banking system as a whole. (See however Chapter 10, Section 1.) Individual banks nevertheless responded by rationing lending, and not by raising the price of loans.

A more general reason for supposing that the banks might react in this way to base control is that monetary policy cannot be conducted in a purely impersonal hands-off manner, as if central bank and banks were not on speaking terms; this would especially be the case with a very strict policy, promising considerable upset to financial markets. The authorities would have to make clear what pace of growth of broad money, and hence of bank lending, they hoped to achieve. The simplest way of achieving what the authorities wanted, and of avoiding the rise in interest rates otherwise inevitable, would be for the banks directly to restrict lending. It is true that a collective decision by the large banks to do so would risk being undermined by non-compliance on the part of smaller banks. But historical precedent suggests that there might nevertheless be an effective restraint of lending. That would cause disintermediation in the same way as officially imposed direct controls on lending.

The alternative of negotiable 'licences to lend'

The Green Paper outlined an alternative scheme which would appear to offer the results that advocates of base control seek without some of the complications that would arise with base control. (This was essentially a simplification of the scheme proposed by Duck and Sheppard 1978.) It was presented as a scheme for 'negotiable entitlements' to take deposits, but it might equally well have been presented as a scheme for negotiable licences to lend.

The authorities (the Green Paper explained) would create 'a supply of such entitlements which banks would be required to buy in proportion to the deposits they wished to take', and would 'increase the supply in line with the growth of deposits that they thought desirable'. If deposits tended to rise above that implied by the stock of entitlements, the price of entitlements would rise. 'This would effectively raise the marginal cost of additional deposits to the banks . . . [who] would raise their lending rates or otherwise restrict their loans . . . to the point where . . . total deposits .

. . were within the total allowed.' The effect would be 'to tax the banks covered by the scheme, obliging them to raise the margin between their lending and deposit rates and/or to pass the business on elsewhere, and so provide an incentive to disintermediation'.

A tight base control, maintained resolutely in face of a persistent tendency for money to grow faster than thought desirable, inevitably implies heavy constraint of the working of the banking system. The above scheme illustrates in simple form the nature of official interference that any control of broad money must involve.

The power of central banks

The power of the central bank over the banks is often said to arise from the fact that the banks' ultimate reserves are their balances at the central bank. This makes it seem simple for the central bank to control the monetary base and thus, via the 'money multiplier', to control the money stock. That account of the determination of the volume of money has a distinguished history, going back to Keynes (1930) and Meade (1934) and beyond. But it is inadequate as monetary theory; and it also fails to locate the source of central-bank power, or to give any inkling of the limits of that power, which also is an important question.

Banks are older than central banks,* and if central banks were abolished, banks would undoubtedly survive. The service that central banks provide is essentially a cheap source of liquidity. As Foot, Goodhart, and Hotson remark,

A banking system as we know it could not have developed had banks not learned how to make loans without collapsing, through want of liquidity, if some depositors wanted their money back. The first line of defence for any bank against such liquidity was traditionally provided by holding a stock of generally acceptable assets — coin or notes — 'behind the counter'. The second consisted of balances with other banks that could be used to obtain additional generally accepted notes. As the Bank of England became increasingly important as a note issuer and as a 'central bank', it became increasingly convenient to hold Bank of England notes and balances at the Bank. (Foot, Goodhart, and Hotson 1979, 150)

By now the most important part of banks' reserves is invisible, like an overdraft facility — the assurance of being able to obtain lender-of-last-resort facilities through the discount houses. Since a strict monetary base control would require withdrawal of that assurance, its first result would probably be to drive the banks to build up alternative reserves. At first

---

* 'Yet central banks are comparative novelties. Even in England central banking history falls well within the last two hundred years, while in the United States and most other countries it is practically confined to the twentieth century' (Sayers 1957, 1).

that might well take the form of aiming to hold larger balances at the central bank. Nevertheless, it should be seen as a step towards lessening banks' dependence on the central bank for the provision of reserves; and actions by the central bank could drive the banks towards greater independence.

It is now mainly large banks that hold balances with the central bank. Many small banks, and all building societies — a major segment of deposit-taking institutions — hold balances at other banks. If obtaining additional reserves from the central bank were made sufficiently expensive, the banks would economize in their reliance on such provision, and could do so for instance by holding larger balances with each other. One or more large banks could indeed in principle provide the services now provided by the central bank, so that the extreme position in which the banking system became completely independent in this respect is not inconceivable.

That situation is not, in practice, likely to arise. For the game is essentially a political one: the central bank could always control the banks in other ways, as all parties are aware. Even if the banks became independent as to reserves, they would not be beyond the reach of regulation. Thus the central bank could make banks hold mandatory deposits with it, or impose other controls on them (not excluding for instance a scheme like that for 'negotiable entitlements' mentioned above). Banks therefore have reasons to seek to conform to the authorities' wishes and to avoid raising questions about the need for more formal control.

Political power, however, is itself inevitably limited. A government if determined can always restrict bank lending, and monetary base control might be one means, though not the most direct or effective. But any effective restriction must either reduce the banks' role (as compared with unregulated institutions) in ways likely to appear unjust and inefficient, or frustrate potential borrowers and reduce expenditure, output, and employment, which might also be difficult to defend. Monetary base control should not be seen as a device that operates in isolation from the economic and political consequences of controlling money.

Base control of narrow money

So far we have discussed monetary base control as a means of controlling broad money. That is indeed arguably the most important context, and also the one most relevant to discussion in the United Kingdom. Nevertheless, it is worth discussing briefly its possible use as a means to control narrow money. Because its effects would be less fundamental and more 'cosmetic', the difficulties would be less. Even so, it seems unlikely to provide a permanent and satisfactory method of control.

We discussed base control of broad money on the assumption that there were no mandatory reserve ratios. But for base control to be able to restrict narrow money, it would have to be accompanied by mandatory ratios: banks would be required to hold reserves in proportion to a specified class of deposits. We can assume that much if not all of the deposits included in the definition of narrow money are non-interest-bearing; much of the effectiveness of the control would come from that.

The authorities would aim to restrict the growth of base money to the rate of increase desired for narrow money. If narrow money on the chosen definition was tending to grow faster than the authorities wanted, that would induce banks to bid for reserves and so drive up interbank rates. It is likely that the banks would then raise rates on deposits that bore interest. That would induce a shift on the part of the public from non-interest-bearing into interest-bearing deposits, so that the target aggregate would grow less rapidly than before, and interbank rates would rise to the point where the growth of the aggregate had been slowed enough for the banks to comply with the specified reserves ratio. To survive, the banks also would have to raise their lending rates.

Base control of narrow money, however, would not seem capable of being indefinitely effective against a persistent tendency for the narrow money aggregate to grow more rapidly than the authorities wanted. The stock of narrow money which the public wants to hold may be assumed to be related to the value of transactions; and, in any economy with rising nominal incomes and expenditure, it may be assumed to grow, at a given level of interest rates, if nominal incomes are rising. A given increase in deposit rates would induce a once-for-all shift from non-interest-bearing deposits (included in the target aggregate) to interest-bearing deposits (mostly outside the aggregate). To counter a continuous tendency for the aggregate to grow too fast, a progressive rise in deposit rates would be required.

That, however, is clearly not a real possibility, so that analysis of movement in that direction again has an unreal air. As in the previous analysis, it is difficult to tell what would happen to market-determined interest rates. Depending on what markets made of policy, flexible rates could rise along with the banks' administered rates: but it also seems possible that they would not rise, or not rise fully in line with the banks' rates. Even, however, if they first kept in step, there is limit (on the argument of Chapter 3) to how high market expectations of interest rates can be pushed by official action. At some stage, then, lending would become uncompetitive with other forms of finance, and banks would start to be driven out of business. It is probably not useful to suppose that policy would be pushed to these lengths.

If base control were pushed hard, it would also become increasingly subject to evasion. Application of base control to a narrow money aggregate means that banks would be required to hold reserves against some classes of deposits and not others. Banks could therefore diminish the cost of conforming by persuading their customers to shift funds from an included to an excluded class of deposit. As with broad money controls, borrowers would also move to institutions not covered by the scheme.

Base control might therefore provide a way of controlling the growth of narrow money for a limited time, depending on the difficulty of the task it was set. But it does not appear to provide a method that could be maintained indefinitely, nor therefore to provide a general answer to the difficulty of controlling even a narrow monetary aggregate.

The practice of other central banks

It is a task of some difficulty (as this study perhaps shows) to discern how monetary policy operates, and this must be especially true of other countries with whose conditions one is relatively unfamiliar. But it appears to be the case that no country now relies on monetary base control, and it is doubtful whether any has placed simple reliance on it over an extended period.

The nearest case was perhaps Switzerland. But the Swiss National Bank appears to have seen movements of monetary base as an indicator of likely future movements of narrow money, rather than as an operational technique (see appendix to Foot, Goodhart, and Hotson 1979). The new operating procedure adopted by the US Federal Reserve System in 1979 may appear to have been a step towards base control. But it was only a small step, for the procedures applied to quite short time horizons (see US Federal Reserve System 1980). Under this procedure, estimates were made of the reserve changes that would be consistent with the growth rates in the target aggregates as targeted at monthly meetings of the Federal Open Market Committee (FOMC), and between meetings the System Account Manager sought to keep the course of reserves to that path. Stronger monetary growth than targeted would then lead the banks, in an effort to obtain additional reserves, to bid up the federal funds rate. But it would also lead them to borrow more at the Federal Reserve discount window, a facility that was not withdrawn. If pressure were sustained, the possibility also remained for the authorities to respond by a discretionary rise in the discount rate. At the next meeting of the FOMC the situation would be reassessed. Thus (as the official account puts it), 'the new procedures entail greater freedom for interest rates to change over the short run in response to market forces'.

The Bundesbank's target of 'central bank money' consists of a total in which the components of broad money are given differing weights. Though sometimes so misinterpreted, its use is not a form of monetary base control. It may be noted that the two countries that may have gone some way towards base control, Switzerland and the United States, both have had narrow money as their main target aggregate.

3. CONCLUSIONS

Monetary base control is often presented as a simple way to control monetary growth. That appears misleading. The conclusion of this discussion must be that, in face of a continuing tendency for the aggregates to grow more rapidly than the authorities regard as desirable, base control would not be an effective way of controlling the growth of broad money, nor for long a practicable way of controlling the growth of narrow money. The basic difficulties in controlling the rate of expansion of banks' balance sheets remain the same under any method. Although the arguments were never fully exposed, the Bank of England's instinctive resistance to monetary base control thus appears well justified.

In the theoretical discussion, monetary policy has usually been discussed in terms of the Hicksian *IS/LM* framework (which has been discussed in Chapter 4, Section 3). That appears to leave it open to the authorities to proceed either by seeking to control the quantity of money or by controlling its price (interest rates), and there has been a considerable debate since (Poole 1970) as to the circumstances in which each is to be preferred. The first might be equated to monetary base control and the second to varying the price at which the banking system can obtain additional reserves by changing central-bank rate. Our conclusion is that neither monetary base control nor the use of central-bank rate provides effective control of the money stock, so that we have no footing in that debate.

10

The Corset, Funding Policy and Banking Supervision

The previous two chapters have discussed what are often regarded as the classical methods of monetary control: the attempt to control the growth of bank intermediation by central-bank rate, which was tried for a decade and a half, and monetary base control, which was never tried. This chapter discusses two other methods of control: in Section 1 the Corset (or, to go by its official title, the Supplementary Special Deposits Scheme), and in Section 2 restraint of public-sector borrowing from the banks and (what may be regarded as its extension) overfunding. Each was used for a time, and was successful at least in a superficial sense; but both had disadvantages, and raise questions as to the purposes of monetary control. Athough both methods have been abandoned, the general lessons are worth discussion. Section 3 provides a short account of banking supervision, whose purposes, while distinct from those of monetary policy, are partially related.

1. THE CORSET, 1973–1980

The scheme of monetary control popularly known as the Corset was a form of direct control with features that permitted greater flexibility than the pre-1971 controls over lending; it was in force intermittently from end-1973 to mid-1980. Although since abandoned and in disrepute, experience with the Corset illustrates the essential difficulty of controlling a broad monetary aggregate, and (as already noted) bears on the possiblities of monetary base control. The details of the scheme are set out in a Bank account of its working (*BEQB* 1982, 74–85) and only the essentials need be considered here.

The Corset applied only to banks; whether comparable control over the building societies would have been desirable or feasible was not considered. Although detailed and precise in its application to individual banks, the scheme rested on no statutory basis. Orders could have been issued under the Bank of England Act, but, as with all other requirements imposed on the banks, the authorities preferred to avoid doing so. It was therefore in form voluntary, although all knew that refusal to comply by even one or two banks could have led to a statutory order.

The way the Corset worked

The scheme was intended to moderate the growth of 'resources available [to banks] for on-lending to other sectors of the economy'. It did not apply to non-interest-bearing deposits on the grounds that the banks 'did not, and presumably could not, vary [these] to accommodate changes in the demand for credit' (*BEQB* 1982, 77); and applied only to interest-bearing 'eligible liabilities' (IBELs) — essentially, sterling deposits. Targets were prescribed for the rate of growth of such deposits, and penalties laid down for banks whose deposits grew more rapidly than the target. These penalties were progressive, becoming more severe the greater the excess rate of growth.

Unlike the previous controls on lending, the Corset thus did not discriminate between lending to the public and private sectors. Furthermore, the scheme was designed to permit competition between banks and avoid freezing the distribution of deposits between them; for deposits placed by one bank with another, or with the discount houses, did not count against the first bank's eligible liabilities. (The corresponding liabilities counted against those of the second bank or the discount houses.) The scheme was designed to operate in conjunction with the existing $12\frac{1}{2}$ per cent reserves/assets ratio applying to the banks (see Chapter 6 above); a parallel capital/assets limit applied to the discount houses. By virtue of the transfer provisions, the scheme in principle imposed a limit only on the scale of the banking system as a whole, not on individual banks; and penalties needed to be incurred only when the system as a whole came against its limit. Penalties were paid on a small scale on other occasions, through inadvertency on the part of some banks. (In practice, however, banks have been unwilling to lend beyond a point on the basis of wholesale (rather than retail) deposits, and may have hesitated fully to avail themselves of the transfer provisions built into the scheme. The control may therefore have constricted individual banks rather than the system as a whole, and thus partially failed in its aim of preserving interbank competition.)

The Corset was first imposed at the end of 1973, remained in force for rather over a year, and was then lifted. It was subsequently reimposed at the end of 1976 for well under a year, and was reimposed again a year later for two years before being finally removed in mid-1980 (details in Table 10.1). For small infringements of the permitted rate of growth (up to 1 per cent; later up to 3 per cent) the penalties were relatively small. Thus, the non-interest-bearing deposits required of banks in the penalty zones amounted to 5 per cent of the excess growth; at money-market rates then ruling, this meant a loss of interest on excess deposits of about $\frac{1}{2}$ per cent at an annual rate (i.e. assuming that the excess over the norm was maintained for a year). Beyond that range the penalties became

TABLE 10.1. Penalties imposed under the Corset

		Penalties imposed		
	Allowable growth of IBELs[a]	On excess growth of	Deposits required	Effective rate of penalty[b]
		(%)	(%)	(%)
1st period:	8% over first	up to 1[d]	5	*0.6*
Dec. 1973[c]–	6 mos. then	1–3[d]	25	*3.0*
Feb. 1975	1½% per mo.	over 3[d]	50	*6.0*
2nd period:	3% over first	up to 3	5	*0.4*
Nov. 1976[c]–	6 mos. then	3–5	25	*2.0*
Aug. 1977	1½% per mo.	over 5	50	*4.0*
3rd period:	4% during	up to 3	5	*0.7*
June 1978[c]–	Aug.–Oct. 1978			
June 1980	then	3–5	25	*3.5*
	1% per mo.	over 5	50	*7.0*

[a] Interest-bearing eligible liabilities (see text).
[b] Loss of interest at average 3-mo. sterling CD rate in period, assuming excess growth was maintained for a year.
[c] Date of announcement
[d] Towards the end of the first period, in Nov. 1974, the limits were widened to those shown for subsequent periods.

Source: BEQB 1982, 78.

severe, involving losses of interest of 2 or 3 per cent a year on excess growth of over 3 per cent (later 5 per cent), and double that for still greater infringements of the allowed rate of growth. Although designed to impose graduated financial inducements rather than outright regulation, the penalties were in fact more or less prohibitive: the effect was thus little different from that of a direct control. The banks managed for most of the time to keep the growth of their liabilities close to the allowed limits. Significant penalties were paid only in the last six months of the Corset's existence, the period following the announcement of its abolition; and the relatively few banks who then incurred penalty presumably aimed to establish a stronger position ahead of the Corset's abolition, and saw the loss of interest as a worthwhile cost.

The effects of the Corset

The course of interest-bearing eligible liabilities and of broad money (£M3) in the years 1973–80 is shown in Fig. 10.1. (The overlap between the two aggregates is partial: IBELs includes overseas sterling deposits, which are not in £M3; £M3 includes non-interest-bearing deposits, and also the notes and coin held by the public, both excluded from IBELs.)

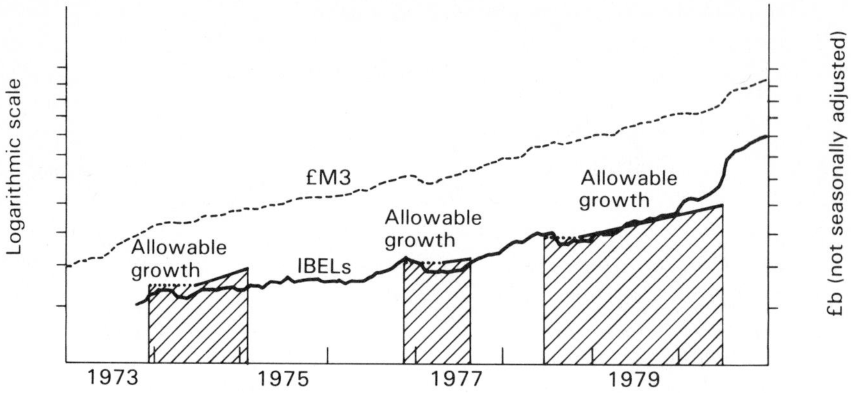

Fig. 10.1 *The course of broad money and of interest-bearing eligible liabilities, 1974–1980*

Source: reproduced by permission from the *Bank of England Quarterly Bulletin* 1982, 80

The fact that the growth of banks' balance sheets was, for most of the time, kept within the penalty-free rate of growth might suggest that the Corset was highly successful. Any such judgement requires a close look at the attendant circumstances, which must be left for Chapter 11; but the broad conclusions relevant to the Corset may be briefly anticipated.

From a superficial inspection, one can get the impression that the growth the banks were allowed within the penalty-free zones was not very different from what they would have chosen anyhow. In particular, immediately after the Corset was first imposed at the end of 1973, the demand for bank loans, previously very buoyant, fell away — so that the new control appeared not to be biting at all hard. But the fact that the scheme was in existence may itself have made banks more cautious in their lending policies. The trends during the three periods when the Corset was in force are perhaps less significant than those over the whole of the six and a half years from first imposition to final abolition; in this period, even when not in effect, it was always known that it could be. There was probably some attempt at forestalling by the banks, at times when the control was off, against its future reimposition. But taking the period as a whole, it is clear that 1974 marked the end of one rapid period of growth of bank credit, and 1980 marked the beginning of another; and after the control was abolished in 1980, it was lending to persons (which the banks had been requested to restrict) that grew particularly fast. This supports the supposition (further examined in Chapter 11, Section 2) that the Corset, together with the 'qualitative' guidance from the Bank, resulted in a general climate of restraint by the banks throughout the five or six years when the Corset was actually or potentially in force.

A general pervasive effect of this sort has not been much considered. Instead, attention has focused on one undoubted, if less important, failing: that some flows were diverted away from the banks and took place via transactions in the money markets. This was probably of most importance at the end of the period, and its scale can be judged by what happened when the Corset was removed: £M3 then rose by nearly 8 per cent in the three following months, perhaps half of which may have represented re-intermediation.

It may be of some detailed interest to note that the effect of the Corset was not quite what its authors envisaged. When it was introduced in 1973, the failure of policy to control the growth of the broad aggregates by means of interest rates was ascribed to the new development of 'liability management' by the banks, that is to their increased resort to the wholesale markets to obtain deposits (see *BEQB* 1982, 75–7), and the imposition of penalties specifically on interest-bearing deposits was meant to stop this. The increased reliance by the banks after 1971 on wholesale deposits must however have been part of a process of re-intermediation of flows previously kept off banks' books. (Companies held larger bank deposits and fewer of each others' bills than before.) The Corset succeeded in checking wholesale deposit taking (which was intended) but necessarily also reversed the earlier re-intermediation (which was not). These were indeed opposite sides of the same process rather than separate developments (as the Bank's subsequent account seems to treat them: *BEQB* 1982, 82).

It will be argued in Chapter 11 that a direct control on lending may have considerable effect on spending, more particularly by consumers; and in Chapter 13, when we come to consider the possibilities of monetary policy in the future, it will be argued that there are circumstances in which this might be useful. Although any direct control of lending must invite some evasion, that may be a cost worth incurring, and not sufficient reason for rejecting such methods. The disrepute into which controls like the Corset has fallen, because of the disinter-mediation they provoke, may be somewhat misplaced.

2. FUNDING POLICY AND OVERFUNDING

Since the end of the war, it has been a general presumption of policy that the government should not rely unduly on borrowing from the banks to meet its borrowing requirement. As part result of this general bias, the stock of public debt held by the banks has since 1971 grown less rapidly than GDP. This can be regarded (for reasons spelt out below) as a factor that has somewhat retarded the growth of broad money over the next one and a half decades — to a point where it would be difficult to make further reductions of bank-held public debt. Overfunding the public-sector deficit, and using the funds so acquired to buy trade bills from the banks, was a way of extending the same approach, and was a policy followed for a few years in the early 1980s. These two lines of policy are considered here together.

Public-sector borrowing from the banks

We have already given reasons (Chapter 6) for not treating total public-sector borrowing — but only public-sector borrowing from the banks — as causing a growth of broad money. The banks help to finance the public sector by acquiring government bonds, Treasury bills, or certificates of tax deposit. In nominal terms the stock of finance so provided has grown continuously, but it has grown less rapidly than nominal GDP; and, expressed as a ratio to GDP, bank-held public debt has fallen each year since 1971. It has thus to some degree offset the tendency of bank lending to the private sector to outpace the growth of GDP, and so has moderated the rise in broad money.

Only in a broad sense can this be regarded as an effect of policy, which was never formulated in these terms. In so far as there was a policy, it was concerned only with how large a proportion of the flow of new borrowing (the public-sector deficit), as it varied year by year, might properly be financed by borrowing from the banks. The authorities' policy about borrowing from the banks gets little mention in public policy statements. But traditional ideas of 'sound finance' implied a presumption that public debt should be long-term, on the grounds that such debt was more 'firmly held' — a form of asset which its holders would find less easy to spend should they later have that desire; and it seems clear that in the 1960s the Bank had come to feel that the average term of existing debt was too short (Bain 1970, 50). The aim, although vaguely formulated, seems to have been to finance 'a reasonable proportion' of the government's current needs by sales of gilt-edged debt (Goodhart 1984, 92).

Before 1971, the rate of growth of the monetary aggregates was not a central control of the authorities, and for some years after that it remained a vague one. The announcement of monetary targets appears to have led to greater emphasis on debt sales to the non-bank public, and gradually to the more or less explicit aim of selling debt (gilt-edged or national savings instruments) on a scale roughly equal to the public-sector borrowing requirement. That could hardly be expected to be achieved year by year, for huge errors are made in forecasting both debt sales and the borrowing requirement. In many years, a significant part of the deficit was met by external borrowing, or as the incidental effect of running down the foreign exchange reserves; in other years additions to the reserves added to domestic borrowing (details in Wright 1984). The proportion of the public-sector borrowing requirement met by bank borrowing was thus highly erratic, and in several years since 1976 a quarter or more of borrowing has been borrowing from the banks.

Nevertheless, since 1971 there has been a continuous tendency for the stock of bank lending to the public sector to grow relatively slowly, in comparison with other aggregates. In nominal terms it more than doubled, but nominal GDP grew fivefold. As a ratio to GDP, bank-held public debt declined with remarkable steadiness (from about 24 per cent of GDP in 1971 to about 8 per cent in 1984: see Fig. 11.3 below). The effect on the monetary aggregates was relatively small and gradual: as compared with a situation in which bank-held government debt kept pace with nominal GDP, the effect was to reduce broad money, as a ratio to GDP, by little more than 1 per cent a year. Although policy was never formulated in exactly these terms, this was the broad result of the policy that was followed — and may be regarded as a rare successful instance of monetary restraint.

The policy of overfunding

For some years in the early 1980s the evident difficulty of controlling bank lending by means of interest rates led the authorities to adopt a policy of overfunding the public-sector borrowing requirement. The rationale was evident: if bank lending to the private sector could not be controlled, its effect on the monetary aggregates could at least be offset by overfunding the central government deficit. 'For [as the Bank explained] other things being equal, an increase in lending by the banks will be reflected in increased deposits — which sales of government debt to the public will reduce' (*BEQB* 1982, 181).

Overfunding had taken place in earlier years, but rather as an accident of forecasting errors than as deliberate policy; the detailed figures are thus not of great significance to this discussion. (They are contained in Wright 1984, who gives variant definitions of overfunding.) The policy of overfunding had however an apparently paradoxical side-effect; in particular, it resulted (for reasons set out below) in the acquisition by the Bank of England of very large holdings of commercial bills (the 'bill mountain'). This made the policy difficult to defend persuasively, and there remained indeed ambiguity as to how fully the authorities were committed to it: it was at times defended, at times unmentioned, and, in June or July 1985, abandoned. Its awkward features are worth examining because of the wider questions they raise.

Overfunding and the banks' reserve positions

Overfunding involves three parties: the government, the banks, and the non-bank public. Up to about 1983, overfunding went along with a reduction of public-sector indebtedness to the banks. To make clear what this involves, assume that the public sector deficit, the total holdings of financial assets by the non-bank public, and bank lending to the private sector all remain unchanged. Each of the three parties — the government, the non-bank public, and the banks — is then involved in trading one form of financial asset for another:

- the non-bank public buys government debt and runs down bank deposits;
- the government, having sold debt to the non-bank public, repays debt to the banks on the same scale;
- the banks thus hold less government debt, matched by smaller deposits from the public.

By 1983 the reduction of public sector indebtedness to the banks had reached a point where it could not easily be reduced further. What the banks hold in the way of short bonds and tax reserve certificates is at their choice. Treasury bills, however, are the government's residual form of finance (which, by convention, the banks supply according to the government's need); and by 1983 the banks' holdings of Treasury bills had become minimal.

This was more important than might appear. Overfunding of the total public-sector deficit tended to mean overfunding that of the central government (see Wright 1984); and since the central government banks not with the commercial banks but with the Bank of England, sales of debt to non-banks in excess of its deficit result — unless the effect is deliberately offset by the authorities — in depleting the banks' reserves, i.e. their balances at the Bank of England. (The qualifications to this statement required to take account of central government lending to other bodies, and of external and foreign currency finance, have already been noted in Chapter 8, Section 1.) So long as the outstanding stock of Treasury bills was large enough, this effect could be offset by running down the stock of Treasury bills — in effect, buying such bills from the banks. When the stock had been reduced to a practical minimum, the depletion of the banks' reserves resulting from overfunding had to be offset by the Bank buying other paper (in particular commercial bills) from the banks.

Under these conditions the triangular set of transactions takes a somewhat different form:

- the non-bank public (as before) buys government debt, and runs down bank deposits;

- the authorities, having sold debt to the non-bank public, now buy commercial bils from the banks (i.e., the government, instead of as before running down debt to the banks, now lends short-term — in the first place to the banks, but in effect to their customers);
- the banks' customers are persuaded to issue bills in place of bank advances, so that the banks lend less to the private sector, that being matched by smaller deposits with them.

(There is here a minor point of statistical definition that needs to be noted. As a matter of practice, it was not the government, but the Issue Department of the Bank of England acting for it, that bought the bills, (paying for them by selling government stock or, after that, by loans from the government. Under the definitions used for statistical purposes, the Issue Department in included in 'the monetary sector'; and its purchases of commercial bills are thus included in the statistics of what may be read as total bank lending. On this presentation, the switch from bank advances to bill finance, although reflected in a reduction of lending by banks other than the Bank of England — perhaps misleadingly — leaves total lending by the 'monetary sector' unchanged.)

The effects of overfunding

Greater sales of debt on balance undoubtedly reduced the public's holdings of bank deposits, and thus the rate of growth of broad money; but there were offsets. It was an essential feature of the policy that the banks should become more willing to accept bills drawn on industry, which they in turn could be sure of selling on a market made more buoyant by the authorities' demand for bills; and that they themselves should lend less to the private sector. The fine terms available on bill finance are thought to have enabled companies on occasions to make a turn by redepositing the proceeds with the banks. For most of the time such a direct profit was probably not available. But the lower cost of bill finance will still have reduced the cost to companies of borrowing to hold a stock of liquid assets. This kind of effect has been discussed in Chapter 2; and Chapter 11 (Section 3) suggests that the desire to borrow to hold liquidity may have been an important reason for the growth of bank lending and of the broad aggregates. This may have been encouraged by overfunding, even though overfunding will have been only one of the factors promoting it. By stimulating borrowing in order to hold liquidity, the policy of overfunding was then — perhaps only to a minor extent — partially self-defeating.

To mitigate this effect, the authorities had by 1985 begun to adopt other ways of employing the proceeds of overfunding — by lending to banks against the security of gilts, and against paper held under official schemes to subsidize credit for exports and shipbuilding. By mid-1985 the authorities had loans outstanding of about £3½ billion against such security, as well as holding around £10 billion in commercial bills. This 'mountain' of bills and other paper, built up in the four years since the autumn of 1981 (Fig. 11.7 below), was equivalent to about 10 per cent of broad money by the time the policy was abandoned.

The effect of overfunding in reducing the growth of broad money may have been only half as large. For the bill mountain resulted from offsetting the effect on the banks' reserves of the central government's transactions, whereas the effect on broad money is to be measured by the extent of overfunding the borrowing requirement of the public sector as a whole; overfunding over these years was equivalent to some 5 per cent of the stock of broad money at mid-1985. The effects of this policy are impossible to estimate exactly: what occurred can by no means be taken as an exact measure of what the authorities intended, nor can the offsetting effects noted above be quantified. As a broad judgement, the policy of overfunding may have reduced the growth of broad money by about 5 per cent over these four years.

Although the authorities pursued the policy of overfunding for a time, they never appeared fully at ease with it. The doubts it provoked were perhaps these. The government was in effect providing short-term finance for industry, although with the credit risk being assumed by the banks: could this be the government's business? For the government had to provide the finance out of debt sales; this presumably raised the cost of financing the public debt, and presumably involved an element of subsidy in the finance provided by the government to industry. Although on the official presentation the bill finance was shown as lending by the 'monetary sector', the policy also inevitably involved official promotion of disintermediation from bank lending into bill finance — something very similar to the disintermediation that, in the case of the Corset, had been branded as merely 'cosmetic' and had led to its abandonment.

That, however, raises fundamental questions about the rationale of policy. The justification for controlling broad money is the belief that excessive holdings of money will later lead to inflation; none of these doubts would matter if it were felt that the volume of money held was the sufficient test of policy. For overfunding is certainly likely to reduce holdings of money; and on this logic, it is difficult to judge that a reduction of money holdings is good if it comes about without official intervention, but bad if it is brought about by one of the few types of official intervention that appear effective for this purpose. If, however, the manipulation involved is regarded as artificial and a distortion, that would seem to imply that the touchstone of policy should shift from the quantity of money to the quantity of bank lending. The questions raised are thus a litmus test for monetary policy; abandonment of overfunding appears in logic to require abandonment of the case for controlling the monetary aggregates.

3. PRUDENTIAL BANKING SUPERVISION

Monetary policy may be regarded as a macroeconomic responsibility of the monetary authorities, and prudential supervision, concerned with individual banks, as a microeconomic responsibility. In the United Kingdom, unlike many other countries, both are undertaken by the central bank. Though the two kinds of official involvement have different aims, these are not completely distinct. Prudential supervision does not aim to affect the course of the monetary aggregates, nor did it probably have a major influence on it in the period since 1971; but it could do so, and perhaps at times has done so. There is then a possible question of whether the processes of prudential supervision could be employed to play a macroeconomic role, and if so whether that would be desirable. That is one reason for discussing prudential supervision at this point. A second reason is that in considering later (in Chapter 13) the role of monetary policy in future, we assume that there will be continuing need for effective prudential supervision.

Our analysis of the behaviour of the banking system in Part I of this book throws light on the rationale of prudential supervision, and on its inherent limitations. We shall confine ourselves here to a general account. We will not attempt to describe in detail the evolution of prudential supervision in the United Kingdom, which was very modest in 1971 and has since then been progressively strengthened. (This is conveniently provided in Gardener 1986, ch. 4, which gives references to the main statements by the Bank of England.) Nor do we discuss the prudential supervision of building societies (described in Boléat 1982, ch. 12). Their activities having been restricted until the mid-1980s to the provision of mortgage finance, supervision has been simpler; it has been handled not by the Bank of England, but until 1986 by the Registrar of Friendly Societies, and since then by the newly established Building Societies Commission.

The rationale of prudential supervision

In all countries, banks are treated as requiring supervision in a way that other companies do not. The shareholders of banks, like those of other companies, necessarily accept risks. Those that banks run are special to banking: their liabilities are less liquid than the assets in which they invest them, and there is always a risk that the assets they hold will fall in value, or the loans they have made will not be repaid in full. Moreover, in the case of banks the risks fall not only (as with other companies) on the shareholders, but also on depositors with banks (to which there is no counterpart with other companies). For two reasons, depositors are thought to require a special degree of protection.

First (as Chapter 2 has sought to bring out), the risks being run by a bank are peculiarly difficult to evaluate. Not only do they depend (as with other firms) on circumstances impossible to predict accurately, but they are often complex and difficult even for bank managements to assess; and, even more than with many other types of company, outsiders can have no good idea of the risks to which a bank may be exposed. Financial markets, therefore, cannot properly discriminate between banks or ensure that banks more risky than the average have to pay more for deposits. Nor can depositors and other creditors, shareholders, or borrowers in general take appropriate account in advance of the risk of the loss and inconvenience that would be caused by the failure of a bank.

Second, the consequences of a bank failure may be especially widespread. As with any large firm, failure may cause inconvenience and loss to many not directly involved. But in the case of a bank, the working of the financial system in general may be disrupted. Given outsiders' degree of ignorance about the true risks, unfounded fears may arise about the safety of other banks and financial institutions. The functioning of banks depends on the maintenance of customary trust, and trust may be destroyed. To quote the Governor of the Bank (speaking in the context of the Johnson Matthey failure):

a failure of a particular participant [can pose] a threat to the system as a whole . . . The ease and speed with which holders of liquid assets can move them from one institution to another has no close parallel in industry more generally. . . . As a result, the failure of certain individual banks or financial institutions can give rise to rumours or fears about other financial institutions and hence put great strain and immediate pressure on such institutions which can if unchecked do them irreversible damage before the full facts can be established. . . . not all banks or financial institutions play a part important enough . . . for their failure to comprise a potential systemic threat. Many do not. But some do. . . . (*BEQB* 1984, 502)

It could be argued that in a mature banking system, as in this country, the risk of serious bank failures is negligible. But in the light of recent developments in the United States, and to less degree in this country, it is impossible to maintain that this is clear and certain.

That is the case *for* official prudential supervision. The case *against* it rests on a denial of the information inadequacies stressed above and an assertion that markets, if left do do so, would be capable of assessing the risks involved and reacting appropriately. It can be argued on these grounds (for instance Mayer 1986) that the present detailed inspection by official supervisors of individual banks' operations is a costly and distracting irrelevance, and that official intervention, particularly if official deposit insurance is provided, creates the 'moral hazard' that banks will then undertake more risky lending than they would without it.

On this view it has been argued (for instance Kareken 1986) that deposit insurance should be privately provided, the fee charged to each bank being based on the insurer's estimate of the riskiness of each bank's portfolio. In that case official supervisors might confine themselves to ensuring in a broad-brush manner that banks avoided undue concentrations on particular risks. It is, however, significant that private institutions offering such insurance have not developed. The factors that Chapter 2 suggests make it impossible for banks to make accurate assessment of the riskiness of their lending to individual customers make it doubly difficult for an outside assessor to do so.

The limitations of banking supervision

These same factors, however, inevitably also limit what official banking supervision can hope to achieve. The regulatory authorities can hope to reduce the likelihood of a bank getting into difficulty; but they cannot hope for complete success, and must therefore also stand ready to limit the damage if a bank does encounter difficulty. These two sides will be briefly considered in turn.

In seeking to limit the riskiness of banking, bank supervisors can follow three approaches. They can require the banks to observe certain ratios. A requirement that banks hold a proportion of their assets as liquid, readily saleable, short-term assets provides some assurance that they will not get into liquidity difficulties. No ratio short of 100 per cent can provide absolute assurance, but the higher it is, the more banking profits are reduced and banking activity restricted. In recent years, minimum liquidity ratios have not been officially prescribed in this country (see Chapter 7). Another sort of requirement normally imposed is that a bank's capital should amount to a certain proportion of its deposits; this gives greater assurance that it will not become insolvent through bad debts, and thus (since liquidity difficulties may reflect market fears of insolvency) also gives greater assurance against illiquidity. Again, no such rule can provide complete assurance.

A second approach is to seek to limit to some degree the riskiness of a bank's lending. But supervisors cannot run banks, and banks would cease to be banks if they did not assume some risks. The riskiness of any particular loan or type of loan is difficult to foresee, and no simple rule applied from outside could discriminate properly between them. The risks in lending to developing countries during the last decade, for instance, were plainly greater than then realized; but it is a question how far bank managements, or bank supervisors, should have seen this at the time. Partial protection can be provided by trying to insist on the spreading of risks, and requiring that not too much of any bank's assets consist of loans to a single customer or class of customers. But 'class' here has to be defined in terms of the joint probability of unfavourable outcomes, which cannot be known in advance. It is therefore impossible to be precise as to how such a rule should be applied, or in assessing how much extra protection it gives.

The third approach is to seek to foster the quality of bank management. Given the need for trust, it seems reasonable that bank supervisors should satisfy themselves (as the Banking Act requires) that banks are run by 'fit and proper' persons. But such judgements have to be legally defensible in case of appeal; and it must be doubtful how far, beyond insisting on adequate experience, they can be applied except in cases of obvious unsuitability.

Supervision of established banks in the United Kingdom nevertheless places considerable emphasis on the quality of management:

The interview is the cornerstone of the Bank's system of supervision. . . . The prime aims of the interview are to build up within the Bank an intimate picture of the institution, its business and its objectives, and to assess the capabilities of its management to control the business and fulfill the objectives . . . management problems and inadequacies have typically provided the first sign of difficulty. (*BEQB* 1978, 384)

Bank supervisors may also be in a position to encourage senior management to provide itself with adequate information about the bank's own operations, and to see that the bank keeps an adequate watch on them.

The difficulties of banking supervision are now evidently being increased by rapid innovation in banking practices and financial instruments (see Cooke 1985). Even without this, as is plain from the above account, the power of supervisors is inherently limited. How much difference supervision makes depends partly on how efficiently and prudently banks would be managed without supervision, so that how much it can contribute must be fairly intangible. But as a practical judgement there can surely be no doubt that it has to be done; though it costs something, this is part of the cost of banks. Official supervision, however, cannot guarantee that banks will not get into difficulty. Occasional failure is inevitable, and is also part of the cost of having a banking system. That needs to be generally accepted, and not necessarily seen as a failure of banking supervision.

Since official supervision cannot ensure that no bank gets into difficulty, monetary authorities in modern times have always felt it necessary to seek to limit the consequences of the failure of a bank. There are three lines of action open to them.

First, since Bagehot's words about the Bank of England as lender of last resort, the central bank has always been willing to provide temporary assistance to a bank, without limit, although on terms of its own choosing and on the security of the bank's assets. Such assistance can be only an interim remedy. It may for a time conceal from the public that a bank is in liquidity difficulties, but when the fact of such assistance becomes public, the bank's difficulties will be known to all and will worsen.

Second, the authorities may institute a system of deposit insurance. Under the Banking Act, an individual's deposits up to £10,000 with an individual bank are protected as to 75 per cent of their amount, the cost being shared between all banks. Although there is no similar scheme for building societies, a society in difficulties has hitherto always been taken over by a neighbouring society. Such arrangements must reduce the likelihood of a contagious run on deposits, but unless 100 per cent, they cannot eliminate it.

The authorities, when the case has arisen, have gone further and arranged for a bank in difficulties to be taken over by a new management and to be given financial support (in practice, provided partly by the authorities themselves but mostly by the large banks). Deposits may thus, *ex post*, acquire total protection; shareholders have not been sheltered. The new owners then have to take responsibility for any loss in excess of shareholders' funds, on a scale impossible to estimate at the time of rescue. The main justification for such rescues must be to avoid contagious withdrawal of deposits. On good grounds, the principle on which they are undertaken and might be repeated in future has deliberately been left unclear.

These last two approaches are to some degree alternatives. If there were 100 per cent deposit insurance, it would be easier for the authorities not to rescue a bank. Both involve an interference with market forces. Deposit insurance in effect transfers potential responsibility for meeting some of the liabilities of a bank to others who have had no say in its operations, and may thus reduce the incentive for an individual bank to behave responsibly. The rescue of a bank (although never certain in advance to take place) also overrides what the market would do. It can be argued that if banks were allowed to fail, this would make the risks involved in banking more apparent, and thus would help to make the cost of funds to banks more dependent on a market evaluation of their individual performance. But if it is accepted that the market lacks information about the risks that banks are running, and that market forces operate very imperfectly, it cannot be claimed that the example of a failure would be salutary. It would be no more helpful than punishing people for mistakes they cannot avoid.

In the past, after the need for support has become evident, the large banks together with the Bank of England have shared the cost of occasional rescue operations, but not on a previously agreed basis. The depletion of Bank of England reserves on such occasions has also raised questions, since it can be seen as a drain on public money. The cost of rescue operations on behalf of banks in difficulty needs to be accepted as part of the cost of having a banking system, for which a contingency fund would be appropriate.

Prudential supervision in relation to monetary policy

Although the purposes of prudential supervision are distinct from those of monetary policy, they appear to some degree to reinforce each other. The rapid monetary expansion in 1971–3 appears to have been accompanied by some relaxation of standards of banking prudence (Chapter 11, Section 2). It may also have contributed to inflationary conditions and excessive levels of demand. More effective supervision might have somewhat lessened the unfavourable macroeconomic effects, although it can hardly be supposed that it would have sufficed to avoid them. A more restrictive monetary (and fiscal) policy might have lessened any imprudence on the part of the banks, but it would not have removed the need for prudential supervision.

To some extent, then, the purposes of monetary policy and banking supervision run together; and it is worth considering whether the procedures of banking supervision could properly assist monetary policy more actively. This could probably be done most effectively by more stringent requirements as to banks' capital adequacy. It is claimed that in the years 1982–5 bank supervisors successfully insisted on a strengthening of banks' capital adequacy. The need to improve capital ratios may to some degree have retarded the expansion of the banks' activities — although it was in those years that monetary expansion was most rapid; and more draconian requirements might have retarded monetary expansion more effectively. But that would have had little to do with the purposes of prudential supervision, and (as Goodhart 1986 has argued) such use of the instruments of supervision might create an undesirable confusion of purpose. Moreover, it would hardly have imposed greater monetary restraint quickly, and might not be the most effective method of doing so. If greater monetary restraint was thought to require strong measures, other steps (such as credit controls or even a tax on banks) could be held to be preferable (see further Chapter 11, Section 2).

11

Monetary Growth Since The Mid-1960s

The analysis of previous chapters was developed as a means of explaining the historical course of the monetary aggregates in the United Kingdom. This chapter seeks to validate the claim that the analysis helps to explain them. Section 1 describes our general approach and treatment of the data, and offers a first survey. Section 2 discusses in more detail the course of lending to the private sector by banks and building societies. Section 3 considers how far additional lending by them resulted in additional spending — an important question for interpretation of the period. Section 4 contains general conclusions about the behaviour of the financial system, and how far policy affected the monetary aggregates.

1. A FIRST SURVEY OF THE DATA

Fig. 11.1 shows stocks of money on various definitions for the years 1963–84, all scaled by the contemporaneous nominal value of GDP. Presented thus in ratio form, the course of the broad aggregates shows five fairly clearly defined phases. Before 1971 (when lending controls were in force) there was rough stability in the very broad money ratio and a gentle decline in broad money. From 1971 to 1973 (after lending controls were removed) there was rapid expansion. There followed two years of marked contraction (1974 and 1975) and then a gentle decline (1976–9): during this period the Corset was intermittently in force (shown by the shaded areas on the chart). Since 1980 there has been renewed rapid expansion.

We attribute these successive phases to the course of bank lending, and thus are concerned chiefly with two pairs of broad aggregates:

- *broad money* (£M3 — since 1987 called simply M3) and its main counterpart, *bank lending* in sterling;
- *very broad money* (PSL2 — since 1987 called M5) and its main counterpart, the combined *lending of banks and building societies* in sterling.

End-year levels for these four aggregates, all scaled by GDP at market prices, are shown in Figs. 11.2 and 11.3 for the years 1970–84.

A statistical reconciliation of bank lending and broad money is given in detail in Table 11.1. Most of bank lending is matched by deposits by

TABLE 11.1. Relations between the broad aggregates, end-1984 (£ billion)

(1) Definition of broad money

Broad money (£M3)	= cash held by non-bank public	+ £ bank deposits[a] of non-bank public
113	= 12	+ 101

(2) Balance sheet of banks

£ bank deposits of non-bank public	= banks' £ lending to UK private sector	+ banks' net £ lending to public sector	+ external[b] factors	− banks' net[c] non-deposit (NND) liabilities
100	= 109	+ 16	+ 0	− 25

(3) Relation of broad money to bank lending

Broad money	= banks' £ lending to private and public sectors	+ cash held by public	+ external[b] factors	− banks' NND liabilities
113	= 125	+ 12	+ 0	− 25

Table continues p.171

(4) *Definition of very broad money*

Very broad money =	Broad money (£M3)	+ building society (BS) deposits of public	− long-term BS deposits	+ other £ short-term assets held by public	− other[e] adjustments
193	= 113	+ 95	− 18	+ 14	− 9

(5) *Balance sheet of building societies*[f]

BS deposits of non-bank UK public	= BS lending to private sector (mortgages)	+ BS lending to public sector
95	= 83	+ 13

(6) *Relation of very broad money to bank/building society lending*

Very broad money =	bank & BS £ lending to private & public sectors	− long-term deposits with BS	+ cash held by public	− banks' & BS NND liabilities	+ other £ short-term assets held by public
193	= 220	− 18	+ 12	− 30	+ 14

---

a Deposits exclude a small quantity held by the public sector and about £45 b of deposits held by monetary-sector institutions with each other. They also exclude about £35 b foreigners' sterling deposits held in the UK and UK residents (small) sterling deposits held abroad.

b This measure of externals is the *level* of banks' net foreign currency assets of all kinds, plus their net lending in sterling abroad. The *flow*, which is called 'the externals' in the familiar 'counterparts' analysis of broad money shown in official statistics, is the flow element of the change in banks' reserves under these headings, minus any increase in public borrowing abroad minus any increase in public-sector net borrowing in foreign currencies from the banks. It thus differs from changes in the levels as here defined because it includes more transactions, and because it includes valuation effects.

c These are, roughly, shareholders' funds less the value of banks' physical assets.

d This is made up as follows:
Liquid National Savings   £9 b.
Money-market instruments   £3 b.
Certificates of tax deposit   £2 b.

e These include building societies' holdings of bank deposits and of cash.

f Excludes building society net lending to banks and building society net non-deposit liabilities: both were small at this date. Building societies have negligible foreign currency business.

the public with banks, but part is matched by government and foreign deposits and by non-deposit liabilities (roughly, shareholders' funds less the value of banks' physical assets). Such liabilities have grown (retained profits and capital issues have exceeded the value of new physical investment and loans written off), and have grown consistently more rapidly than deposits. Broad money, unlike bank lending, includes the public's holdings of cash, and another reason for the divergence between bank lending and broad money is that holdings of cash have tended to fall in relation to national income.

The combined lending of banks and building societies is, similarly, matched as to the greater part by deposits with these institutions. Their total lending is shown in Fig. 11.3 along with very broad money. We take very broad money to be represented by PSL2 because that is a familiar aggregate, although in some ways it is inappropriate. It excludes long-term building-society deposits (which the building societies have succeeded in expanding), but includes holdings of money-market instruments (which more recently have grown less rapidly than incomes). For these reasons, and also because of the growth of non-deposit liabilities, the combined lending of banks and building societies, which was previously about equal to PSL2, now comfortably exceeds it.

Despite discrepant tendencies of this sort, the large cycles in bank lending (Fig. 11.2) are reflected in those of broad money. Cycles in combined bank/building society lending are — to a somewhat lesser extent — similarly reflected in those of very broad money (Fig 11.3). Lending by banks has throughout the period been rather greater than that of building societies, and their respective shares, though varying, have not varied very greatly. The broad and very broad aggregates have thus shown similar cycles.

The narrower money ratios, by contrast, have been more stable. Holdings of M1 declined in relation to national income for much of the period, but the fall was partly reversed in the 1980s (Fig. 11.1). The decline in the 1960s may have reflected a less-than-unit income elasticity (as income rises, agents may increase transactions balances less than in proportion), high interest rates, and in the 1970s the spread of credit cards. Its renewed rise in the late 1970s owed much to the fact that banks, faced with competition by the building societies, began increasingly to pay interest on sight deposits (in 1980 only 20 per cent of the deposits included in M1 bore interest: by 1984, over 60 per cent). The ratio of cash to national income has declined gradually and almost uninterruptedly, and has halved since the mid-1960s (Fig. 11.1). This must reflect the increasing use of banks by wage-earners and the increasing use of credit cards (see Trundle 1982a, 1982b).

The stock of bank lending to the public sector, as a ratio of GDP, has fallen rather steadily since 1971 (Fig. 11.2). This trend has already been discussed in Chapter 9, Section 2 (and is to be further considered in Section 4 below). It has to some extent offset the effect on broad money of the growth of bank lending to the private sector; and that influence has been almost continuous. The analysis of Section 2 therefore concentrates on lending to the private sector, which has varied much more.

Our interpretation of the lending institutions' lending behaviour is based on the analysis of Chapter 2. It was there argued that, because of the information problems arising in assessing credit risk, lending institutions ration loans to individual customers. They assess a customer's creditworthiness by criteria such as his past and prospective income or profits, or the value of his assets. These magnitudes rise continuously in an economy where real incomes or prices are rising. Thus, with unchanged credit standards on the part of lenders, lending is likely to rise in line with the rise in money income, and in that case the rise in lending may be regarded as a passive response by lending institutions.

We therefore make the general assumption that the criteria that lenders use in assessing creditworthiness can be proxied by nominal GDP. An expansion of lending in proportion to the rise in nominal GDP is taken as a first indication that lending criteria remain unchanged. We have argued that the conventions that banks adopt in lending are a collective phenomenon: each bank is able, and feels impelled, to maintain what it takes to be the general rule. But the collective convention can, and does, change. As a first approximation, we take a rise in lending faster, or slower, than in proportion to the rise in nominal GDP to indicate that lending criteria have been relaxed, or made more stringent. (This implies that any effect of such a change in lending on nominal GDP is minor in the year in which the change occurs — an assumption we believe valid in the present context.)

The indications of lenders' attitudes provided by this procedure are at best rough. They appear most reliable in respect of lending to persons; and it is chiefly in regard to this class of lending that we are able to cite independent evidence that lending criteria in fact changed as we hypothesize. We will be much more cautious in applying this procedure to evaluating banks' attitudes in lending to companies. Banks must be concerned to assess the likely future trend of companies' profits, which may be imperfectly reflected in their recent trend. Moreover, banks are likely to take a long view of their customers' needs, and at times of difficulty may continue for a time to accommodate them. The effect of their customers' demand for loans in such cases must be difficult to distinguish from banks' underlying willingness to provide finance.

Our account of money creation in Chapter 2 envisaged that easier lending by banks at first accelerates monetary growth, and that relative interest rate changes later induce borrowers to repay bank loans, so that the actions of banks in creating money later induce actions by non-banks which reverse that result. But we also argued that for various reasons the self-reversing process was likely to be both delayed and only partial; and we will show in Section 4 that this indeed seems to have been the case.

The last two decades have seen a rapidly expanding role for lending institutions. Persons borrow much more than previously. Lending to the personal sector by banks and building societies has grown in relation to GDP particularly rapidly in the 1980s, and now equals sterling lending to industrial and commercial companies (Figs. 11.4 and 11.6). Companies also have become much more dependent on the banks as an external source of finance (Fig. 11.10).

Most intermediation by UK banks is between borrowers and lenders abroad, not borrowers and lenders at home; and most is denominated in foreign currency, not sterling (Table 11.2). We shall be concerned only with the banks' role *vis-à-vis* residents. That is chiefly in terms of sterling, although foreign currency lending to industrial and commercial companies has grown continuously and now accounts for about a quarter of what banks lend to them (Fig. 11.5 and Table 11.2). The long runs of

TABLE 11.2. UK banks' deposits and lending by sectors, end-1984

	Deposits from sector (£ b)		Lending to sector (£ b)	
Sterling				
UK private sector		100		109
of which:				
Personal sector	57		51	
Industrial and commercial companies	25		59	
Non-bank financial companies	19		19	
UK public sector		3		19
Overseas		30		25
		133		153
Foreign currencies				
UK private sector		21		36
UK public sector		0		2
Overseas		424		412
		445		450
Net non-deposit liabilities		25		—
All currencies		603		603

Source: Financial Statistics

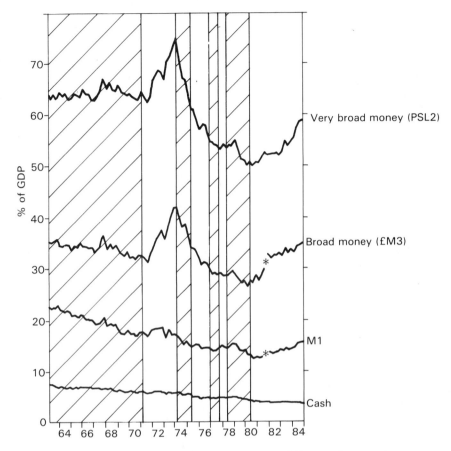

FIG. 11.1   *The main monetary aggregates, 1963–1984: stocks at end-quarter as a percentage of GDP*

Note: 'cash' comprises notes and coin held by the public. Shaded bands indicate periods when lending controls or the Corset were in operation. Asterisks indicate a break in the series: see statistical note at end of chapter.

figures shown in the charts have required a good deal of minor estimation by methods that are decribed in the Statistical Note to this chapter.

2. FLUCTUATIONS IN LENDING TO THE PRIVATE SECTOR

The main phases of expansion in lending to the private sector have already been indicated. Lending by banks to companies, and lending by banks and building societies to the personal sector, both expanded rapidly (in relation to GDP) in 1971 and the next two years, contracted in

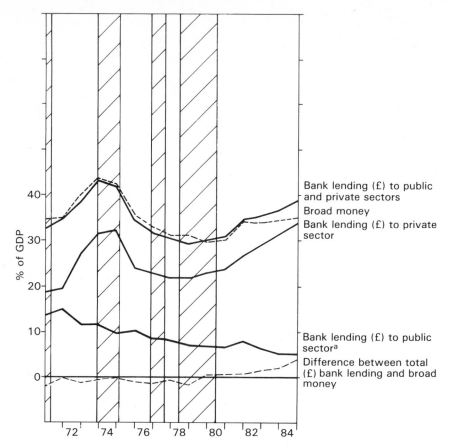

Fig. 11.2   *Bank lending and broad money, 1970–1984: stocks at end-year as a percentage of GDP*

Note: vertical bands indicate periods when lending controls or the Corset were in operation.
a Net of public sector deposits.
b The main reason for the difference was that an increasing proportion of bank lending was matched not by deposits but by increases in the banks' capital: see text.

the following two years, and then became more stable. Then about 1980 there began a new phase of rapid expansion, which continued over the next five years (Figs. 11.4–11.6). In this section we offer an interpretation of these successive phases. We argue that the removal of lending controls (first in 1971 and again in 1980) permitted greater competition among lending institutions, which led to a progressive relaxation of their lending criteria; and one purpose of this review is to see how far this interpretation can be supported by independent evidence that lending criteria were relaxed or made more stringent in these phases.

The analysis of previous chapters led to the conclusion that officially induced changes in interest rates provided little if any incentive to switch

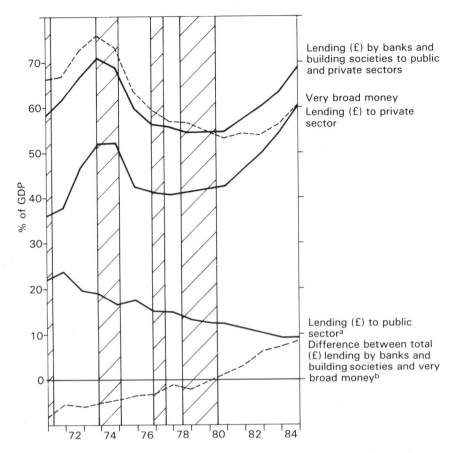

Lending (£) by banks and
building societies to public
and private sectors

Very broad money
Lending (£) to private
sector

Lending (£) to public
sector[a]
Difference between total
(£) lending by banks and
building societies and very
broad money[b]

FIG. 11.3   Very broad money and lending by banks and building societies,
        1970–1984: stocks at end-year as a percentage of GDP

Note: vertical bands indicate periods when lending controls or the Corset were in operation.
[a] Net of public sector deposits.
[b] An increasing proportion of lending was matched not by deposits but by increases in the
banks' capital.

borrowing from banks to other sources. Periods of rapid growth in bank
lending are not associated with low interest rates, or vice versa; and the
lack of connection between the level of interest rates and monetary
growth is perhaps attested (but see Section 4 below) by the well
documented failure of demand-for-money equations (Goodhart 1984) to
explain or predict monetary growth in the United Kindgom since 1971.
Although interest rate policy seems to provide no systematic explanation
of the main phases of lending, steep increases in interest rates could at
times have affected — positively or negatively — borrowers' desire to
borrow.

    Chapter 10 (Section 2) has argued that public-sector borrowing from

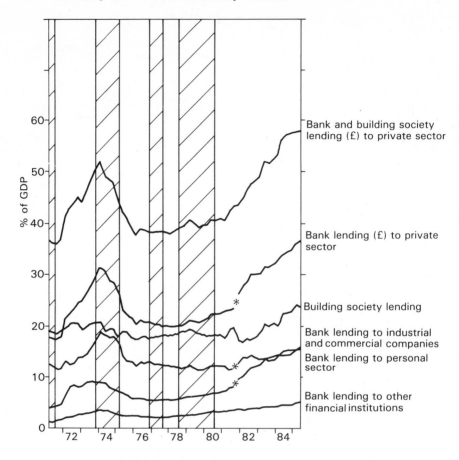

Fig. 11.4   *Lending in sterling to the private sector, 1971–1985: stocks at end-quarter as a percentage of GDP*

Note: vertical bands indicate periods when lending controls or the Corset were in operation. Asterisks indicate a break in the series: see statistical note at end of chapter.

the banks, and the policy of overfunding, affected the rate of growth of broad money to some degree. They did so, however, by offsetting the effect that bank lending to the private sector would otherwise have had on monetary growth, not by controlling such lending. Thus, apart from the effect of direct controls, we have regarded the course of bank lending as unaffected by the influence of monetary policy, and in that sense as an endogenous process.

This section does not aim to provide a detailed history of monetary developments, but only to present a simplifed account of the development of monetary aggregates, and to discuss the possible reasons why they behaved as they did. It will be evident that we can hope to carry

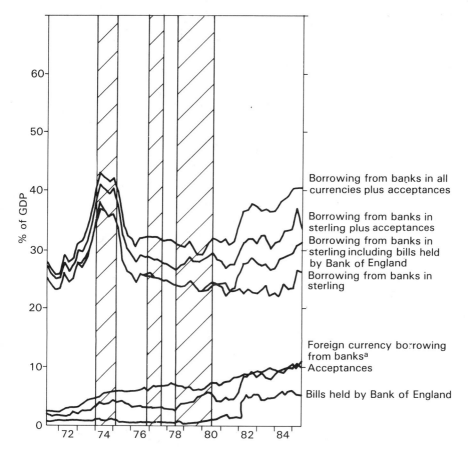

FIG. 11.5 *Borrowing by industrial and commercial companies, 1971–1985: stocks at end-quarter as a percentage of GDP*

Note: vertical bands indicate periods when lending controls or the Corset were in operation.
[a] Roughly adjusted by use of a smoothed index of the dollar/sterling exchange rate to exclude major changes in valuation.

explanation only a little way. Thus, while we have stressed the importance of the behaviour of lending institutions, we have no precise hypothesis as to how fast they will modify their lending criteria in various circumstances, and thus have no hypothesis that could be tested econometrically. Without that, interpretation is bound to be imprecise and tentative.

The last decade and a half has been a period of unusual turbulence, with deepening recession, wide fluctuations in the rate of inflation, and large swings in real interest rates and exchange rates; and it is perhaps surprising that monetary developments were as smooth as they were. A further series of charts, to which we refer in detail below, shows the

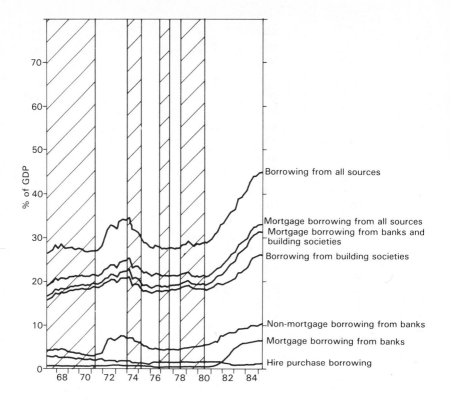

FIG. 11.6   *Borrowing by personal sector,ᵃ 1967–1985: stocks at end-quarter as a percentage of GDP*

Note: vertical bands indicate periods when controls on lending or the Corset were in operation.

ᵃ Includes only borrowing in sterling, but personal borrowing in foreign currencies is negligible.

fluctuations in output and the real exchange rate (Fig. 11.7), the rate of inflation and bank base rates (Fig. 11.8), selected asset prices (Fig. 11.9), and the sources and uses of industrial and commercial companies' funds (Fig. 11.10).

The expansion of lending after 1971 and subsequent contraction

In the years 1971–3, lending to the private sector grew significantly more rapidly, and in the next two years significantly more slowly, than GDP (Fig 11.7). It will be argued that this contractionary phase was partly a reaction to the preceding three years of rapid expansion.

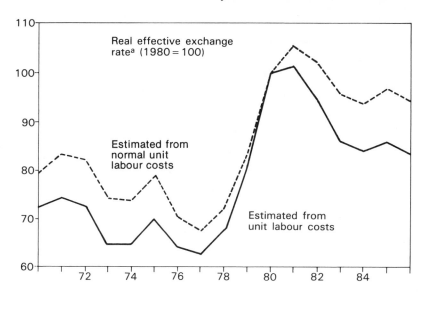

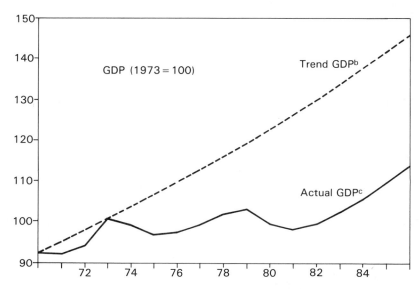

FIG. 11.7 *Output and real exchange rate, 1970–1986*

a Effective exchange rate deflated by relative unit labour costs (annual averages: UK compared with 7 major competitor countries).

b Pre-1973 trend in GDP projected forward.

c Output measure omitting output of oil: annual averages.

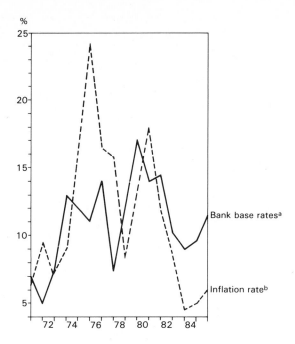

FIG. 11.8   *Inflation rate and bank base rates, 1970–1985*
[a] Up to 1971 (Q4), Minimum Lending Rate
[b] Change in retail price index over preceeding 12 mos.

The big expansion of lending came when direct controls on bank lending were removed in 1971. Bank lending had been limited since the war by appeals to the banks for 'restraint' in how much they lent. From 1965 onwards these had taken the more definite form of 'ceilings', which specified the rate of increase at which banks were expected to allow their lending to grow. Bank lending in relation to GDP in fact remained fairly constant in the 1960s. (Although our charts of bank lending do not go back so far, this is reflected in the flatness of the broad money ratio shown in Fig 11.1.)

It was thought at the time that the main effect of the restraint of bank lending was to cause growing disintermediation, which was merely 'cosmetic', so that controls in a true sense were ineffective. The most obvious form that evasion could take was by inter-company lending (on which a bank would normally take the credit risk by accepting a commercial bill, a contingent liabilitiy not subject to control). This route does not in fact appear to have been important, as it was to be later with the Corset; bank acceptances on behalf of UK residents were equivalent

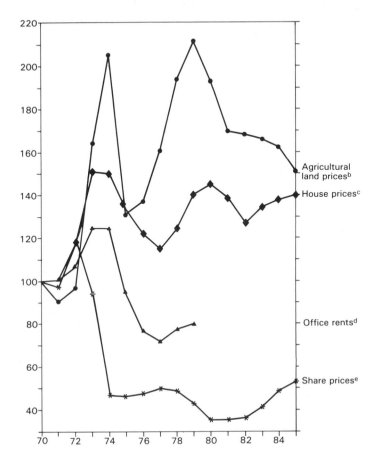

FIG. 11.9   *Selected real asset prices, 1970–1985ᵃ (1970 = 100)*

ᵃ Price indices deflated by retail price index, yearly averages.

ᵇ From *Farm Incomes in the United Kingdom*, Ministry of Agriculture, Fisheries, and Food.

ᶜ Price of new houses estimated by Halifax Building Society.

ᵈ From *Commercial and Industrial Property Statistics,* 1979, Department of the Environment (not available after 1979).

ᵉ *Financial Times* index of (30) industrial ordinary share prices: The FT-Actuaries (500) share index gives considerably higher figures in more recent years.

to only 4 per cent of GDP, and varied little in the period 1966–70; nor did they fall much when controls were removed (Fig. 11.5).

On our interpretation, the main effect of the removal of direct control was indirect; by opening the way to greater competition between banks, it led to a progressive relaxation of their lending criteria. Under the

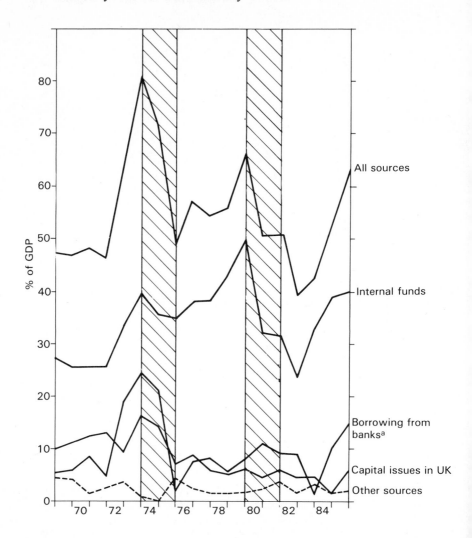

FIG. 11.10(a)   *Industrial and commercial companies' sources of funds, 1968–1985*

Note: vertical bands indicate periods of recession, i.e. years when output fell.
a Includes Bank of England purchases of commercial bills.

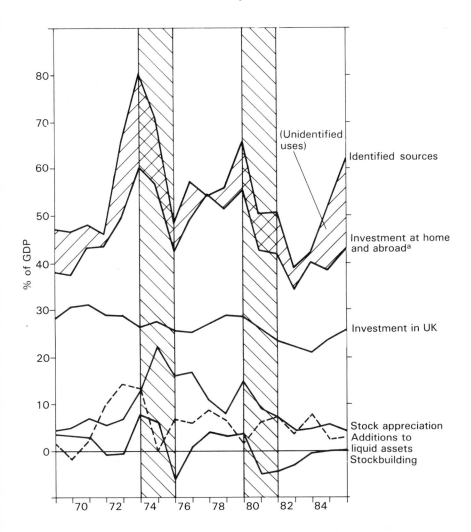

Fɪɢ. 11.10(b) *Industrial and commercial companies' uses of funds, 1968–1985*

Note: vertical bands indicate periods of recession, i.e. years when output fell.
a Direct investment overseas plus purchases of foreign currency financial assets.

previous regime, ceilings were supposed to apply to each bank individually; i.e., all were to expand at the same pace. The abolition of ceilings thus allowed individual banks to expand their lending as they wished. A main motive for the removal of the controls (Chapter 7) was indeed to permit greater competition between banks. A further impetus was given by the abolition of reserve requirements on interbank transactions (Chapter 7). These had previously acted as a kind of double tax on any intermediation involving final lending by one bank matched by non-bank deposits taken by another; by discouraging any bank from expanding its lending faster than the growth of its own deposits, they had held down the volume of lending. In this new world the banks had little to guide them as to how fast to expand. They seem to have learnt as they went along, and borrowing grew progressively.

Since banks had previously been requested to restrict lending to persons particularly severely, an expansion of such lending was to be expected. Lending to persons was in fact the first category to show rapid expansion, and in the year to mid-1972 accounted for much of the total rise in bank lending (Fig. 11.4). Lending for purposes other than housing, expressed as a ratio to national income, doubled in this period (Fig. 11.6). Banks also gradually became more active in providing mortgage finance, although their share of the mortgage market remained small.

Building societies also increased lending rapidly, and in this case there is clear evidence that they eased their lending criteria. Their practice has been to limit lending to a multiple of borrower's income, and the average size of new loans rose from 80 per cent of average earnings in 1972 to 90 per cent in 1974. Building societies previously had not been officially controlled and thus were not directly affected by decontrol; but it must be supposed that they were affected by the atmosphere of easier lending, and stimulated by the competition of the banks.

The expansion of lending in 1971–3 coincided with a rapid expansion of output (Fig. 11.7) and thus in real incomes. That is sometimes attributed to the monetary expansion itself. But there were certainly other factors, in particular the expansionary fiscal policy adopted by the government at this time, and the strong rise in world demand (see Saville and Gardiner 1986); and there are reasons to doubt how important monetary factors were (see further Section 3). Inflation too, accelerated after mid-1972 — but much more markedly in 1974 and 1975 (Fig. 11.8); and that also has been attributed to UK monetary expansion. But here too there were other factors, in particular the rise in world commodity and oil prices and the fall in the exchange rate (Fig. 11.8); and these must explain much of the rise in the UK price level (again see Saville and Gardiner 1986).

The housing market was one sector where bank lending most clearly exacerbated the boom. House prices rose rapidly (by over 30 per cent in both 1972 and 1973: Fig. 11.9). Some of this might have happened anyway as a result of consumers' rising incomes; and once house prices were rising, houses appeared both attractive to buy and good security on which to lend. The rise in loans for house purchase (in relation to GDP) thus probably represented not only banks' and building societies' increased willingness to lend, but also an increased eagerness on the part of borrowers to borrow; and it must have contributed to the emergence of speculative conditions in the housing market.

Similar conditions developed in the market for industrial and commercial property, and there is reason to think that banks' lending standards were here relaxed for a time and later had to be tightened. The large banks were often involved only indirectly in lending for investment in property; much was undertaken by specialist institutions, using deposits taken from the public by the clearing banks and on-lent through wholesale markets. Some of these institutions became listed banks during 1972 and 1973, while others remained 'fringe' banks. Much of the investment was of a speculative character, as was revealed at the end of the boom. The falls in asset prices towards the end of 1973 reduced the security offered by some borrowers from fringe banks, making the latter less attractive customers of the banking system; this in turn undermined the position of a few listed banks, some of whom also had heavy direct exposure to property companies (a detailed account is given by Margaret Reid: see Reid 1982). To prevent contagion, the 'lifeboat' rescue operation had to be mounted in 1974, in which large banks provided stable funding to a number of fringe banks; there was also a series of forced or arranged takeovers and mergers of financial and property companies.

Bank lending to industrial and commercial companies rose more gradually (Fig. 11.4) to a peak in early 1974. This may have reflected both the removal of controls on bank lending and the pressures arising from the financial situation in which companies found themselves; the latter were temporary, which probably helped the subsequent contraction of lending. Profits increased rapidly in the boom, allowing a big increase in internal sources of funds (Fig. 11.10), which however met only half of companies' needs. The world rise in commodity prices forced them to set aside large sums to meet stock appreciation (a factor that went into reverse in 1974). Although their fixed investment increased less rapidly than GDP, there was a large build-up of stocks in 1973, presumably mainly involuntary, as demand slowed down (this also reversed in 1974). Despite these pressures, companies seem to have added largely to their holdings of liquid assets in the years 1971–3 — a possibility that lending controls may previously have denied to them (discussed further in Section 3).

This narrative of events is consistent with the view, suggested by the ratios in the charts, that banks' lending standards were relaxed. That interpretation looks the stronger if one accepts the view that lending standards were tightened again in the subsequent phase.

In the two years 1974–5 the lending ratios did not merely stay flat, as they might have done if lenders' attitudes had ceased to become easier and been frozen at their end-1973 posture: rather, they fell, and reversed the whole of what we have interpreted as easing in the years of expansion. This is the only occasion in our period when that occurred. We suggest that the reasons were threefold: in part an effect of the recontrol of lending, in part a reaction by the banks against earlier imprudent lending, and in part a reaction to the recession that then set in, which was in fact to mark a radical change in the economy's performance and prospects.

In the course of 1973 the authorities had become increasingly alarmed at the continued rapid rise in broad money and the growth in lending that underlay it. This led them to call for Special Deposits, and to raise interest rates sharply; and fear (well-founded, in our view) that these steps should prove insufficient led them also to impose the newly devised control, the Corset (details are in Chapter 10, Section 1). But there is reason to think that the course of lending may have already been on the turn by then. Although the penalty-free zone under the Corset allowed an increase in lending only half as great as that experienced in 1973, the prescribed limits were not reached, and there was a clear impression among those operating it that there was little pressure behind the control. However, the Corset may well have been important in crystalizing a new attitude on the part of the banks. In face of the speculative conditions in the housing and property markets, the banks may have already come to feel that they had lent too open-handedly; and official alarm at the course of events may have matched their own awareness that all concerned needed to review their lending and borrowing policies.

The economy, too, was at a turning point. Signs of recession became evident at the turn of 1973; and it is clear from contemporary commentaries that it was at this point that there was a marked break in industrial confidence. One reason for recession was the downturn in international trade; in part this was a result of the first large rise in the price of OPEC oil, but in addition, domestic demand had been rising at a rate that could not have been sustained. As recession developed, this too must have made the banks more cautious in their lending.

The sudden transition from boom to recession at the end of 1973 was soon to place companies in a position of great financial stringency. Investment could not be quickly adjusted — spending on manufacturing investment continued to rise in real terms during 1974, reflecting orders placed earlier during the boom. Disappointed sales expectations similarly left companies with higher stocks. Equally important, continued rapid inflation meant that stock appreciation remained extremely large (Fig. 11.10). The account of the sources of companies' funds shown in Fig. 11.10 is incomplete, but it appears that internal funds ceased to grow in relative terms as they had done in the boom years, partly because the rise in interest rates greatly increased interest payments on the debt that companies had incurred earlier, much of which carried floating interest rates. Companies seem to have ceased to add, as they had added earlier, to their liquid assets. Even so, the increase in their bank borrowing in 1974 was almost as large (in relation to GDP) as in 1973.

Recession thus delayed — but only delayed — the slowdown in bank lending. In the abstract, given the worse prospects of their clients, the banks would no doubt have preferred not to lend much more to companies. In practice, being already substantial creditors of companies, they had little option but to lend more to ensure their debtors' survival — the alternative being bankruptcy and a delayed, problematical, and perhaps only partial settlement of debt. And for what it is worth (which is something), the authorities certainly encouraged banks, where possible, to keep their customers afloat.

The financial situation of companies eased in the following year. By then they had succeeded in running down their excess stocks. They were also given generous tax reliefs (announced in November 1974); because of their financial straits, firms were relieved of tax on the element in their trading profits represented by the increase in value of stocks. It was thus only in 1975 that their bank borrowing (in relation to GDP: see Fig. 11.10) started to fall. By the end of the year, lending to companies in relation to GDP (both from all sources and from the banks) was down to where it had been in early 1971 before the great expansion. It is difficult to make sense of so large a retrenchment except as a sign of increased caution on the part of lenders and borrowers. In part it probably represented increased stringency by the banks in lending; but it also reflected an unwillingness by firms to be so heavily in debt — since recession and fast inflation had each greatly reduced their ability to service it.

Depsite rising prices and wages, personal-sector borrowing in nominal terms hardly changed in 1974 and 1975, and as a ratio to GDP (Fig. 11.6) it thus declined: by the end of 1975 it, too, was back to the level of early 1971. There are similar puzzles as to why it did so. The Corset, during the first year or so it was in operation, may have been more important in limiting lending to persons than in limiting lending to industry. The banks, as we have seen, had to allow the latter to continue to rise; and in order to make room within the confines of the Corset for the needs of industry, the banks must in effect have been forced to cut back on personal credit (which was indeed what the Bank of England requested).

The cutback continued when the Corset was suspended, so that the Corset alone cannot have been the reason. The answer may in part be that, for various reasons, the banks had become more stringent with personal lending. It may also be that by now persons' creditworthiness appeared significantly less good; thus, real personal incomes, which had grown by over 10 per cent in the two years 1972 and 1973, was now on an erratically falling trend (Table 11.4 below). These considerations, together with the falling trend of real house prices, may well also explain the similar behaviour of building society lending.

It is noteworthy that when later (in 1980–1) there was a further, equally large, deepening of recession, there was no similar dip in the lending ratios — either for lending to persons or for lending to companies. This perhaps supports the conclusion that in 1974–5 there was a widespread general tightening of lending criteria, partly in reaction to imprudences committed earlier, in the first experience of banking freedom, and partly in reaction to the first traumatic experience of serious recession, after decades of fairly steady growth.

Restrained growth in lending, 1976–1980

For the first two years after 1975, lending grew roughly in line with GDP. (The ratios shown on Fig. 11.4 were roughly flat.) Then began an acceleration which in the next two years was very gradual, but from about the end of 1980 was again to become rapid. Interpretation of this period must be coloured by what came after it. The main reason for the restrained growth of lending in these four years was, we suggest, the Corset — which, having been suspended eighteen months earlier, was reimposed at the end of 1976 for what was to prove a brief period and imposed again in mid-1978 for a further two years before being finally abolished in mid-1980. To the Corset control we again attribute not only a direct effect, but a wider, more pervasive, effect in discouraging the kind of competition between financial institutions that later became so evident.

From the Olympian standpoint of our ratios, the years up to 1980 appear uneventful. That is not the impression they made at the time, nor is it probably now the recollection of those who remember them. Before evaluating the effects of the Corset, therefore, it may be useful to recount the sequence of events that led to its being twice reimposed.

The year 1976, the year of its first reimposition, was a year of exchange crisis. (For greater detail see Chapter 7.) Between March and early December the effective exchange rate fell about 20 per cent and then, following agreement with the International Monetary Fund, started to recover.

It was against this background, with broad money appearing to be starting to rise more rapidly, that the Corset was reimposed in November. In Fig. 11.1 the rise in broad money in the course of 1976, expressed in ratio terms, shows up as a very small blip, but contemporary discussion was in terms of nominal aggregates. Even in ratio terms, 1976 clearly marked a turning point: it was the end of the two-year phase, after the excesses of 1973, of banking consolidation and retrenchment, a phase during which nominal monetary growth had been very moderate despite rather rapid inflation. As already noted in Chapter 7, a formal monetary target, foreshadowed in July, was also declared for the first time in October 1976. The target rate of growth for M3 (12 per cent in the current financial year) was in the event comfortably met, earlier signs of disproportionate monetary growth proving very short-lived. The Corset at this stage appeared not to impose tight constraint, and was suspended in the following August. General guidance remained in force; banks were still asked to give preference to lending to industry, and to restrain personal lending and lending for commercial property.

The behaviour of broad money in the next three years, in the ratio form shown in our charts, looks very restrained (Fig. 11.1). But the target ranges for these years (Table 7.1 and Fig. 7.1) pointed at most to monetary growth proportionate to the increase in GDP; and judged by these standards, in the first part of 1978 monetary growth appeared to be becoming excessive. The Corset was therefore reimposed, for the third and last time, in June 1978.

Reactivation of the Corset implied a further waning of faith in high interest rates as a method of control; nevertheless, Mininum Lending Rate was raised progressively — and at this date the aim continued almost solely to be a domestic monetary control. (The rise is reflected in the rise of bank base rates shown in Fig. 11.8. MLR was raised — almost continuously but with some interruptions — from 5 per cent in October 1977 to 17 per cent in November 1979, where it stayed until June the following year.)

On this occasion, the Corset remained in force for two years. The banks kept close to the limits laid down, and in the last six months of their being in force significant penalties for excess growth were paid (Chapter 10, Section 1). On this occasion, too, there was a significant disintermediation through the 'bill leak', as companies shifted to borrowing directly from each other through the issue of bills accepted by a bank: total credit extended could rise, without bank lending and bank deposits rising. Thus bill finance increased in 1978, and became important in late 1979 and early 1980 (Fig. 11.5). When the control was lifted this disintermediation went into reverse, causing two months of especially rapid growth in broad money in the summer of 1980.

Compared with what came later, the first years of monetary targets (from 1976 on) appear on our charts as years of restrained growth in lending, both to persons and to companies. In this, the Corset — when in force (or, when not, the constant possibility of its reimposition) — must, together with the official guidance given to banks, have played a major part. The control had strong teeth, and this must have affected the banks' actions directly. More generally, it must have discouraged the banks from even thinking of being truly expansionary. For this (we have argued in Chapter 2, Section 1) would have required a consensus among banks to move in that direction, and such a consensus must have been prevented from building up.

In the light of subsequent developments, what seems most remarkable about the years up to 1980 is not so much the restrained growth of lending to companies as the failure of the banks and the building societies to exploit more fully the profitable opportunities of lending to the personal sector. Lending to persons in particular was discouraged by the authorities, and official views, backed by controls, were at this stage heeded. The Corset, in short, probably lived up to its popular name. By sanctioning the conventional caution of lenders, it must have strengthened the conservative element among bank and building society managements, who preferred to follow the ways in which they had been brought up. After 1980, on our reading, forces for change became more important.

The great expansion of lending after 1980

The new phase of rapid expansion that started around 1980 was more sustained if less rapid than in 1971–3, and was to carry the lending ratios well above the 1973 peak. The greater part of increased lending was to the personal sector. Most was for housing (at least nominally: see Section 3); and in providing mortgages, the growth of building society lending was even more rapid than that of the banks.

We attribute the expansion of lending to a progressive change in lenders' attitudes, arising not only from the removal of the Corset — a permissive step — but also from positive encouragement by the authorities. After the election of mid-1979, the new Conservative government not only put monetary control at the centre of its policy, but was equally dedicated to the removal of restrictions on competition in all spheres. Exchange controls were promptly abolished in October. By opening the way to increased disintermediation, this would have made it difficult to retain the Corset even had that been desired. When the Corset was removed in June 1980, its removal was clearly permanent. In August the reserve/asset ratio was removed: although this had not proved to be of much effect (Chapter 7), it signalled that the banks could expand with less risk of being caught out by future policy changes.

The change in attitudes may also in part be ascribed to the increasing internationalization of financial markets. The abolition of exchange controls made possible a major diversification into foreign assets by non-bank financial institutions, and a more rapid rise in foreign currency lending (Fig. 11.5). Banks were exposed to potential competition from banks abroad from whom their customers could now borrow. The by then considerable presence of foreign banks in London must have diluted the Bank of England's power to rule by moral suasion. Increasing competition in financial markets was positively encouraged by the government, although the most dramatic step came only in the summer of 1983, with the undertaking by the stock exchange to remove restrictive practices by the end of 1986. That prospect had a widespread effect; it led to major regroupings of financial institutions and to a further major change in attitudes, in which the banks have shared.

Building societies, too, became more competitive, both with banks and among themselves. This was partly a response to the banks' return to mortgage lending in 1981 (when they made 25 per cent of all new housing loans) and partly a reflection of the modernization and expansion among the bigger building societies, which now began to offer chequing accounts in competition with the banks.

Having started as local friendly societies, the building societies had traditionally been more concerned to keep down the cost of mortgage finance to existing borrowers than to expand its availability. They therefore tended to follow fluctuations in market interest rates only with some delay, and not to bid actively for deposits, to accept somewhat passively the increase in deposits with which the general expansion of the economy provided them, and to restrict their lending to the growth of deposits that this pattern of behaviour gave them, rationing lending when necessary by imposing tighter standards of creditworthiness and accepting longer mortgage queues. With a few large building societies in the lead, the societies now began to shift from this traditional ethic towards meeting the existing demand for mortgages, and towards keeping more closely in step with banks' deposit rates so as to compete with them for deposits. Under competitive pressure from the banks, they became more willing to offer larger loans on more costly houses, and increased the proportion of the purchase price they were willing to lend. (The average deposit required from first-time buyers in relation to annual earnings almost halved between 1980 and 1984.)

The building societies were previously organized in a tight and rather docile cartel, which had a standing arrangement to consult with the authorities. Given the political sensitivity of mortgage rates, the government was reluctant to abandon this system, but acquiesced in its gradual disintegration. In October 1981 the cartel agreement became applicable only to deposit rates on 'shares' (which accounted for less than half of total deposits). From October 1983 societies ceased to be required to give notice of changes in deposit rates. Official regulations were also changed then to allow building societies to pay interest gross of tax; this enabled them to obtain additional funds by borrowing on wholesale markets, rather than raising their deposit rates to attract small deposits away from banks. Competition by the building societies, in turn, stimulated increased competition by the banks, evidenced for instance by the rapid spread of payment of interest by the banks on sight deposits with them. (As already noted, the proportion of sight deposits bearing interest rose from 20 to over 60 per cent in the four years after 1980.)

There is, then, ample evidence of a much more competitive spirit among the major lending institutions, which by itself would make it quite likely that access to credit was eased; and there is some evidence that the criteria relating to lending to persons were in fact relaxed. It seems reasonable to believe that that helps to explain its rapid rise. Bank advances to persons, other than on mortgage terms, rose rapidly after 1980 and, as a ratio to national income, rather less than doubled in the four years 1981–5 (Fig. 10.9). However, that was a much less important component of the rise in personal borrowing than the rise in mortgage lending by both banks and building societies, which doubled between 1980 and 1984 (Fig. 11.6).

Bank lending to industrial and commercial companies in sterling terms remained remarkably flat in relation to GDP after 1980, but lending in foreign currencies grew more rapidly (after 1981: see Fig. 11.5). As a consequence of the overfunding policy (Chapter 10, Section 2), the Bank of England's holdings of commercial bills, and bank acceptances of bills not (or not yet) acquired by the Bank, both grew rapidly after 1980. These substituted for bank lending and, like bank lending in foreign currencies, should be included. With these additions, lending to industrial commercial companies grew quite rapidly, to a level in 1985 as high relative to national income as in 1973. It is however less clear than with lending to persons (where the rise was much greater) that this can be taken as an indication that lending standards were relaxed. (In interpreting developments we make some use of the statistics of sources and uses of companies' funds shown in Fig. 11.10, although these show a large residual between total sources and uses which makes their evidence defective.)

It is worth looking first at companies' experience during the second major stage of recession, which came in 1980 and 1981 (and thus largely preceded the new expansion of lending to companies). Output, having staged a partial recover after 1975, dipped further, and as sharply as in 1974–5 (Fig. 11.7). The real exchange rate had risen over 30 per cent between 1978 and 1980 and stayed high in 1981 (Fig. 11.7). That was one of the causes of the recession, and it put a dramatic squeeze on profits (and thus on companies' internal sources of funds: Fig. 11.10). This in turn probably forced companies to react more quickly and drastically to this second stage of recession than they had to the first; stock levels, investment, and employment all appear to have been cut much more promptly than on the previous occasion.

Although financial stringency might have prompted greater borrowing, companies' ability to service debt was also heavily impaired. In fact, their borrowing from banks hardly changed (in terms of the ratios shown in Fig. 11.5) until the end of 1981. In contrast to what happened at a similar state of recession in 1975, bank borrowing then increased.

Bank lending to companies, therefore (as a ratio to GDP), continued to rise gradually (Fig. 11.5). Neither fixed investment nor stockbuilding nor stock appreciation (in ratio terms: Fig. 11.10) appear to have called for greater finance. What is remarkable about the rise in borrowing in the years 1980–5 is that it was largely matched by the quantity of companies' bank deposits. While at the end of 1980 companies' bank deposits stood in aggregate at under half their outstanding bank debt, over the next five years the increase in deposits amounted to 90 per cent of the increase in bank debt.

Ex post facto, this made it safer for banks to lend, but individual banks can have had little idea that this would be the result. It is therefore difficult not to see this process as one in which the banks made it easier for their customers to borrow, and companies used their greater freedom to add to the holdings of liquid assets. The process is further discussed in the next section.

The banks' internal administrative arrangements

In the course of this account, we have had cause at points to qualify the assumption that changes in the ratios of lending to nominal GDP can be taken to indicate changes in the stringency of banks' lending criteria. But we would claim that this interpretation nevertheless remains generally plausible in the light of the changing economic and policy environment in which banks were working. We have been able to cite other evidence that changes in lending criteria in fact took place: this was most clear in the case of mortgage lending, which was a large component of the total rise in lending.

It may be asked what means the banks had to implement such decisions about lending. In the large banks, detailed decisions about lending to individual customers are made by branch or regional managers. Although broad decisions on lending policy are made at headquarters, it is clear that the large banks had no elaborate machinery whereby decisions at the centre could be transmitted to the operational level. That, however, would not have been necessary. What was needed to comply with the Corset, or with the authorities' wish for restraint in lending to particular types of borrower, could be conveyed in broad terms by occasional letters of general guidance or in other ways, and practice evidently varied from bank to bank. Given that the large banks had only broad control of the lending sanctioned by local and regional managers, it would be natural if they played for safety and at times overreacted to changes; this may help to explain the severity of the cutback in lending after the Corset was imposed at the end of 1973. When the constraints were removed in 1980, and as banking became progressively more competitive. the concern of bank managements shifted from seeking to ensure restraint towards encouraging expansion, and in particular towards maintaining market share in a situation where all banks were expanding. In accordance with this more competitive atmosphere, it would seem that the performance of individual managers came to be assessed rather less in terms of bankerly prudence and more in terms of ability to earn profits. The building societies also have plainly developed a much more commercial attitude towards their operations.

What has to be explained is not frequent changes of course, but rather the few and progressively large changes in the trend of lending. This picture of the changing ethos of banking, impressionistic as it is, accords with what can be observed from the statistical aggregates.

3. THE CONSEQUENCES OF INCREASES IN LENDING

At first sight it may be natural to suppose that if people borrow they will increase their spending by an equivalent amount, but that is by no means so obvious as might appear. When persons or companies borrow from banks or building societies they must either spend more than they otherwise would, or increase their holding of financial assets, or reduce other forms of debt. In the second case, there is merely a shift in the composition of borrowers' portfolios of financial assets and debts. We will argue that the big increases in lending by banks and building societies resulted quite largely in portfolio shifts, not in increases in expenditure. But they may well also have some effects on spending.

If the increases in lending by banks and building societies had produced equivalent changes in spending, the effect on GDP would have been very large. Table 11.3 shows for years 1971–84 annual changes in the real stock of loans to the private sector by banks and building societies, expressed as a percentage of real GDP. Had the extra lending been spent in full, the additional spending would in several years have amounted to as much as a third of GDP; and in 1975, when lending fell heavily, it would have resulted in as great a fall in spending. (The previous analysis in this chapter has been in terms of the ratio to nominal

TABLE 11.3. Increases in lending by banks and building societies, 1971–1984a
(Percentages of GDP)

	Total increase in real lending			Increase in lending more or less than in proportion to change in nominal GDP			
	By banks	By building societies	Total	By banks	By building societies	Total	Increase in real GDP
1971	3.0	4.0	7.0	0.8	1.9	2.7	1.5
1972	26.9	7.8	34.7	24.4	5.8	30.2	2.5
1973	31.4	6.4	37.8	21.7	0.04	21.7	7.3
1974	10.2	− 2.9	7.3	11.3	− 2.3	9.0	− 1.7
1975	− 26.6	− 5.7	− 32.3	− 25.7	− 5.2	− 30.9	− 1.1
1976	− 6.4	− 0.3	− 6.7	− 10.1	− 3.0	− 13.1	2.6
1977	0.2	2.5	2.7	− 0.7	1.8	1.1	2.6
1978	3.7	5.0	8.7	0.2	2.4	2.6	3.0
1979	4.1	2.0	6.1	1.9	0.5	2.4	2.7
1980	3.9	− 3.2	0.7	6.2	− 1.7	4.5	− 2.4
1981	9.3	1.7	11.0	10.6	2.6	13.2	− 1.7
1982	29.9	5.1	35.0	28.0	4.1	32.1	2.1
1983	16.6	10.5	27.1	11.2	7.6	18.8	3.3
1984	22.9	13.3	36.2	19.3	11.3	30.6	2.6

a The table shows increases in lending in all currencies by banks and building societies to the UK private sector. The first three columns show the increase in the real stock of loans expressed as a percentage of real GDP, or $\Delta \left(\frac{L}{P}\right)\left(\frac{P}{GDP}\right)$, where L = the nominal stock of loans, P = the GDP deflator, and GDP = nominal GDP. The next three columns show the changes in the borrowing ratio, or, $\Delta \left(\frac{L}{GDP}\right)$. Since most of the changes in nominal GDP reflected a change in prices rather than a change in real GDP, the two series are of the same order; the first exceeds the second when GDP is rising. Changes in real GDP are (for comparability with the lending figures) changes in constant market prices, and are for changes between averages for calendar years. Changes in borrowing are on a similar basis and show changes between the average stock of debt in one calendar year (calculated from quarterly figures) and that in the previous year.

GDP of the stock of loans by the lending institutions, which may be called the 'borrowing ratio'; and for comparison, the table also shows annual changes in the borrowing ratio of the private sector. These are broadly similar in scale to the changes in real lending.)

The fact that the changes in borrowing, although usually in the same direction, were altogether larger than actual changes in GDP makes it impossible to believe that all — or even a considerable fraction — of the additional borrowing resulted in additional spending. If one supposes it had done so, one would also have to suppose that other opposing factors happened to be at work keeping changes in GDP to their modest actual size. This is contrary to what existing evidence suggests. The standard explanations of changes in GDP as embodied in econometric models, although not perfect, explain the behaviour of total expenditure fairly well without taking account of this kind of effect, and appear to leave little room for it. This does not rule out the possibility that borrowing had some effects on spending although on a much smaller scale.

The effects of lending on spending

Banks are intermediaries. If they lend they create deposits; and if they lend for instance to companies, and if persons hold the additional deposits, this is equivalent to lending by the personal to the corporate sector. On the face of it, such a transfer from one sector to another may appear to have no effect on spending in total. There are nevertheless two ways in which intermediation may affect spending, which are likely to appear in combination but are analytically distinct. They are conveniently illustrated by considering first bank lending to companies, and then bank lending to persons.

Consider, first, additional investment by companies financed by borrowing from the banks, and assume for simplicity a closed economy. The additional spending must *ex post* generate additional income, accruing either to other companies or to persons, and additional saving. The additional bank deposits generated by the additional bank lending are (we may suppose) the only additional financial assets to have been created by this process; they must be held by companies or persons, and in aggregate must be equal to their additional *ex post* saving. The additional income may be supposed subsequently to generate a second round of expenditure increase, as a result of which the additional deposits are typically transferred to other agents in the system, and so on to the end of the multiplier process. By the end of the process, the additional financial assets are what agents at their *ex ante* incomes (now equal to *ex post* incomes) will wish to hold. (There may be a question of whether they will then wish to hold them in the form of bank deposits: this has already been discussed in Chapter 2 (Section 2), and we do not need to consider the question further here.)

The essential function of bank intermediation in this process is to ensure that the unplanned additional saving that arises at numerous unpredictable points within the system in the course of the expansionary process is made available to finance the initial investment. Banks make funds available to lenders simultaneously with the generation of saving in the course of the expansion, but without it being clear in advance who it is that will hold the additional deposits. A very similar process takes place if, instead of borrowing from the banks, companies finance additional spending by drawing on 'idle' bank deposits; the deposits are then held elsewhere in the system by those to whom unexpected income accrues. But without either the prior existence of 'idle' deposits or the intervention of banks who make available this sort of 'instant finance', the expansionary process could not take place.

This must make it difficult to say how far expansion is 'due' to bank lending and how far to 'real' factors. In a normal year the economy expands, and the expansion will normally be explicable, let us suppose, in terms of the aggregates contained in an econometric model. But these mechanisms probably can operate only on the proviso that the banks are normally accommodating. If the rate of expansion accelerates, it will thus be the joint result of the desire of agents to spend more, and of continued provision of 'instant finance' by means of bank intermediation. But one can perhaps distinguish two cases.

1. The banks (as argued in Chapter 2) are normally faced with excess demands for loans. If they relax their lending criteria, they will permit extra spending to take place, and the relaxation by banks may be regarded as the 'cause' of the acceleration. But it would not take place if there were not also the desire, hitherto frustrated, to spend more.
2. There may be an increase in the desire to spend, for instance because of improved investment opportunities or an increase in overseas demand. The banks may accommodate this demand because they share their customers' assessment that the additional spending is likely to be profitable.

It can be argued that in this latter case, there is not true relxation of banks' lending criteria — even though it will show up in an increase in lending in relation to GDP, which we have taken as an index of relaxation of lending criteria. In the case of companies, then, the ratio of lending to GDP, contrary to our general presumption, may not provide a good index of change or constancy in banks' lending criteria. In the case of lending to persons, the ratio of lending to GDP is likely to provide a more reliable guide to constancy or inconstancy of lending criteria.

We must now consider the effects on spending of a relaxation of banks' lending to persons. As compared with companies, persons have limited access to credit, and only a restricted ability to spend now on the strength of future income prospects. They have little access to credit apart from borrowing from banks or building societies. A relaxation of the lending institutions' criteria in lending to persons appears capable, therefore, of having a particularly marked effect on spending.

Consider then the sequence of events following additional lending to one category of persons (borrowers), and again for simplicity assume a closed economy. The 'borrowers', we here assume, spend — so their saving falls. The additional expenditure and output is reflected in simultaneous additional *ex post* income, accruing to other persons and companies, and in additional *ex post* saving by them, equal to the fall in saving of the 'borrowers'; and these other persons or companies must hold the additional deposits created by the additional lending (since these, we may again suppose, are the only additional financial assets created). The additional income will subsequently generate further rounds of expenditure increase, in which the additional deposits will (as before) typically be transferred to other agents in the system.

What banks do in this process is, first, to permit greater expenditure by relaxing lending criteria towards agents whose access to credit is particularly limited, and whose expenditure would otherwise be constrained by that, and second (as in the case of companies), to provide 'instant finance' for the additional expenditure.

A closer look at historical experience

We must now take a closer look at events since 1971 to see how far lending by banks and building societies may be supposed to have played a positive role in expenditure fluctuations. We start with lending to persons and then discuss lending to companies. We have taken a growth of lending proportionately greater than the growth in nominal GDP to be an index of a relaxation of lending criteria. Table 11.4 shows how greatly such 'disproportionate' increases in lending would have added to consumers' expenditure if the whole of the additional lending to persons had been spent.

It is necessary to take account not only of non-mortgage bank lending, but also of a part of mortgage lending (by both banks and building societies). Since the early 1970s, new mortgage borrowing appears to have exceeded by a growing margin owner-occupiers' expenditure on acquiring new and existing houses and on house improvements (see Davis and Saville 1982; Drayson 1985). Those providing mortgage finance had earlier sought to limit finance to what was needed to make up the purchase price of a house *less* any proceeds from the sale of a previous house. This rule later came to be relaxed, and loans for house improvements also became easier to get, so that houseowners were able to borrow more freely against their equity in housing (even though lending institutions will still have remained opposed to their doing so too directly). This 'mortgage leak' has in course of time become very considerable: in each of the three years 1982–4, housing expenditure by owner-occupiers appears to account for not much more than half of net new mortgage borrowing. The result (equivalent to 3 per cent of personal disposable income) could thus in effect be used for current expenditure — or to acquire financial assets. This is shown in Table 11.4 along with banks' non-mortgage lending to persons. The attraction of borrowing on

TABLE 11.4. Lending to and spending by persons, 1971–1984 (Percentages of GDP)

	Increase in lending to persons more or less than in proportion to change in nominal GDP			Increase in real disposable income	Increase in real consumer spending[b]
	Non-mortgage lending	'Mortgage leak'[a]	Total		
1971	0.6	0.9	1.5	0.8	1.9
1972	12.4	1.5	13.9	5.5	3.5
1973	3.4	0.3	3.7	5.1	3.0
1974	−2.2	0.3	−1.9	−0.6	−0.8
1975	−5.8	0.5	−5.3	−0.1	−0.2
1976	−2.9	0.5	−2.4	−0.4	0.2
1977	−0.3	0.5	0.2	−0.7	−0.3
1978	0.5	0.5	1.0	4.4	3.1
1979	2.1	0.1	2.2	3.5	2.5
1980	1.8	−0.3	1.5	1.2	−0.2
1981	4.0	0.5	4.5	−1.5	−0.1
1982	6.3	1.6	7.9	0.2	0.6
1983	3.7	1.4	5.1	1.7	2.4
1984	3.0	1.8	4.8	1.6	1.3

[a] Mortgage lending by banks and building societies *less* owner-occupiers' expenditure on acquiring new or existing houses and on home improvements (as estimated by Drayson 1985).

[b] These, like the figures in other columns, are expressed as percentages of GDP and thus show the contributions of consumer spending to the change in real GDP.

mortgage was that interest payments on mortgage borrowing for house purchase or improvement (up to a limit, raised in 1983 to £30,000) were eligible for tax relief; this made it by far the cheapest form of credit available to personal borrowers.

As will be seen from the table, lending to persons of a sort that may be considered to have been potentially available for non-housing expenditure increased in most years considerably more rapidly, but in four years less rapidly, than nominal GDP. The 'disproportionate' lending was usually of the same sign as the change in consumer spending, but was quite frequently considerably larger. If the hypothesis were accepted that such lending resulted in equivalent additional spending, it would be more than enough in many years to account for the observed fluctuations in consumer spending. That appears highly implausible, for reasons similar to those already stated in commenting on Table 11.3.

The question here, however, is somewhat more complex than might appear and concerns more than the nature of the consumption function.

Changes in consumer spending are fairly adequately explained by accepted econometric models in terms of changes (along with some other factors) in persons' real disposable income (whose magnitude is also shown in the table). That, however, does not dispose of the matter; for on the hypothesis that extra lending resulted in equivalent spending, this extra spending would have increased national income, of which much would have accrued to persons. Thus, what this hypothesis implies is that 'disproportionate' increases in lending had a dominant effect in the generation also of disposable income; and it is that which is difficult to accept. For accepted models explain economic fluctuations fairly well without taking account of this kind of shock; and although there is much room for improvement, they hardly leave room for additional effects of this order of magnitude.

It seems likely, none the less, that part of the additional lending resulted in additional spending. Evidence as to the size of the effect could perhaps be obtained only indirectly, by numerous experiments with complete models to see whether the explanation they offered of the behaviour of the economy could be improved by incorporating different scales of lending effect. The proportion of lending that gets spent may well have varied, and the results might well not be very conclusive. This we have not attempted. Nevertheless, even without detailed evidence, this general line of reasoning suggests that the effects of lending by the lending institutions on consumer spending may have been relatively small, and that much of 'disproportionate' increases in lending to persons may have been absorbed by portfolio adjustments.

One reason why persons would wish to borrow in order to change the composition of their assets and debts is that much of the increased borrowing was in the form of mortgages on which the interest cost was low — more especially because it attracted tax relief. This must have made a redistribution of portfolios more attractive; in some cases the return on assets that could be bought by borrowing have been, even after tax, larger than the interest cost incurred on the borrowing.

There are, similarly, reasons to query how far the increase in bank borrowing by companies in recent years can be considered as a cause of increased spending by companies. The reasons for doubt derive from an inspection of what has been happening to companies' financial position. We first set out some of the evidence and then discuss the interpretation to be put on it.

It has already been noted that, in aggregate, the increase in companies' holdings of bank deposits since 1980 has almost matched the increase in their bank debt. The increase in their total liquid assets — including other liquid assets as well as bank deposits — has very comfortably exceeded the growth in their bank debt (first and second columns of Table 11.5). The increase in their bank deposits has largely been in wholesale deposits, which have grown dramatically since 1980 (see estimates in Goodhart 1986, 86): this indeed accounts for much of the total growth of deposits (and without it there would have been no growth in the ratio of broad money to GDP).

Companies in aggregate have thus become more liquid. Although companies vary greatly as to their holdings of liquid assets, the typical picture is not of some companies being heavily indebted to the banks, with other companies having large liquid assets. Table 11.5 shows that, in the most recent years, two-thirds of companies' bank debt was matched, company by company, by liquid asset holdings; of these, the bulk consist of bank deposits.

TABLE 11.5. Companies' bank debt and liquid assets; *stocks at end of accounting year*, 1973–1984

	Stock of short-term bank debt	Stock of liquid assets	Portion of individual companies' bank debt that was matched by holdings of liquid assets[a]	
	(£b)	(£b)	(£b)	(as % of bank debt)
1973	3.36	4.15	1.70	51
1974	4.75	4.53	1.88	40
1975	4.28	5.51	2.10	49
1976	4.51	7.18	2.25	52
1977	4.93	7.90	2.59	53
1978	5.39	8.93	3.06	57
1979	6.25	8.24	3.11	50
1980	6.91	8.49	3.48	50
1981	8.87	11.41	4.72	53
1982	8.58	12.33	5.07	59
1983	9.73	15.32	6.16	63
1984	12.43	16.70	8.54	69

[a] The sum of the lesser of individual companies' bank debt and holdings of liquid assets. A comparable table was previously published in Allen (1982).

Source: Bank of England selection from Datastream tabulations for 979 UK large and medium-sized companies reporting for each year between 1973 and 1984: trust funds and financial companies were excluded. Companies' accounting years are for years ending at various end-quarters; bank debt and asset holdings are as at the end of the accounting year, and are here shown against the calendar year covering most of the accounting year.

A similar analysis of changes in bank debt and liquid asset holdings (Table 11.6) shows furthermore that a good proportion of increases in companies' bank debt was matched, company by company and year by year, by increases in their holdings of liquid assets. In the last five years for which figures are available, this matching within the accounting year approached 30 per cent. (For companies repaying bank debt, a smaller

TABLE 11.6. Changes in companies' bank debt and liquid assets, 1974–1984
(Change through accounting year to year shown)

	Total net increase in companies' short-term bank debt	Companies increasing bank debt		Companies decreasing bank debt		Total net increase in companies' liquid assets
		Increase in bank debt	Proportion matched by liquid asset accumulation	Decrease in bank debt	Proportion matched by reducing liquid assets	
	(£m)	(£m)	(%)	(£m)	(%)	(£m)
1974	1 390	1 625	9	−234	23	381
1975	−472	657	17	−1 129	4	983
1976	234	986	36	−752	9	1 664
1977	416	924	24	−508	20	718
1978	464	1 257	33	−793	13	1 037
1979	862	1 516	14	−653	34	−689
1980	655	1 573	22	−918	17	249
1981	1 965	3 040	20	−1 074	6	2 915
1982	−294	2 551	31	−2 845	14	927
1983	1 148	3 468	35	−2 320	9	2 896
1984	2 699	4 025	28	−1 326	18	1 465
Total for 1980–4	6 173	14 657	28	8 483	13	8 452

Source: as for Table 11.5.

proportion of reductions in bank debt was matched by reductions in liquid asset holdings.) Over the longer term, moreover, borrowing and acquisition of liquid assets at the level of individual companies tend to a large extent to match each other.

Some part of companies' acquisition of liquid assets may have resulted from unexpected accruals of profits. But a consistent tendency of this sort suggests, rather, the growing tendency for companies to undertake borrowing from the banks with the intention of increasing their bank balances. (In that case it would seem wrong to regard the growth of wholesale deposits simply as a growing tendency towards 'liability management' on the part of the banks, as for instance suggested by Goodhart 1986.) Unless it was clear that the whole of companies' marginal borrowing was undertaken with the purpose of building up liquid balances, there would be no reason to think that it had no effect on their expenditure. If access to borrowing is limited, the two purposes must be competitive. But the evidence may suggest that the desire for liquidity was a main motive, and that in the 1980s, given the ease of access to borrowing, the effect of marginal borrowing on expenditure may in this period have been relatively small.

There is one piece of evidence that may appear to contradict this last deduction. At times there has been a close relation between companies' bank borrowing and their expenditure on stocks (see Moore and Threadgold 1980). This however may have been a short-term phenomenon. Thus, we have already suggested (Section 2) that in 1974 banks had little choice but to finance spending that companies could not quickly adjust, but that the return to lower lending and spending in 1975 owed something to the banks imposing a restraint on them, as well as (perhaps) to companies imposing it on themselves. The observed relation between bank borrowing and stockbuilding may thus be a transitory one, and a temporary exception only to the proposition that the major expansions of bank lending may have had relatively little effect on expenditure by companies.

There are two sorts of reason that might account for the apparent tendency of companies since 1980 to borrow in order to hold additional bank deposits. In recent years, competition among deposit-taking institutions has driven deposit rates much closer to banks' lending rates, so that the cost of simultaneously maintaining a bank loan and holding liquid assets is much less than it was; and it now seems to be comparable with the cost of maintaining unused drawing lights under an overdraft facility, which is an alternative way of satisfying the same need. A second sort of reason (suggested in the Governor's Loughborough lecture: *BEQB* 1986, 504) is the upsurge in takeover and merger activity, frequently involving the cash purchase of shares, in preparation for which companies may wish to hold larger bank balances.

A loan that is used by a bank's customer to increase his liquid assets involves little extra risk to the lending bank, because the risk of default is small. In any individual case a bank may have little reason to believe that this will occur. But since there was a general tendency for companies to increase their deposits, banks may have had less than the usual hesitation about lending. There may then be relatively little obstacle from the side of the banks to an indefinite simultaneous extension of bank lending and broad money. This may help to explain the rapid growth of lending since 1980. It should also colour what one thinks of it. A monetary expansion of this form is much the same as an extention of overdraft facilities — something that previously would have taken place unobserved.

4. IMPLICATIONS FOR MONETARY ANALYSIS AND MONETARY CONTROL

Chapter 2 sought to show how the monetary aggregates are likely to grow in an economy with a rising trend of output or price level; and it presented growth in the aggregates primarily as a response of the banking system to the evolving preferences of lenders and borrowers in such an economy. That presentation now needs to be considerably modified. If it were a complete account, the aggregates would have tended to grow more or less in line with nominal GDP. In fact, monetary growth has tended to expand considerably more rapidly. That, we have suggested, resulted from the relaxations of banks' and building societies' lending criteria. We have also suggested that, in some large part, the additional borrowing was undertaken not for the purpose of financing additional expenditure, but as part of an adjustment of borrowers' portfolios of financial assets. This rather different picture has a number of implications both for monetary analysis and for monetary control, which we discuss in turn below.

The power of banks to create money, and the demand to hold money

In Chapter 2 we considered how far banks had unlimited power to create money — in Tobin's phrase, possessed a 'widow's cruse' (Tobin 1963b), and we admitted Tobin's objection to that view, although only in a rather long-term perspective. There are now additional reasons, which we will list below, to qualify the importance of the general equilibrium considerations that Tobin adduced. These have implications for demand-for-money functions, some of which we have already touched on in earlier chapters but which it is now convenient to look at together. These considerations can best be illustrated by examining the consequences of an easing by banks of their lending criteria, which results in an increase in the ratio of bank lending and deposits to national income. We will consider the consequences under three alternative assumptions.

We will first assume that the extra lending results in extra spending. That starts an expansionary process, in the course of which there will be unexpected increases in income and savings. To summarize the argument of Chapter 2, the additional deposits will, for a time, be willingly held at the current pattern of relative interest rates. But by the end of the expansionary process, the public finds its holdings of money excessive, seeks to purchase other types of financial assets, and thus drives up their price. The consequent reduction in yields on such assets reduces the cost of raising finance by issue of equities or bonds, and that leads borrowers to repay bank loans. In this case, the action of the banks is reversed by the subsequent reaction of non-banks. This is the kind of reaction that Tobin had in mind.

It is to be noted that, during the expansionary process, the public has abnormally high holdings of money in relation to income and interest rates; but at the end of the process, a normal relation is restored. A demand-for-money equation (assuming it took appropriate account of interest rate relativities) could hope to capture the end result. But it would not capture what happened in the transitional stages, and, even assuming rapid reactions by borrowers, these must be assumed to last a year or more. There have been several major fluctuations in income in the years since 1971, and, even though these did not result primarily from fluctuations in bank lending, they must be presumed to have resulted in a series of transitional periods in which normal demand-for-money relationships were suspended.

In the second place, this account has to be qualified to allow for some major lags and frictions. Borrowers will take time to adjust to changes in interest relativities, and will not immediately repay bank loans when stock market finance becomes relatively cheaper. Second, small borrowers have little access to sources of finance other than borrowing from banks or building societies, and will not therefore repay bank loans in response to changes in the relative cost of different sorts of finance.

Similarly, small holders of deposits, finding themselves with abnormal holdings of deposits, are more likely to switch to other relatively liquid assets with inflexible interest rates (e.g. National Savings) than to stock exchange securities, so that the shift in interest relativities may be much muted. These frictions must in fact have been severe; for instance, most of the increase in bank lending since 1980 has been to persons, and no subsequent contraction of bank loans and bank deposits will probably have occurred. These lags and frictions, too, have important consequences for the likely stability of demand-for-money functions. If the frictions are severe, such functions will fail to capture even the end result. Each individual may have a demand to hold money of the form that theory postulates without the relationship being manifest in the aggregate data.

Finally, assume that when banks ease their criteria and increase lending the result is not to increase spending, but to permit a rearrangement of borrower's financial portfolios. In that case there will be no expansionary process set in train. It must be assumed furthermore that borrowers are switching to a preferred composition, previously denied them by restricted access to borrowing, of their financial assets and debts. There will therefore be no pressures making for a subsequent contraction of bank lending. Demand-for-money equations must also fail to capture this sort of adjustment, for the starting point was in a sense a disequilibrium position. But it is this sort of adjustment, we have argued, that probably underlies much of the expansion of the broad aggregates in recent years.

The conclusions of this recapitulation are then as follows. The factors to which equilibrium analysis points must impose some limits to the power of the banks to create money, but, in the range within which the banks have operated, these must have been very weak. After the first major expansion in the money/income ratio (1971–3), there was indeed a reversal. But that was not due to any significant revival of stock market issues (Fig. 11.10); in Section 2 we ascribed the contraction of lending in 1974–5 to other factors — a combination of official control, reaction against earlier imprudent lending, and the onset of recession. The second expansionary phase (1981 onwards) has proceeded for five years without reversal. There has been some revival of stock exchange issues, without which the expansion of broad money might have been even greater; but it was not on a scale that could offset the other factors making for an expansion of bank lending. The conclusion is that the 'widow's cruse', though not indefinitely reliable, allowed the banks large leeway to expand.

A second conclusion is that major relaxations of banks' lending criteria are likely, for the various reasons set out above, seriously to disturb the regularities that demand-for-money functions seek to model. It was about 1971 that the previously established equations broke down; and it is since 1971 that there have been major fluctuations in bank lending of a sort we have ascribed to changes in banks' lending criteria. In their study of monetary trends in the United Kingdom in the century or so before 1975, Friedman and Schwartz (1982) claim to have demonstrated the stability of the relation between money stock and national income. That claim has been vigorously contested by Hendry and Ericsson (1983) on the grounds that the statistical methods used are insufficiently rigorous. These authors go on to comment that the clear instability of that relation is, on the contrary, 'massive evidence' against the view (held by Friedman and Schwartz) that money determines prices — but, equally, evidence against the view that nominal incomes determine money. Although we hold that view, we do not suppose, as will be clear, that the relation of money to incomes is rigid.

The limited power of the authorities to control money

We have regarded bank lending to the private sector as the driving force behind monetary expansion, and have treated the growth of lending as limited by direct controls but otherwise untramelled by policy. Throughout the period of this study, the authorities sought to control the rate of monetary growth by varying central-bank rate. We have argued (Chapter 3) that, although the authorities have power to influence the general level of interest rates, they have little influence over relative interest rates, and thus little power to encourage the funding of bank loans and to reduce the growth of bank lending by this route. This chapter has added to the previous analysis the suggestion that much of the increase in bank lending since 1970 represented a portfolio adjustment by individual companies and persons. Officially induced changes in the general level of interest rates can similarly have had little effect on the advantages of borrowing to undertake such adjustments.

Although lending by the banks — and building societies — was in our view unaffected by interest rate policy, we have suggested that the authorities were able to offset its effects on monetary growth by debt-management policy, and by the policy of overfunding. These have been discussed in detail in Chapter 10 (Section 2), and we may now put them in perspective.

In most years since 1971 the banking system continued to increase its lending in nominal terms to the public sector (in the form of holdings of government stock, certificates of tax deposit, and, to a decreasing extent, Treasury bills). But the stock of such lending increased less rapidly than nominal national income, so that as a ratio to GDP (Fig. 11.2) it fell almost continuously, from 15 per cent in 1971 to 3 per cent in 1984. The rate of increase of total public debt (public-sector borrowing) was relatively low (about 3 per cent of GDP) in the conditions of fairly steady growth and full employment up to 1971. Although the scale of public-sector borrowing grew in the following years of recession, it was accompanied by an increased emphasis on containing the scale of borrowing from the banks. The result was to produce a continuous minor offset to the buoyancy of bank lending to the private sector, which reduced the growth of broad money on average by 1 per cent a year over the period since 1971, as compared with a situation in which bank-held government debt increased in line with nominal GDP (see Chapter 10, Section 2).

Overfunding may be regarded as an extension of this same approach. Sales of debt to non-banks had sometimes previously exceeded the total public-sector borrowing requirement by accident, but for some years after 1981, such overfunding was adopted as deliberate policy to moderate the pace of monetary growth. To avoid draining banks' liquid assets, the proceeds of this overfunding were used, first, to run down the banks' holdings of Treasury bills, and later (when these had been reduced to a practical minimum) to buy commercial bills and other paper from the banks, so that the Bank of England acquired a growing 'mountain' of bills. The effect of overfunding was that the public held government debt rather than bank deposits. The scale on which lending was transferred from banks' balance sheets is known, but no exact estimate of its effect on bank deposits is possible. (The favourable terms on which bill finance became available, even when not such as to lead to 'round-tripping', will have reduced the cost of holding liquid assets, and that will have tended to increase lending and broad money.) But as a broad judgement, by the end of the three or four years when the policy was in operation, the stock of broad money may have been reduced by about 5 per cent as compared with what it would have been had the banks themselves done the lending to companies (Chapter 10, Section 2). In that sense it could be regarded as having been a success. Because of the distortions it involved to financial flows, the policy was abandoned in the middle of 1985.

Even so, neither of these methods was enough to offset the momentum of lending to the private sector. Monetary expansion proceeded relentlessly, regardless of the aims of monetary policy, and it is ironic that the second period of pronounced monetary expansion should have coincided with a period when large hopes were built on monetary control. We have regarded both bursts of monetary expansion as being permitted by the removal of lending controls, and have argued that this resulted in a progressive erosion of conventional restraints on lending, as competitive forces were unleashed. We have suggested, too, that this processs must have been stimulated after 1980 by the government's encouragement of competition among financial institutions: policy in effect operated in segmented compartments, with competition policy not being regarded as related to the purposes of monetary policy.

We will discuss in Chapter 13 the morals for policy in future. But it is useful here to consider how long the sort of increase in lending experienced in recent years might continue. It seems unlikely that the stock of lending could increase indefinitely at a rate significantly in excess of the growth of incomes. We have suggested that, to some large extent, easier access to borrowing has resulted in companies adding to their liquid assets, and to persons rearranging their portfolios; but, if so, these must in principle be once-for-all adjustments, even though possibly not yet completed. Most concern probably attaches to consumer lending, and here there could well come a point where the lending institutions were reluctant on prudential grounds to increase lending further. But although there are grounds for thinking that terms for mortgage lending were eased excessively, the bulk of the extra lending cannot have been to the least creditworthy borrowers; and although the banks have incurred bad debts, they have not typically been incurred in lending to persons. Comparison with consumer–debt ratios (as usually measured) in the United States could suggest that the phase of rapid lending growth has a long way to go.

STATISTICAL NOTE ON BANKING STATISTICS

The quarterly series of bank lending for the period from the end of 1971 shown in the charts in this chapter are derived from the CSO published data, but with numerous detailed adjustments necessitated by incompleteness of the data as published.

The estimates of financial balance sheets by sector published in *Financial Statistics* provide quarterly data only from 1982 Q1: quarterly information for earlier years is available on printout, but without the disaggregation into sterling and foreign currency components available for later years in *Financial Statistics*.

For the period 1970 Q1–1975 Q4, quarterly estimates were obtained as follows. What are known to be rough estimates are available of the quarterly paths of bank lending by currency and borrowing sector (*Financial Statistics*, December 1973, Table 39). Those shown for 1975 Q2 differ markedly from the more accurate figures that become available from that date. Leaving the total for all lending unchanged, the sectoral allocation for quarters before 1975 Q2 has here been corrected by the proportional error at that date. Since these total lending figures are higher (by 3–10 per cent) than those in the printout, all figures have then been scaled down to make them compatible with the latter.

For the period 1975–81, the end-year data in the printout are in some cases quite different from the most recently published balance sheets, (*Financial Statistics*, October 1985 and January 1986, Table 14). The end-year figures in the latter have therefore been used, and figures for intervening end-quarters have been interpolated by use of estimates of changes in 'banking sector liabilities and assets outstanding' in the table of that name in various issues of *Financial Statistics*. (The end-year figures in these two sources diverge, but by only relatively minor amounts, the discrepancy being proportionately largest — up to 25 per cent — for the relatively small category of non-bank financial lending in sterling.)

There are several breaks in the banking statistics, the most important of which occurred at the end of 1981 when the Trustee Savings Banks, the National Girobank, and the Banking Department of the Bank of England were included in the banking sector (subsequently called the monetary sector). This reclassification is thought to have raised £M3 by about £8 billion (10 per cent), three-quarters of which was due to the inclusion of the TSBs. Estimates of bank lending were similarly affected, both in total and even more by sectors: lending in sterling to the public sector was raised by nearly 30 per cent; that to industrial companies and to the personal sector was reduced. The reclassification affected foreign currency lending, reducing lending to industrial and commercial companies and the personal sector and raising that to non-bank financial institutions — by an amount that is indeed difficult to explain (for details, see *BEQB* 1981, 531–2). There is a less important break in the series at 1975 Q2, and minor ones at 1975 Q4 and 1983 Q1. The first of these reduced sterling lending to the private sector by £0.9 billion ($3\frac{1}{2}$ per cent), within which lending to industrial and commercial companies was reduced by £1.4 billion (8 per cent).

An attempt has been made in the data presented in the charts to smooth out its effects, except in Figs. 11.1 and 11.4, where the major break in 1981 is shown. Elsewhere smoothing of this break was based on the data in *Financial Statistics* relating to the Trustee Savings Banks' deposits and lending for earlier years.

The figures for foreign currency lending shown in the charts are derived from estimates of the change in the value of stocks held between different dates, which include valuation changes. Rough adjustment is made for valuation changes arising from exchange rate movements. The figures shown on the charts are intended to exclude such valuation effects and thus in principle measure the value of additional loans made by the banks.

PART III

Conclusions

12

The Limitations to the Role of Monetary Policy

Different schools of thought, though differing radically in their conclusions, agree in attributing to the monetary authorities decisive power over the behaviour of the economy. The present study, by contrast, has concluded that the powers of the authorities are in various ways considerably limited. This should perhaps not be surprising. Monetary policy, to be effective, must affect the behaviour of banks; but banks flourished before central banks came on the scene, and it should be expected that the power that central banks have since been able to establish over them, and over the financial system generally, should extend only a certain way. This chapter considers the general implications for the role that monetary policy can hope to play, before we turn (in Chapter 13) to make proposals for future monetary policy.

- The arguments of earlier chapters led to the conclusion that the stock of money is not, by and large, something that the authorities can control. If accepted, this conclusion has major implications for the role of money in the economic system, and in particular for control of money as a means of controlling inflation (Section 1).
- The authorities' control over interest rates is also (we have argued) limited. This limits their effectiveness in influencing the level of investment in the way that is given importance in neo-Keynesian doctrine (Section 2).
- The authorities' power to determine exchange rates is (we have argued) also limited. This has implications for hopes of using the exchange rate as an anchor against inflation (Section 3).

We are here considering the wider implications of the arguments developed in the ten preceding chapters, and Sections 1–3 start with a summary of what the relevant arguments were. Finally, Section 4 states some conclusions about the kind of monetary policy followed since the mid-1970s.

1. MONEY AND INFLATION

Both monetarist and Keynesian macro theory frequently hold that the stock of money determines the price level, either fairly proximately or at some perhaps remote equilibrium point; that the stock of money can be controlled by the authorities; and hence that monetary policy can control the course of inflation. Any argument on these lines is in opposition to our own conclusion that by and large the authorities are not able to control the stock of money. Before confronting these arguments more closely, we will first set out briefly the essential elements of our own argument about the nature of monetary growth, the limited power of the authorities over interest rates, and their limited power of monetary control. For the present purpose it is convenient to assume a closed economy; exchange rates are considered in Section 3.

The nature of monetary growth

- Most money is bank deposits, and when the stock grows both sides of the banks' balance sheets must expand. Similarly, a fall in the money stock can take place only in banks loans are repaid. A theory of monetary growth thus must rest on an account of the macroeconomic behaviour of the banking system.
- We argue (Chapter 2) that the difficulty banks encounter in assessing risks forces them to apply conventions or rules of thumb in deciding how much to lend to individual customers. Bank credit is thus limited by a rationing process, and the rate of interest at which banks lend is an administered rate, in contrast to the flexible yields on securities.
- Although within limits banks can decide how much to lend, they cannot expand lending indefinitely. A continued expansion of lending, it was argued, would create a progressively increasing incentive for borrowers from banks to repay bank debt. (Thus, when banks lend they create deposits; and as the public finds itself with greater deposits, it will tend to substitute other assets for deposits in its portfolios. That will force up the price of other assets such as equities and bonds, and reduce the yield on them; and that in turn will induce borrowers to issue securities as an alternative source of finance, and repay bank loans.) There is therefore an economic limit or equilibrium point to the scale of bank intermediation — dependent in part on banks' assessment of risk as reflected in their lending criteria, which may change.
- The corrective reaction of the non-bank public to an increase in the money stock will however be incomplete and slow. The public will not seek to diversify out of money straightaway; borrowers will take time to switch borrowing from banks, and perhaps only a minority of borrowers have an effective alternative to borrowing from banks or building societies. Because of these lags and frictions, the equilibrium scale of bank intermediation is thus a fuzzy area rather than a precise limit. Within a range, therefore, the banking system can vary the scale of its lending without setting up counter-forces through the reaction of non-banks.

- The criteria that banks use in setting limits to their lending include the incomes, past and prospective, of personal borrowers and the profits, past and prospective, of borrowing firms. With unchanged lending standards, therefore, the banks will tend progressively to increase the scale of their lending, and with it the total of bank deposits, as nominal national income grows. When broad money grows in proportion to nominal national income, we take that as a rough indication that banks' lending criteria are remaining unchanged; and when it grows more than in proportion to nominal income, we take it as a rough indication that banks' lending criteria are being relaxed. In the first case the banks' balance sheets may be said to expand 'passively' to the expansion of the environment in which the banks operate, and the growth of money may be regarded as fully endogenous. In the second case, the disproportionate growth of money may be seen as being due to the 'active' behaviour of the banks in relaxing their lending criteria, and in this sense as exogenous.
- When borrowers borrow, they do so either in order to spend more than otherwise, or to acquire and hold additional financial assets; and the latter may have been the predominant motivation (Chapter 11, Section 3). In the first case a relaxation by the banks of their lending criteria will increase total demand; in the second there is no effect on demand.

The limited power of the authorities over interest rates

- We argued (Chapter 3) that there is a considerable area within which interest rates are free to vary in response to expectational factors. (Fundamental factors relating to the profitability of the capital stock and the desire of savers to maintain or extend their holdings of wealth, and market perceptions of these factors, set limits to this range: see Section 2 below.)
- Interest rates are determined by expectations of future interest rates. We argued (Chapter 3) that, because of the unpredictability of the future, fundamental factors impinge on markets only weakly. Interest rate expectations are diffuse and weakly held; operators operate chiefly on a short-term basis, and are influenced by what they expect the opinion of other short-term operators to be.
- For the same reasons, markets may also be strongly influenced by what they infer of the views of the authorities, and are ready to follow the lead provided by changes in central-bank rate. The banks' administered rates follow central-bank rate, partly because that also influences interest rates more generally; the fact that the banks follow it, in turn, magnifies the influence of the central-bank rate over interest rate expectations.

- Although the authorities thus can make bank lending more expensive, they then also raise interest rates in general. Hence they can do little or nothing to raise the relative cost of bank loans as compared with alternative sources of finance, and thus to encourage bank customers to repay bank loans.

The limited power of the instruments of monetary control

- Broad money cannot be controlled by variations in central-bank rate since (as noted above) a rise in the rate provides little or no incentive to fund bank loans (Chapter 8). Variations in central-bank rate do induce switches between a narrow monetary aggregate (if largely or completely non-interest-bearing) and interest-bearing deposits. A persistent trend in narrow money, faster or slower than the authorities judged appropriate, could not however be corrected by this means.
- The Corset, like any direct control, caused disintermediation into close substitutes more money. More important, it made the banks more conservative in their lending attitudes, and hence prevented pressure from building up behind the control. (This became apparent in the rapid growth of broad money after the Corset was abolished.)
- The reduction of public-sector borrowing from the banks over the decade after 1971 offset a small part of the growth of private-sector borrowing, and thus somewhat slowed the growth of broad money. By the early 1980s, the point was reached where the process could not easily be carried further.
- Overfunding was also effective in reducing the growth of broad money: the public ended up holding less of its wealth as bank deposits and more in public debt. This involved (1) a substitution of bill finance for bank lending in companies' financing, and (2) the government's buying bills that companies issued, and borrowing to do so. That made the method seem unacceptable.
- With the above exceptions, the authorities thus lacked effective means to influence the rate of growth of broad money. Monetary targets notwithstanding, the monetary growth that took place must, by and large, be regarded as the result of market forces, not of government policy.

The ineffectiveness of monetary base control

- Monetary base control would not on our view provide a practicable method of control (Chapter 9).
- Monetary base control with mandatory reserve ratios geared to broad money would be equivalent to a direct control of bank lending, with the same effect in causing disintermediation.

- Without mandatory reserve ratios, restriction of the growth of banks' reserves against strong pressures for monetary expansion could cause high (in principle, increasingly high) short-term interest rates. But these would be no more effective in controlling bank lending, and hence the growth of broad money, than extreme levels of central-bank rate. The attempt would cause serious disruption of financial markets, and one possibility is that in such conditions banks would ration lending, causing disintermediation as with a direct control. Banks might also evade the control by holding reserves with other banks, as small banks and building societies do now.
- Monetary base control with mandatory reserve ratios would, we argued, be more effective in controlling the growth of narrow money; for high interest rates would cause a diversion from non-interest-bearing deposits to those that bore interest. But in face of a persistent tendency for narrow money to grow more rapidly than the target rate, an indefinite progressive rise in short-term interest rates would be required — which beyond a point would be impossible.

For these reasons is appears inappropriate, in building a long-term theoretical model of the economy, to assume that monetary base control provides the authorities with a permanent means to determine the size of the stock of money.

The implications of our arguments for equilibrium analysis

Both the monetarist and the Keynesian arguments that the money stock determines the price level derive from consideration of the equilibrium position of the economic system. Even though our analysis has been concerned with the short term and not directly with long-term equilibrium, it would seem to undermine these equilibrium arguments.

We may start by comparing our analysis with a monetarist position. Despite differences between different writers, the essentials of what may be called a monetarist position can perhaps be stated as follows.

1. The demand for money in real terms is a stable function of real output and the real rate of interest; and in equilibrium real output and the real rate of interest are determined by real factors.
2. The supply of money is independent of the demand for money, and can be controlled by the authorities.
3. Hence if the 'money supply' is increased, the price level in equilibrium is higher than otherwise.

This picture appears to be consistent for instance with that in Milton Friedman (1956). It implies that additional money can in some sense be 'injected' into the system, so that the public then holds more money than it would in equilibrium wish to hold. It is implied that, when an existing equilibrium is upset in this way, the public spends more than otherwise. Given full employment and a limit to real output, prices must rise to the point where the larger stock of money is willingly held. Different writers vary as to whether it is broad money or narrow money that determines the price level.

The idea that money can be injected into the system appears unsatisfactory, in part because it is incomplete. It seems to imply either that the stock of money can be increased without anything else happening, or that, if other changes are implied, they are left unspecified. In fact, the non-bank public can acquire an additional holding of money only if it spends less than otherwise, or sells some other financial asset, or enjoys an increase in income; any of these has its counterpart in actions by other parties, the consequences of which need to be traced. What is money to the non-bank public is debt to other parties, namely, the authorities or the banks; furthermore, what they do with the sums thus borrowed, which will also have consequences, needs to be specified. Divorced from these necessary attendant circumstances, an increase in money holding appears like a windfall gain.

Chapter 2 attempts to analyse the process of monetary growth along with both the changes in debt/asset positions that must accompany it, and the changes in income/expenditure that in some cases accompany it or result from it. Its central conception is that the money stock increases as a result of evolving preferences of lenders to or borrowers from the banks as nominal incomes rise, or can change as a result of change in such preferences or changed attitudes to risk on the part of banks. The structure of debts and assets (including bank deposits and bank debt) tends towards an equilibrium position in which preferences are fully met. In the course of establishing that position, there may be disequilibria in debt/asset positions (reactions to which produce the movement towards equilibrium) which may persist for a period of years. These reactions have some similarity with those assumed on a monetarist view; the differences are worth spelling out.

Positions of disequilibrium arise most clearly in our account when banks relax their lending criteria. In that case something that may be regarded as an injection of money occurs. (Indeed, if we saw monetary base control as effective, we might picture an easing of control, otherwise an increase in the 'money supply', as resulting in a relaxation of banks' lending criteria, and taking effect in precisely that form.) The initial effects of such a relaxation have to be distinguished from the secondary further effects.

The initial effect of easier access to credit is either an adjustment of borrowers' portfolios (of which the simplest case is a parallel rise in both their bank debt and their bank deposits), or an increase in spending. In the first case, there is neither disequilibrium in debt/asset positions to be corrected, nor secondary effects on income and spending. In the second case, if spending is increased it is to be noted that, while additional deposits are indeed created by additional lending, the additional spending results from the easing of credit, and is undertaken by those who borrow, not by those with additional holdings of money.

The initial impact will leave two sorts of disequilibria. First, the initial additional spending will have increased incomes, which will lead to a train of subsequent (multiplier) increases in income and spending. Second, the initial increase in lending may result in a higher stock of money than the public will permanently wish to hold at existing relative interest rates. These secondary effects on spending, it is to be noted, are the delayed effect of the increase in income, not the effect of abnormal money holdings — even though it is in this form that agents temporarily hold unspent income.

By the end of the process, either incomes will have increased enough for the larger stock of money to be willingly held at existing relative interest rates, or it will still be in excess. That will reflect not an unsatisfied demand to spend (which we take to be governed primarily by income-type variables), but dissatisfaction with the form in which wealth is held. Hence it will cause not extra spending but a rise in the prices of other financial assets — to the point where the stock of money is willingly held. The associated changes in relative interest rates will, in turn, cause bank debt to be replaced by other debt, and when that process has run its course, asset/debt equilibrium will have been re-established. (We have argued that in practice there are many frictions in the way of repayment of bank debt. This means that an easing of credit may result — contrary to what a simple monetarist account might assert — in a rise (at the aggregate level though not at the micro level) in the equilibrium relation of money holdings to income. But although important as a matter of short-term realism, this is perhaps not of fundamental theoretical importance.)

At the new short-term equilibrium, output will be higher than before; and as a consequence of that, prices may be higher and perhaps rising more rapidly than before. However, this does not mean that either the behaviour of the banks or monetary policy can be seen as long-term determinants of the price level.

Although our account of the short-term behaviour of the financial system has some similarities with a monetarist view, the features described above must be seen as important only in the short term. The banks could not relax their lending criteria without limit, and in the long term bank intermediation should be assumed to be at some equilibrium scale. Thus, on a long-term view, we see market forces tending to keep bank lending and broad money rising more or less in line with nominal GDP. If prices rose, this would cause the aggregates to rise with it. That might appear superficially similar to what would happen on a monetarist interpretation, which also sees the money stock on a long view rising in line with nominal incomes. But on such an interpretation, the former determines the latter, whereas on our view the reverse is true.

Our crucial departure from a monetarist view is thus that we believe the authorities lack power to control the market forces that produce monetary growth. The use of central-bank rate, we have argued, is ineffective as a control over broad money, and in the long term also over narrow money. More direct means, whether by monetary base control or controls on lending, would merely divert holdings from money to close substitutes; nor can they be regarded as tenable methods in the long term. Much the same applies to a manipulation of the composition of the public-sector debt. On a long view, the authorities are not in a position to make members of the public hold more, or less, money than they want.

On this view, then, the decisive objection to the monetarist position is to the assumption (assumption (2) above) that the stock of money is an exogenous variable subject to control by the authorities. Our contention is that a price rise produces both an 'increase in demand for nominal money holdings' and an 'increase in the supply of money to meet it' (Friedman 1956, 17) — a contention that Friedman himself has noted as a possible line of argument against his view. The same objection applies to models of the Keynesian type, based on the Hicksian *IS/LM* synthesis, which likewise assume that the stock of money is exogenous and under the control of the authorities, and which treat the price level in equilibrium as a function of the money stock.

This does not mean that monetary policy could not on occasion be used to influence demand and thus, indirectly, prices (see Chapter 13, Section 1). But that would be a short-term measure, and would be far from providing full control of the price level. The case for it would have to be based on judgements about the economic situation — the sort of probablistic and contingent judgements that monetarism sought to replace.

2. LIMITATIONS TO INTEREST RATES AS A MEANS TO INFLUENCE INVESTMENT

In contrast to the inability of the authorities to control the money stock, our analysis suggests that they have considerable power to influence interest rates — but only within a range. In some strands of neo-Keynesian thinking, the authorities' power of interest rates is regarded as a means whereby they can determine the share of national output going to investment. Our analysis suggests that their power in this respect is at best very limited. In developing this argument, we first summarize our conclusions of our discussion of interest rates.

The determination of interest rates (summary from Chapters 3 and 4)

In many models of long-term equilibrium it is the rate of interest that brings into equality the stock of the capital that managers of capital wish to employ with the stock of wealth that the community wishes to hold; and the rate of interest is determined by the marginal return on capital and the preferences of the community as between present and future consumption.

- These fundamental forces, we argued, fail to dominate the short-term behaviour of market interest rates because the stocks of capital and of wealth respond only slowly to changes in interest rates. In the short term, therefore, the rate of interest does not play an equilibrating role in bringing the desire to add to wealth (i.e. to save) into equality with the desire to add to capital (i.e. to invest).
- The necessary equality between saving and investment in any period is thus brought about not by the rate of interest, but by adjustments of income. Since market interest rates are not dominated by the fundamental factors, they can be dominated by speculative forces. Prices and yields are thus determined day to day by the expectations of short-term operators, each engaged in guessing what other operators will think (Keynes's beauty contest), and are unstable and erratic.
- Nevertheless, fundamental factors limit the range of interest rate expectations, and hence the range of interest rate fluctuations. Within this range, interest rates may be said to be indeterminate.
- The fact that interest rates are indeterminate within a range also makes it possible for the authorities to influence market expectations, and thus to have a direct influence (without extensive operations on their part) within that range on the general level of interest rates. Central-bank rate determines the banks' lending and deposit rates and also goes far to determine interest rates generally.

Implications of our analysis for the determination of investment

The idea that interest rates are a powerful determinant of investment figured quite largely in earlier Keynesian discussion of policy, and is retained for instance in Meade's 'New Keynesian' prescription (Vines, Maciejowski, and Meade 1983). Interest rate policy is here seen as a means of determining the share of investment in national output. In a different, and weaker, guise, it appears in Tobin's advocacy of public-debt management as a means of influencing investment (see discussion in Chapter 6, Section 2). (It also underlies recent British monetary and fiscal policy: see Chapter 6, Section 3.)

Although we have not in this study attempted a comprehensive discussion of the determinants of investment, the analysis of previous chapters suggests that the influence that the authorities can bring to bear on interest rates provides relatively little power to control private investment.

We have argued, first, that the authorities' power to manipulate interest rates is itself limited in various respects. The authorities can influence interest rates only within a certain range, and only because of the range of indeterminacy within which the fundamental forces do not dominate them. If investment responded quickly and strongly to changes in interest rates, that would not be the case. Thus, the reason why the monetary authorities are able to influence interest rates at all is precisely that investment is affected only slowly, and in any period only slightly, by variations in interest rates that are within the range the authorities can bring about. They have influence over interest rates only because interest rates themselves have little immediate influence.

Our analysis of the determination of interest rates in many ways parallels our analysis of exchange rate determination (to be summarized in Section 3 below). But the observed range of fluctuation of exchange rates appears considerably wider than that of interest rates, probably because the authorities have continued to play an important role in the latter, whereas exchange rates have been left largely to market forces. When we come to draw policy conclusions (in Chapter 13), therefore, we give priority to the avoidance of undue fluctuations in exchange rates, in order to keep real exchange rates as far as possible to a long-term sustainable level.

But the sustainable level cannot be precisely judged, so that there is some range of choice, and there may be good reasons to opt for a somewhat high or a somewhat low rate. In the same way, there is some range of choice as to the level of interest rates. Since the range is limited, we argue not that private investment cannot be influenced at all by interest rates, but that their power is weak. If a higher level of investment appeared desirable, that would be one reason for seeking to keep interest rates low.

3. LIMITATIONS TO THE AUTHORITIES' CONTROL OVER EXCHANGE RATES

For a decade or so — say, from the mid-1970s to the mid-1980s — it became orthodox to argue that exchange rates were uncontrollable and had to be left to market forces, and that price stability could be ensured by an appropriate domestic monetary policy. More recently, opinion seems to be moving against domestic monetary targets and towards targets for the exchange rate, and also towards reliance on the latter to ensure price stability. That view implies that the authorities can have their way with exchange markets. We take a middle view, and thus have to guard our position on both flanks. In Chapter 13 we make the case for an exchange rate policy, and argue against those who doubt its feasibility. Here we are concerned to stress the limitation to the authorities' power over exchange rates, and to discuss the implications of such limitations for the hope of using exchange rate policy as an anti-inflationary weapon.

The determination of exchange rates (summary from Chapter 5)

- We argued that, while extreme fluctuations in the exchange rate are limited by fundamental factors, within a considerable range the exchange rate is not determined by such factors. Exchange rates thus can be (and have been) highly erratic. Since future exchange rates are highly uncertain and expectations about them are weakly held, few operators take long-term positions. Markets are dominated by short-term operators, whose actions are determined in effect by expectations of what other short-term operators expect.
- The authorities may influence the exchange rate either by buying or selling foreign currency in exchange for domestic currency (intervention); or by varying central-bank rate in order to influence the level of domestic interest rates as compared with those abroad (interest rate policy).
- Such action may also affect expectations about exchange rates, and thus have further, indirect, effects on rates. This is because the authorities are potentially large-scale operators; and if their actions are thought to be in pursuit of an exchange rate aim, any action implies that further action may be taken in pursuit of that aim. Since private operators' expectations are weakly held, they are likely to follow a clear lead from the authorities — always provided that official policy is believed to be practicable and likely to be pursued.
- Provided that such credibility is retained, the international mobility of capital, far from being an obstacle to an exchange rate policy, assists the authorities in their exchange rate aim — to the point where action on their part is scarcely needed. But credibility is hard to establish, easily damaged, and quickly lost. A level of the exchange rate too far from the vague centre of market opinion will cease to appear to markets to be sustainable, and capital flows may then easily overwhelm the actions of the authorities.
- The possible scale on which the authorities may act to influence the exchange rate is itself limited. Intervention to support the rate is limited by the size of the reserves and by how much the authorities can borrow in foreign currencies; and intervention to keep down the rate

is limited because the authorities will not wish to acquire an indefinitely large stock of foreign currency.

• The use of interest policy is also limited. If an interest rate differential is created, it will provoke a shift into (or out of) the currency; but to provoke a further shift (for instance, to finance a continued current account deficit), an additional differential will be required. Beyond a point, that is not possible; for there is a limit to how far the authorities can vary domestic interest rates (Chapter 3). Too high a level of interest rates, moreover, may be read by markets as a sign that it is proving difficult to prevent a decline in the exchange rate, and in that case may undermine confidence rather than reinforce it.

The conclusion to emerge from Chapter 5 was thus essentially two-faced. On the one hand, so long as exchange rate policy appears credible, the authorities appear to have great power over the rate. On the other hand, if their policy ceases to appear credible, they can rapidly become almost impotent. Nor is there means of telling what will destroy confidence or when it will go. Exchange rate policy thus rests on a fragile foundation, and to try to accomplish too much by means of controlling the exchange rate risks destroying its foundation.

The implications for the hope of using the exchange rate to counter inflation

A rise in domestic interest rates is likely to raise the exchange rate, to make imported goods (and the import content of home-produced goods) cheaper, and, for a period, to reduce the rate of increase of an index of domestic prices that includes the price of such goods. While evidence that the rate of growth of the monetary aggregates affects prices has been hard to come by, it was clear that monetary restraint affects prices via the exchange rate in this way; and the argument has shifted to the proposition that it is by that route that monetary restraint can control inflation. This is clearly not a remedy that could be applied to all countries: if one country gains that way, some other country or countries must lose. The argument rather suggests that, as a local solution, countries with higher-than-average inflation should tie their exchange rate to the currency of a country with lower-than-average inflation. But it will be argued below that, if a country has serious inflationary problems, the relief to inflation by this route is likely to be obtained only for a time, after which the benefit must at least in large part be undone.

Consider first two countries, in one of which (country A) inflation is proceeding steadily more rapidly than in the other, and where the exchange rate between them is changing in such a way as to maintain purchasing-power parity. In country A, the prices of foreign goods in foreign prices rise less rapidly than domestic goods in domestic prices, but in domestic prices, because of the falling exchange rate, they rise at the same rate as domestic goods; and export prices in domestic currency rise faster than foreign goods, but in foreign currency they rise at the same rate. In country B, with faster inflation, the reverse will be true. In both countries, therefore, wages and import costs in domestic prices, the two major components of domestic prices, increase in line with each other; and real wages must increase as rapidly as productivity. If wage-earners are content with that, the situation will be stable: there is no reason why such a situation should not continue indefinitely, nor why inflation in the more inflationary country (as sometimes argued) should have to accelerate. This picture provides a reference point, against which variant situations can now be considered.

We now need to consider the possibilities for the more inflationary country (country B) of using the exchange rate to slow down inflation. Suppose first that country B intervenes to hold the exchange rate stable; and suppose further that price flexibility is so great that the mere exposure to competition with foreign goods whose prices rise more slowly is itself enough to ensure that from now on prices will rise in line in the two countries. The object then would be accomplished in full, and the stable exchange rate would be sustainable indefinitely. That however is clearly an unreal case. (On such assumptions one could, indeed, say little about the effects on inflation: one could as well assume that convergence was brought about through acceleration of inflation in country A, as by deceleration in country B.)

Suppose then, as before, that country A intervenes to keep the exchange rate stable, but that, while the price rise slows down, it slows down insufficiently. The exchange rate will not then be sustainable indefinitely. When later a downward adjustment is made to the rate, some or all of the gain in slowing down inflation will be reversed. During the period before the rate is slowed down, there will be a reserve loss. If that loss has to be recouped (by running with an undervalued currency for a while), the whole of the gain in slowing down inflation will be reversed. If the loss of reserves can be accepted, part of the gain will be retained. Thus it is possible to trade a lower rate of inflation for a once-for-all reserve loss. Even in that case, if there is a persistent underlying tendency for domestic costs in country B to rise more rapidly than in country A, a new divergence of costs will progressively emerge, and the new lower exchange rate will again not be sustainable indefinitely.

Two conclusions may be drawn. On the practical plane, there may be occasions when it is sensible to make such a trade, and try for a while to hold the exchange rate constant. But, unless additional steps are taken as well to moderate the underlying inflationary trend, this cannot be a permanent policy. The possibilities of using either intervention or interest rate policy are finite. At some point, given that differential inflation persists, reversion to a policy of allowing the exchange rate to decline will be necessary. If continued too long, market forces may necessitate a downward step adjustment of the rate. That not only would undo the benefits of the policy, but would undermine general market confidence in the ability of the authorities to manage the exchange rate. As a general rule, it seems best that governments should seek to stabilize real, rather than nominal, exchange rates.

On the plane of economic theory, the conclusion is that the exchange rate cannot provide a long-term anchor to the price level. Governments do not have the power to fix nominal rates in perpetuity. Section 1 has argued that control of the money stock was not available as an anchor to prices on the essentially similar grounds that governments lack power to prevent increases in the stock of money in the face of an upward trend in prices and incomes. These conclusions run counter to a long strand of academic thinking about money and about monetary policy, and, perhaps, also to the deeply ingrained feelings of practical men. Economists hanker for equilibrium solutions, and practical men for reassurance. But absolute answers seem not to be had.

4. SOME CONCLUSIONS ABOUT MONETARY POLICY SINCE THE MID-1970s

It may finally be worth considering how the kind of monetary policy followed in this country since the mid-1970s appears in light of this discussion. A balanced assessment requires that monetary policy be seen in the context of economic developments and of policy as a whole; and this is all the more difficult because the view taken in this study about how the economy operates differs in many respects from that underlying official policy.

The operation of monetary targets has to be regarded, more especially since 1979, as a serious and prolonged attempt to deal with inflation, and as part of a general economic strategy, since the reduction of inflation was intended to create the basis for sustained economic growth. Although the exchange rate was not the main focus of monetary policy, it was foreseen that attempts to maintain a tight policy might result in a high exchange rate, and this was regarded as useful for reducing inflation. Fiscal policy was in effect subordinated to monetary policy (Chapter 6, Section 3); in order to maintain monetary control without undue reliance on interest rates, a progressive reduction of the scale of public-sector borrowing was thought necessary. The effects on demand and output, both of high exchange rates and of a restrictive fiscal policy, were either less regarded or seen as a cost worth paying.

The debate that has taken place about economic policy since 1979 has been concerned less with monetary policy in the narrow sense than with these demand effects of the policies that went along with it. Since we have not discussed these questions in this study, we confine ourselves here to noting opposing views. The fact that the recession was so deep, and that growth continued to be insufficient to reduce unemployment, has been attributed in part to fiscal and exchange rate policy (see for instance Buiter and Miller 1981[b], 1983). That can be seen as a defect of policy or, to a degree, a success; thus Fforde (1982) has argued that monetary targetry enabled the authorities to 'stand back from output and employment as such' and to stress the importance of containing the rise in costs. On the other hand, the resumption of output and productivity growth after 1981 has been seen as an economic renaissance, attributable to greater industrial confidence; and that in turn has been seen as attributable to restrictive financial policies and in particular to the containment of public-sector borrowing (see Walters 1986).

The major apparent success for the policies followed is that inflation has been reduced. By 1983 inflation had fallen, although erratically, to about a third of what it was in 1976 and 1977 (Fig. 11.8 above). The rise in retail prices was somewhat above 15 per cent in 1976 and 1977 and fell to under 10 per cent in 1978; it was significantly above that in the next three years, since 1981 has been mostly in the range of 5–7 per cent, and in 1986 reached a low of $3\frac{1}{2}$ per cent.

There was no notable success in achieving monetary targets (see Table 7.2 above), and we have argued that the authorities in fact lacked generally effective means of controlling monetary growth. That view makes it impossible to see control of the aggregates as the reason why inflation slowed down. This study has not sought to explain price movements. But reasonable alternative explanations of the slowdown of inflation would be, first, low levels of demand and, second, the effects of the fall in world oil and commodity prices, both direct and indirect via their effect in reducing wage increases. Both of these factors have operated also in other industrial countries, where there has been a parallel slowdown in inflation. In the United Kingdom, the rise in the real exchange rate since 1978 (Fig. 11.7) must also have contributed substantially to the deceleration of inflation. That was probably only in part an effect of policy: in so far as it was, it came not from control of the aggregates but from high interest rates.

If monetary control was (as we have argued) ineffective, it cannot itself have been positively harmful and may even have helped to some small degree to slow down inflation simply because it was widely believed that it would. But any such effect depends on the policy being credible; a policy whose first step is to control the monetary aggregates cannot continue to be credible if it becomes clear that the authorities are unable to achieve that first step. Since that, we argue, is now evident, monetary targetry no longer appears tenable. The conclusion is that a new start has to be made with a monetary policy conceived on quite other lines.

13

Monetary Policy Without Monetary Targets

This study has been concerned with the type of monetary policy that aims to control the growth of the monetary aggregates, and that has been attempted in the United Kingdom throughout the decade since the mid-1970s. Its increasingly evident lack of success has led to the continued value of monetary targetry being widely questioned (as for instance in the Governor's Loughborough lecture, already cited), and in the 1987 Budget targets for broad money (although not for monetary base) were abandoned. It is the contention of this study that the failure of monetary policy has been not superficial, but basic. Without adequate means to control any of the aggregates, the extensive hopes built on such control need to be set aside, and the rationale of policy thought out afresh. Although there might be some agreement on the need to recast monetary policy, there has been much less disposition to re-examine its underlying philosophy — an evolution of thought to which this study may perhaps contribute.

Analysis of the past, as in previous chapters, contains important pointers to what alternative lines of policy might be. What remains to be done is to try to put these together, and that is the aim of this chapter. Monetary policy has to be seen as part of economic policy as a whole, and this is briefly discussed in Section 1. Section 2 outlines what we see as the future domestic role of monetary policy; we suggest however that its chief role should be as part of exchange rate policy, which we discuss in Section 3. Section 4 completes the discussion with comments on the mix of monetary and fiscal policy.

1. MONETARY POLICY AS PART OF GENERAL ECONOMIC POLICY

It is impossible to define the role of monetary policy without indicating its relation to other instruments of policy. Nor is it possible to consider the role of policy without also discussing the problems with which policy has to deal; of these, we see the problem of inflation as the most intractable, and a serious constraint on what policy can hope to accomplish. To discuss these questions comprehensively would take us far outside the limits of this study; and we confine ourselves to the minimum required as background to our proposals for the role of monetary policy.

We see fiscal policy as capable of influencing total demand and output (Chapter 6, Section 1), and as having larger effects than monetary measures. But there are important limitations to its use for this purpose. First is the debt constraint: the ratio of public debt to national income could not in practice be raised indefinitely, and public borrowing beyond a point difficult to determine in advance would damage the government's credit standing (Chaper 6, Section 1). Second, and at least as important in practice, there is an inflation constraint. Fiscal stimulus to the economy (like any other stimulus) may directly put upward pressures on costs and prices; it will also worsen the current balance of payments, reduce the exchange rate, and thereby indirectly put pressure on costs and prices.

Despite the severe constraints this places on fiscal policy, we do not see prudent demand management by fiscal policy as providing a full solution to the problem of inflation. Much discussion of inflation is based on the idea that, at a sufficiently low level of demand and high level of unemployment — the 'natural rate', or 'non-accelerating inflation rate of unemployment' (NAIRU) — inflation would be kept to a low and stable rate. But experience has clearly shown that undesirably high inflation can persist despite very high unemployment. One way of saving the theory is to suppose that the critical level (NAIRU) has risen along with the rise in unemployment (Layard and Nickell 1985). But it may also be argued, and perhaps more plausibly, that there are no good grounds for supposing that the rate of inflation is rigidly determined by the level of demand, and that high inflation may persist even at a very low level of demand (for instance Dow 1964, 333–4).

To be complete, we should also say that we do not see a major role for incomes policies of one sort or another. There are doubtless longer-term means of reducing inflationary pressures, by promoting greater competition and greater mobility of labour — or perhaps by limiting the power of trade unions (Dow 1986). But these would probably fall short of providing a full answer to the problem. When, therefore, we argue (as in Chapter 12) that neither monetary targets nor exchange rate policy is capable of providing a barrier to inflation, we do not imply that another method would be more effective.

If that is the case, it may seem surprising that inflation has not been even more rapid than it was. One partial explanation is that much of the fluctuations in the rate of inflation have been due to fluctuations either in world commodity prices or in the exchange rate, and that such fluctuations are in large part self-righting. Going beyond that, one might perhaps attribute to the economic system a degree of resistance to accelerating inflation. Nevertheless, there seems no absolute protection against an acceleration of inflation, which at some point could become cumulative and self-reinforcing; and that possibility appears dangerous because there are no easy and sure ways of containing it. This suggests a picture of inflation in normal times as an iterative process, governed by habitual modes of response, but beyond some trigger point governed by expectations of future inflation. One may perhaps compare inflation to a sleeping giant beside which policy must tread warily lest it be roused; once roused, the bluntest instruments have to be used to break the speculative climate.

Such a view greatly limits the possibilities of economic policy. The academic discussion of policy generally assumes a tidier world, in which the powers of the authorities, properly used, are adequate to attain the goals of policy, and in which the use of different policy instruments can be clearly assigned. In Meade's 'New Keynesian', for instance, the discussion of stabilization policy rests on the prior assumption that the danger of inflation has been removed by 'near compulsory' arbitration (Vines, Maciejowski, and Meade 1983). That world seems at least some distance away.

A dominant recent strand in the discussion of economic policy has been concerned with the search for an optimum way of conducting monetary policy; this approach requires mention, since it rests on assumptions about the potency of monetary policy which our analysis has denied. The approach (as in Poole 1970) assumes the *IS/LM* construction and a 'natural rate' of unemployment. As subsequently modified (by Barro and Gordon 1983, following Sargent and Wallace 1975), it assumes also that the public can foresee the results of policy action, and alters its behaviour as a result; and that the authorities take account of such reactions by the public. The result is to produce not advice to the authorities so much as a description of the authorities' behaviour: prescription is confined to seeking ways of altering the regime in which they operate in order to improve the authorities' performance — for instance by specifying rules rather than allowing them discretion, or, on one argument (Rogoff 1985) by the appointment of a not-too-conservative conservative as governor of the central bank. Such trains of argument depend not only on the assumption of fully informed rational agents, but also on the assumptions (which we have more particularly disputed) that the authorities can control the stock of money and by so doing determine the price level. Without that, we are reduced to a much messier world, in which the rules of policy are much cruder because the powers of policy are so restricted.

For this reason, we have not gone into many questions that figure in recent discussion of monetary policy. It is, for instance, often argued that a monetary expansion permitted by the authorities will affect output only if its more fundamental affects on prices are not foreseen: rational agents will foresee this, however, and therefore will not respond by spending more in response to the monetary stimulus — so that in this sense monetary policy is impotent. In our view it is impotent for the more basic reason that the rate of monetary expansion is not amenable to control by the authorities.

It is often argued that the monetary authorities will not (or should not) seek short-term effects on output, because, on the above argument, this depends on the more fundamental price effects not being foreseen by the public; hence, if the authorities make a habit of resorting to such actions, they will lose the reputation for acting long-sightedly, and with that lost, output effects will not be obtained. That argument, too, is irrelevant if (as we assert) the authorities are in any case able to control neither the rate of growth of the money stock, nor therefore the price level by this means. Control models designed to show how control of the money stock may best be used to keep the system stable in the face of unexpected outside shocks are similarly irrelevant if, as we assert, the growth of the money stock is not amenable to control by the authorities.

It is often also argued that fiscal policy is impotent to affect output. We have already, in Section 1, given reasons for rejecting that argument. The argument depends on the powers of foresight of rational agents and we have rejected it basically on the grounds that the future is so uncertain that rational agents cannot be supposed to foresee it with the certainty and in the detail predicated. Our nihilism about monetary policy does not, however, extend to denying that interest-rate changes may affect demand; and although this study is not directly concerned with fiscal policy, it is appropriate to indicate how we conceive of it being employed along with interest-rate policy. (That of course is interesting only to those who accept it has effects.)

In accord with the preceding remarks on inflation, we distinguish — for clarity of presentation no doubt over-sharply — between 'normal' periods, in which inflation does not appear an overriding problem, and other times, when it is. If fiscal policy is capable of influencing demand, it is appropriate that it be used to manage demand. We assume it is so used subject always to the constraints created by the potential danger of accelerating inflation. Although interest rate policy might be used as auxiliary to fiscal policy in restricting demand (Section 2 below), its main use would be in relation to exchange rate policy (Section 3 below). At times when inflation was an overriding problem, the aim of managing the economy smoothly might have to be superseded (Section 4).

2. THE DOMESTIC ROLE OF MONETARY POLICY

Under the regime of monetary targets, monetary policy was allotted the dominant role in guiding the evolution of the economy, and an abandonment of these pretensions must leave monetary policy with a much more modest domestic role. We have argued that, public-sector financial operations aside, the growth of the monetary aggregates has to be regarded as the response of the banking system to market forces. There is a general presumption that market forces should be left free to operate, unless there are good reasons to override the presumption. There is therefore a general case for an accommodating monetary policy, but a need also to identify the possible occasions where intervention is required. Such intervention might be appropriate when a rapid growth of bank lending seemed to be contributing to a level of demand in the economy as a whole that appeared excessive, or where clearly speculative conditions were developing in particular markets. There are however costs to invervention, which we discuss further below.

An exceptionally high rate of monetary growth does not in itself appear to provide grounds for intervention. This might result from a progressive relaxation of banks' lending criteria. Even though the effect on spending was far less than equivalent (Chapter 11, Setion 3), it might still contribute to a rate of economic expansion that may be judged too fast, given the economy's capacity to expand. Equally, it will not always do so. A phase of rapid monetary growth may also occur (even in the absence of a change in the banks' lending criteria) when the prospects of borrowers improve. Thus, improved profit expectations, stemming for example from a rise in foreign demand, could warrant fresh lending, and that would induce an unusually rapid growth in broad money. In such cases, too, the economic expansion thus facilitated may in some circumstances be judged too fast — but again, in other cases, not. We suggest below the types of monetary measures that could be used, in place of or in support of fiscal measures, to slow down the rate of economic expansion.

In both cases, the grounds for intervention by the authorities are not the rate of monetary growth as such, but whether or not the rate of economic expansion, present and forecast, is to be judged excessively rapid. That has to be assessed in the light of the traditional considerations: the direct effect on domestic costs and prices, and the effect via the balance of payments on the exchange rate. A rapid growth of broad money may serve as a warning signal, though not an infallible indicator, which at least points to the need for a close evaluation of the state of the economy.

The second sort of contingency against which the authorities, it is suggested, should be on guard is the onset of speculative price rises. The danger of such a development is normally limited to the areas where the stock is large in relation to potential flow, and where present prices can accordingly be dominated by short-term extrapolative expectations. The main areas are exchange rates (to be discussed in Section 3), commodity prices (where one country could hardly act alone), stock exchange prices, and property and house prices (where speculative conditions were important at least in 1971–3).

Despite the limited areas where there is normally a possibility of speculative price developments, official concern nevertheless seems appropriate, for various reasons. Although speculative price bubbles are temporary, they can persist long enough to divert the allocation of resources frolm the pattern sustainable in the longer run — and that involves some cost and waste of resources. The temporary increase in demand for particular resources is likely to create inflationary pressure in some areas (e.g. for building labour), which may strengthen inflationary pressures more generally. Finally, despite the best efforts of official supervisors, there would be some risk to the stability of financial institutions when prices fall after a speculative boom. Such occasions may be rare, but they are nevertheless to be guarded against. (Given the general inflationary bias of the economy, speculative price falls seem to carry less danger, and are in any case difficult to counter.)

Given the discussion in Part II of the limited effectiveness of most sorts of monetary policy action, it seems that only two sorts of monetary action would be effective in restricting aggregate demand. The first is by means of a rise in interest rates, which however would be a weak instrument; the second is by controls on lending, which it will be argued would be more effective than has recently come to be assumed. (In both cases, the effectiveness of intervention can be seen to stem largely from the facts that small borrowers have only limited access to credit, that the banks' role in providing it is not easily replaced, and that the authorities can, within limits, have a strong influence on banks' behaviour. The effect of such interventions is in each case somewhat asymmetric: they could be used to restrict total demand, but are likely to be less effective in expanding it.)

A rise in interest rates has two effects which need to be distinguished. First, it makes debt-financed spending more expensive. Most expenditure or borrowing for expenditure is not highly interest-sensitive (for reasons discussed in Chapter 3). This effect — within the limits within which a rise in interest rates can be induced by the authorities — is therefore likely to be small. Second, a rise in interest rates makes the service of existing debt more costly. If borrowers are unwilling or unable to draw on past savings or to borrow more, they will have to cut spending when income available after paying interest on existing debt is reduced. What borrowers lose is matched by what lenders gain. But lenders may well have a lower propensity to consume out of unexpected income than borrowers, since they are less likely to have been previously constrained in their consumption by lack of access to borrowing. A sharp rise in interest rates might thus possibly have a significant effect in cutting spending — the impact depending on the financial positions of agents in the economy, on how long the rise is expected to persist, and on how far the rise comes as a shock to expectations.

The effect is none the less limited in various ways. Some debt is on fixed-interest terms. Borrowers from building societies are cushioned because the societies are slow (though less so than earlier) to raise mortgage rates in line with a general increase in rates. Moreover, the societies are willing to extend repayment periods. Banks adopt the same procedure in respect of mortgage lending; and in lending to business borrowers, banks often in practice have little choice but to grant additional credit when interest rates rise. The effect on total spending is thus likely to be rather limited. High interest rates are in any case not a way of exerting great continued restraint on spending, for much of the effect here under discussion comes from an unexpected rise in rates.

If stronger monetary restraints appeared necessary, the earlier analysis suggests that the most effective route would be a return to direct lending controls — for which, although much out of fashion, there remains a case. Experience up to 1971, and with the Corset control, is commonly taken to show that evasion is so easy that controls on lending are likely to be completely ineffective. Large firms with access to the money markets may indeed be able to find alternative sources of finance, particularly if they are able easily to borrow abroad. Such escape routes however are less readily available to small firms, and hardly at all to most personal borrowers, whose importance in the total of bank lending has greatly increased. The reimposition of direct lending controls might therefore be highly effective in curbing some sorts of bank lending, and that would probably curb expenditure to some degree.

Lending controls certainly have many disadvantages. Their reimposition would involve a substantial retreat from the recent policy of encouraging competition in banking. If applied to business borrowers, there would be great unfairness as between firms of different sizes, since large firms could evade control by issuing debt; in practice, control might have to be confined to personal borrowers. Controls on personal lending if applied to banks might also have to apply to building societies; and although they themselves have habitually rationed credit, official control would be unprecedented. In controlling mortgage lending, it might be possible to avoid arrangements that froze the pattern of lending as between different lending institutions; thus, it might be possible to regulate lending criteria, e.g. the maximum proportion of the purchase price to be covered by a mortgage. It would hardly be possible, however, to apply the same principle to personal non-mortgage lending by banks, and a return to the old system of seeking to restrict the growth of lending by individual banks might be inevitable. An informal type of control might be possible; a call for voluntary restraint by banks could perhaps be effective for a while, and might be worth considering.

The need for a return to such methods may appear a remote and unlikely contingency. Stricter prudential requirements for capital adequacy may now prevent extremely rapid growth of lending (Chapter 9, Section 3). But the case for monetary restraint of this sort rests not so much on the pace of lending as on general demand conditions; and not only may total demand remain relatively low for many years, but even an unduly rapid growth of demand may seem unlikely. Predictions of this sort are highly fallible, however, and a rapid, continuing growth of bank lending is certainly a possibility. While reliance could be placed instead on fiscal policy, the possible need for a return to lending controls seems therefore something that should be kept in mind.

The same two methods of monetary restraint might be used if the authorities felt the need to counter speculative price rises. A sharp rise in interest rates affects the price of financial and other marketable assets including house or property prices, and might be enough to break a cumulative speculative rise in prices. Second, the authorities could seek to limit finance for activities in markets where conditions have become speculative. In the case of large borrowers, perhaps no more could be done than to call on banks to restrict the scale of lending likely to be used for such purposes. In the case of lending for house purchase, a more formal direct control of lending might in some circumstances come to seem required. It is an accident that the scale of mortgage lending has been restricted in the past not by policy but by the conservatism of the building societies, and it is quite possible that a rapid growth of mortgage lending could at some stage put undesirable pressure on house prices.

Interest rates and public debt

The circumstances discussed above are likely to be exceptional. At other times there is a general case for keeping interest rates low in order to minimize the cost of servicing the public debt. In recent years that aim has not had priority. Interest rates have been increased with the aim of restraining monetary growth (an attempt that was not effective), or keeping the exchange rate high (an aim to be questioned in Section 3 below). Public-sector financing has shifted towards borrowing from the public and away from borrowing from the banks (Chapter 11, Section 4), which probably increased the average interest rate paid. Even before the adoption of monetary targets, it was the general philosophy that the public debt should in considerable part be long-term: that too may have raised the interest cost.

The main argument for long-term funding appears to be that, if the public holds its accumulated savings in long-term form, that is a protection against a future surge of spending on the part of the public; a general attempt to dispose of long-term assets would depress their price, which would act as a deterrent. But it is questionable whether a future possible change of spending plans on the part of the public is a major danger to be guarded against; if it were, steps should also be taken to limit borrowing for the purpose of holding additional liquid assets, stocks of which have been greatly increased (Chapter 11, Section 3). It is also questionable whether there can be any effective safeguard against the danger; for the public always has considerable liquid and capital-certain financial assets, and it hardly conceivable that these could be reduced to a level so low that spending could not be increased. It might also be difficult to increase holdings of long-term public debt except by taking additional steps to encourage saving through the financial institutions, which buy most of it; and that might be questionable policy on other grounds.

The argument for seeking to keep interest rates low is a strong one. It is generally argued that there are dangers in the public sector being continuously in very large deficit; for beyond a point, it must add progressively to the cost of servicing the debt, in relation to national income (Chapter 6, Section 1). This argument is not easy to apply in a mechanical fashion, since the tolerable debt burden cannot de defined exactly. But, whatever weight the argument has, the same considerations point to the desirability of reducing the servicing costs of the public debt by keeping interest rates low. In recent years the rate of interest on public debt has come to exceed the rate of growth of nominal GDP. If that continued, it would clearly exacerbate the debt-burden constraints, imprecise though they are, on fiscal policy.

It is sometimes suggested that the cheapest way for the state to finance itself would be to print notes. But what matters is not the quantity of notes printed but the quantity of notes the public holds; and that the public decides, not the government. However, if cheap finance was the aim (and assuming that control of the monetary aggregates was no longer an objective of policy), greater resort to borrowing from the banks might well be one among other possibilities. Given the uncertainties, an instruction to the managers of the public debt to finance it in the cheapest way would not be easy to apply. But if that had been the aim in recent years, it seems likely that ways would have been found to keep the interest cost of the debt lower.

Conclusion

The domestic role proposed above for monetary policy may seem unduly modest in comparison with that allotted it by monetary targetry. But, despite the way it was presented and the effort to achieve it, the policy followed in the last decade was much closer to *laissez-faire* than might appear. Not only, as has been argued, were the means by which the authorities sought to control broad money ineffective, but the deposits of the building societies, although almost as large, were almost completely outside the purview of monetary targetry. Not surprisingly, the domestic role suggested here for monetary policy is not unlike what was expected of it in days before monetary targets; the above prescriptions for policy may indeed appear somewhat similar to those in the Radcliffe Report.

The generally *laissez-faire* approach is admittedly put forward as a doctrine for 'normal', fairly stable, times. It rests on the belief that the pace of inflation is determined mainly by factors such as the pressure of demand and independent pressure from wages or import prices, and that, although the growth of the monetary aggregates may, on occasion, be one factor causing over-fast expansion of demand, the relationship is not strong or systematic. It may be instructive to qualify these assumptions by considering what would happen under extremely inflationary conditions. All prices would then tend to become progressively more flexible, potentially more unstable, and more sensitive both to demand pressures and to monetary policy. The situation envisaged above as an occasional possibility in a few markets dealing in flexibly priced assets would then become the general one. Steep rises in interest rates, or controls over lending, might have to be employed to break the inflationary mentality. That sort of solution would clearly not be a monetarist solution; nevertheless, control of the general price level would then become, as monetarists always see it, very directly a task for monetary policy.

3. MONETARY POLICY AND THE EXCHANGE RATE

In contrast to the relatively unambitious domestic role we have assigned to monetary policy, we suggest that in future it should be determined chiefly by exchange rate considerations. This would be a move at least some way back to the fixed-rate regime that prevailed up to the early 1970s, in which interest rates were adjusted chiefly to protect the stability of the exchange rate. In Section 4 we consider how far the use of interest rates for this purpose would conflict with the domestic role we have suggested for them, and also the role of fiscal policy. In this section we give reasons for believing that an active exchange rate policy could produce a reasonable stability of the exchange rate — provided always that it was used with proper awareness of the limits to the authorities' power over exchange rates. The argument is put chiefly in terms of a single country, such as the United Kingdom, attempting to maintain stability in its rate; but later we consider the case of a group of countries attempting to do this.

The feasibility of an active exchange rate policy

It is usual to think of the years since 1973 as being a period of floating rates. In fact, the majority of currencies have remained subject to managed regimes of some form. Many are tied to the US dollar or to a basket of other currencies, in some cases with provision for frequent updating according to an index of price movements. The European Monetary System and its predecessor have operated with some success; the periodic adjustments of rates within it, often regarded as a failure of the system, may be seen rather as providing a necessary degree of flexibility. The regime of floating rates has thus operated chiefly in the relation between the currencies of major industrial countries or areas.

In the early 1970s proponents of floating rates argued that markets, given their head, would adjust smoothly to the evolving situation of different countries, and that, in contrast to the step changes required under the fixed-rate regime, exchange rates would be relatively stable. That has proved not to be the case. In addition to much short-period fluctuation, there have been prolonged swings in major countries' rates that have sometimes lasted for years, and that may have been 10 or 20 per cent on either side of any sustainable smooth course of the exchange rate (Chapter 5, Section 3).

In the decisions that firms make as regards their international trade, a distinction can be drawn between decisions as to the destination of output produced by existing capacity and decisions involving a modification or extension of capacity. Decisions of the first sort require a relatively short lead time, and the risk of exchange rate fluctuations can in part be avoided by use of forward markets or in other ways. Decisions of the second sort may often require a lead time of many years, over which the risk of exchange rate fluctuations cannot be hedged. Long-period fluctuations on the exchange rates between major currencies of the sort that have occurred thus make longer-term planning by firms of their international sales greatly more hazardous; they must create major distortions in the siting and scale of production of internationally traded goods (a real loss), and put serious impediments in the way of balance-of-payments adjustments (a loss to policy flexibility).

We argue that exchange rate policy should have the relatively modest aim of providing as much stability as possible. That alone would be a major gain, and may itself be quite difficult to attain. An exchange rate policy operated by a single country could hope to stabilize only the average of its exchange rates with its trading partners (i.e. its effective rate); within the average, its exchange rate *vis-à-vis* individual countries would still fluctuate. That, although imperfect, would however reduce the risks of international trade. Greater stability could be obtained only by all trading partners operating a similar policy.

Despite the erratic fluctuations that have characterized floating rates, it has until recently been the ruling orthodoxy that markets could determine exchange rates better than governments, and also (a double-clinch to the argument) that governments could not for long go against market forces and thus had no power to determine exchange rates. On this view, the breakdown of the Bretton Woods regime was inevitable; and the vast increase in the international mobility of capital since the early 1970s is seen as making it more and more impossible to return to a managed regime. If fluctuations in exchange rates have occurred, they were an inevitable part of reality, reflecting the changing collective perceptions about future world developments of those who managed funds: no one could improve on or go beyond that.

The analysis of Chapter 4 took a less idealized view of market behaviour. Since the future course of exchange rates is (within wide limits) extremely uncertain, operators in exchange markets do not for the most part take long-term positions. The market is thus dominated by short-term operators, and the level of exchange rates by their short-term expectations (and these in turn, in an incestuous way, are determined by what operators think other operators will think).

In the longer term, a country's current balance of payments must be limited to the size of sustainable capital flows, and the exchange rate must be such as to produce that balance. These long-run fundamentals (we argued) set limits to the short-term fluctuations of exchange rates. But the limits are wide. Within them, exchange rates are indeterminate and erratic; although markets' day-to-day response to news is sensitive, it is determined less by an evaluation of long-run fundamentals than by short-run factors; it may therefore be exaggerated, and expectations unstable.

Since expectations are footloose, markets are disproportionately influenced by clear signals of the sort that everyone is likely to take notice of. Among these are the actions of the authorities, who tend to be credited with stable views and are seen as potentially large-scale operators. Any observer must be struck by how ready markets often are to fall in with an official lead — not only in response to acts or stated aims, but often to what is merely inferred about unstated aims. This influence via expectations may thus greatly magnify the effect of the authorities' acts — provided always that the market believes that the rate the authorities are aiming at can be sustained.

The actions that an authority can take to influence the exchange rate are buying or selling its own currency in exchange for foreign currency, or raising or lowering central-bank rate and thus raising or lowering domestic interest rates relative to those in other countries. (We argue that in practice fiscal policy is unlikely to have an active role in exchange rate policy: see Section 4). Neither intervention nor variation of interest rates can however be employed on an indefinite scale. This implies (as argued in Chapter 11) that the authorities do not have power in the long term to put the exchange rate where they like, but can hope to smooth out its fluctuations about some median course.

The operation of a managed system thus requires the authorities to take a view about the average sustainable course of the exchange rate, i.e. a view about what the equilibrium level of the rate is going to turn out to be. It is often argued that governments are not qualified to make such a judgement. But the judgement is at least as difficult for market operators and they are less equipped for, and less interested in, taking such a view. There is probably a significant range at any point within which an official view would appear plausible. Once established, markets would thus find an official rate within this range credible; and therefore, unless conditions changed, it would in fact prove tenable.

If the authorities are able to establish credibility for their policy and thus carry market opinion with them, capital flows will reinforce their actions: the mobility of capital will be not foe but friend. But credibility is slow to be established and can be quickly lost; and, if lost, capital flight can overwhelm any action the authorities can take. In some circumstances markets are very malleable and the authorities have great power over exchange rates; in other circumstances markets are implacable. Exchange rate policy must thus always be essentially fragile.

These are reasons for dismissing the view, until recently very widespread, that governments had no power over exchange rates. But in correcting one exaggeration, it is important not to fly to the other extreme, and assume that governments have unlimited power to fix exchange rates where they wish. Governments can successfully operate exchange rate policies only on the proviso that they do not rely on their powers too much.

The present is a particularly difficult time to judge the possibilities. The regime of floating rates has for over a decade allowed free rein to powerful and erratic forces, and it is not possible for anyone to say how quickly and completely they can be brought back under control. This is a bigger unknown for sterling than for the currencies that have been inside the EMS arrangements. For sterling, along with the US dollar and the yen, has been subject to the largest fluctuations in the last decade. There are also major imbalances in the world economy, and thus major uncertainties — for instance, about the price of oil or the US dollar — which might affect sterling and which may persist. It thus remains to be seen how far sterling's exchange rate can be stabilized.

In face of these large uncertainties, there appears a strong case for a gradual and experimental way back to managing the exchange rate. It may be that a less cautious approach will be attempted, but it is still worth illustrating what form a cautious approach might take. The process would best start in a period when sterling seemed likely to strengthen, and in the first phase upward movement in the rate would be subject to some restraint, without any fixed upper limit being announced. The aims at this stage would be to get interest rates down to levels ruling elsewhere, and to allow the reserves to be built up considerably; foreign currency borrowing might also be desirable. At some later point an upper limit on the exchange rate would be set; at a later stage still, when confidence in the system had been built up, lower limits to the exchange rate would also be announced. The width of the band might be wide at first and narrowed only later.

No system, however, could be proof against all possible pressures. The large rise in the exchange rate in the period 1978–80 may in part have reflected a realization of the strengthening of the UK's external position provided by North Seal oil. If a managed exchange rate system had been in operation, the upward pressures might have been less; but it might well have been both necessary and desirable to allow it to move up some distance before attempting to hold it. The rise might also have been due in part to the advent of a new government, and political uncertainties will always remain. A change in government might, for instance, bring heavy downward pressure on the rate, and it might well seem necessary to allow it to move down before repegging; even so, the expectation that a managed system would be reimposed might limit the degree of volatility. The possibility of sustained shifts in capital flows arising in other ways, which might also have to be accommodated, has been discussed in Chapter 5 (Section 3). Only in the event will it be possible to find out whether such pressures will prove important or trivial.

If exchange rate management proves possible, however, the general objective should be not to avoid all adjustments of the rate, but rather to avoid large sudden adjustments, and to make small frequent adjustments in the right direction where this can be judged. It has already been argued (Chapter 12, Section 3) that the exchange rate should not be used as a means to reduce inflation; for reliance on such means in face of persistent inflationary pressure is likely after a while to prove unsuccessful. The attempt to maintain an unsustainable rate would tend to discredit the attempt to manage the exchange rate, and the end result is likely to be an increase in exchange rate volatility. To avoid this, it would be better if the effective exchange rate were adjusted at fairly frequent intervals in accord with relative price movements in the United Kingdom as compared with those in major competitor countries — in the hope that adjustments could then be kept small, so offering speculators only trivial gains. An exchange rate policy of this sort could be operated by a single country acting on its own.

It is necessary, finally, to comment on the possibilities of international collaboration. If many other major countries were attempting to manage their exchange rates in this way, it would be necessary for them at least to agree among themselves as to their exchange rate aims to ensure that they were not inconsistent. It would probably also be necessary for them to have a degree of understanding, in order to avoid contradictory policies, as to how they would vary interest rates; and it would be possible and advantageous if they also agreed on ways to increase the funds available for intervention, either by swap arrangements or in other ways, to supplement national reserves. It would not appear necessary (though this is often asserted) that they should agree on how they would use fiscal policy, so long as the policy they followed was consistent and predictable. A more restrictive fiscal policy in one country than in others, and a consequently lower level of activity, would mean that the sustainable level of its exchange rate would be higher than otherwise: provided this consequence was accepted, other countries could adapt to it.

The potential advantages to an individual country of a collective attempt to manage exchange rates are twofold. First, if successful, it would (as already noted) give greater stability not just to its average or effective exchange rate, but also to the cross-rates within the group. Second — especially if extra finance for intervention were provided — a collective attempt to manage exchange rates might have greater credibility than an attempt by one country on its own. Participation by the United Kingdom in the exchange rate arrangements of the EMS would not secure great advantages in these respects. If successful, it would provide greater stability for the exchange rate as against EMS currencies, but not as against other currencies; and the additional finance available from participation in EMS is relatively trivial.

It is possible that the movement of opinion away from the floating-rate regime will lead to a general attempt among major countries at exchange rate management, perhaps on the lines of that outlined above for a single country. An effective international attempt at exchange rate management would have to rest on agreement at least among the three most important countries, the United States, Japan, and Germany; given that, other countries also could participate. Under a world wide scheme, the potential advantages of international collaboration would be realized much more fully (by providing greater stability not just to average or effective exchange rates but also to cross-rates). To be effective, more finance for intervention would probably have to be made available than individual countries' existing reserves provide.

Given that Germany would have a key role in any such international attempt, other countries participating in the EMS exchange rate arrangements would face a choice. One possibility is that they should leave active participation in the wider arrangements to Germany, maintain their parities with the Deutschmark, and accept the joint exchange rate that would result between the EMS bloc and the rest of the world. The alternative is that EMS member countries should develop arrangements, now largely lacking, for operating a joint exchange rate policy for the bloc as a whole. That step might prove difficult, and the need to take part in it might be held to diminish the attractions of UK participation in the EMS exchange rate arrangements.

4. THE MIX OF MONETARY AND FISCAL POLICY

The general argument of this study has been that the powers of monetary policy are subject to severe limits; and in setting monetary policy in the context of economic policy as a whole, we had also to note the limitations we see to the use of fiscal policy. The first of these is contrary to recent fashion, and can be regarded as a return to an old-fashioned view. The second is, in its general thrust, in accord with fashion — but is unfashionable in grounding the limited power of policy largely on the authorities' lack of full control over inflation. Given this general view, the aims we propose for policy have perforce to be unambitious. For that reason, the allocation of roles to fiscal and monetary policy is relatively straightforward, and in brief may be stated as follows.

This study has not been concerned primarily with fiscal policy, and the role we see for it must be indicated only briefly. At times when inflation is not a large problem, we see a role for fiscal policy in demand management — always subject to the constraint of not undermining the stability of prices. That constraint is one-sided: it rules out undue stimulation of the economy, but does not limit action to prevent excessive levels of demand. In 'normal' times, with prices relatively stable, the aim of fiscal policy would be to help promote a rather smooth and orderly growth of demand — since this provides conditions favourable to the preservation of relative stability of prices, though by no means a certain guarantee. In this task monetary instruments can also play a role, although, we argue, a subsidiary one.

The main aim we see in 'normal' times for monetary policy is to preserve the relative stability of the exchange rate. That alone, without any more ambitious aim, would be a major gain; and even that might be achievable only imperfectly. In particular, we have counselled against attempting to use the exchange rate as a means to reduce domestic inflation, arguing that that is likely to prove ineffective, that it would be possible only in the short run, and thus in the end that it would be disruptive of exchange rate stability. If inflation more rapid than in our trading partners persists, we argue for a gradual adjustment of the exchange rate to that faster rate. How great a degree of exchange rate stability is possible may depend in part on whether other major countries follow similar policies; we would hope that after a period of transition it might be possible to keep fluctuations in the rate to rather narrow limits.

Central-bank rate (along with intervention in exchange markets) would, then, be used primarily to moderate fluctuations in the exchange rate. We would not see fiscal policy being used in the same way as a short-term means to maintain exchange rate stability. However, its employment to preserve orderly demand conditions, as above, would provide an essential condition for exchange rate management; and the choice of what growth of demand to aim at would necessarily be constricted by the likely consequence for the balance of payments.

We have argued that monetary policy should also be used for domestic reasons — at times as a means along with fiscal policy to restrict total demand, and at times to counter speculative conditions in particular markets. This might conflict with its use for exchange rate policy. However, the possibilities of conflict are limited in three ways. First, it is only on occasion that we would see fiscal policy having to be supplemented in this way. Second, on such occasions, exchange rate considerations might also counsel such action. Third, if a major effect were needed, this would have to come not by raising interest rates, but by resort to direct lending controls; here, the effect on the exchange rate is probably fairly minor.

Under the gold standard, the chief business of the central bank was to vary interest rates in accord with movements in the gold reserve — and thus in effect to maintain the stability of the exchange rate. If the latter again became the chief operational aim of interest rate policy, that would in a limited sense be a return to a very old-fashioned type of monetary policy. But our proposal differs crucially, in that accommodation to differential rates of inflation in different countries would be built in. In the days of the gold standard, countries were not subject to the inflationary bias that has been manifest since the Second World War; and we in effect have taken the view that nowadays inflationary forces are so entrenched that official management of the exchange rate is impossible unless it makes allowance for differential inflation rates. It is possible that, earlier in the century, countries' price structures were more flexible, so that interest rate policy could play a role in maintaining domestic price stability. One could say that, if the gold standard then provided an 'anchor' against inflation, it could do so only because that was then hardly needed, and was an easy task.

We restrict ourselves to doing the best that is possible in the light of present conditions; and even then, as we have stressed, we are unable to propose an adequate answer to the problem of inflation. All the above proposals are fair-weather proposals, on the assumption that inflation is not an overriding problem. But there is always a possibility that it may become one. What, then, do we propose?

Faced with what seems serious excessive inflation, governments have usually felt forced to take some spectacular action; and that instinct can hardly be dismissed as mistaken. The action is usually such as to deflate the economy. The effect on inflation may not be clear-cut, but must usually be helpful; and a collective demonstration of concern and intent itself has value. If such a situation arises, there is no reason why monetary policy as well as fiscal policy should not be used. In such circumstances, it might make sense to promote a temporarily high exchange rate even at the cost of creating problems later. The preservation of orderly financial conditions, here proposed as the proper normal aim of monetary policy, may have to be suspended for the sake of administering a salutory shock. The capability of monetary policy is not all-extensive; and it would be a deception to believe that there is always an orderly smooth-working solution to hand. If there is not, then disruption of the economy in one form or another may be inevitable, and a price that has to be paid to avoid the danger, if that seems in prospect, of rapidly accelerating inflation, and the disruption that that would entail.

Bibliography

References in the text to articles in the *Bank of England Quarterly Bulletin* are referred to with the date only (as '*BEQB* 1985') and generally are not listed separately below. However, where an author's name was given, articles are referred to in the text by name and are included in the Bibliography.

Allen, W. A. (1982), 'Intermediation and pure liquidity-creation in banking systems', *Greek Economic Review.*

Artis, M. J., and Lewis, M. K. (1981), *Monetary Control in the United Kingdom,* Oxford, Philip Allan.

Bain, A. D. (1970), *The Control of the Money Supply,* Harmondsworth, Penguin.

Bank of England (1984), *The Development and Operation of Monetary Policy, 1960–1983: A Selection of Material from the Quarterly Bulletin of the Bank of England,* Oxford, Clarendon Press.

Barro, R. J. (1974), 'Are government bonds net wealth?', *Journal of Political Economy.*

_____ and Gordon, D. B. (1983), 'A positive theory of monetary policy in a natural rate model', *Journal of Political Economy.*

Blackaby, F., *et al.* (1978), *British Economic Policy 1960–74,* Cambridge, Cambridge University Press.

Blanchard, O., and Watson, M. (1982), *Bubbles, Rational Expectations and Financial Markets,* Harvard Institute of Economic Research Discussion Paper 877.

Blinder, A. S. and Solow, R. M. (1974), 'Analytical foundations of fiscal policy', in *The Economics of Public Finance,* Washington, Brookings Institution.

Boléat, M. (1982), *The Building Society Industry,* London, Allen & Unwin.

Britton, A. J. C. (1983), 'Public sector borrowing', *National Institute Economic Review.*

Buiter, W. H. (1977), 'Crowding out and the effectiveness of fiscal policy', *Journal of Public Economics.*

_____ (1985), 'Government deficits reinterpreted', *Economic Policy.*

_____ and Miller, M. (1981a), 'Monetary policy and international competivity: the problems of adjustment', *Oxford Economic Papers* (Supplement).

_____ and Miller, M. (1981b), 'The Thatcher experiment: the first two years', *Brookings Papers on Economic Activity.*

_____ and Miller, M. (1983), 'Changing the rules: economic consequences of the Thatcher regime', *Brookings Papers on Economic Activity.*

_____ and Tobin, J. (1979), 'Debt neutrality: a brief review of doctrine and evidence', in G. M. von Furstenberg (ed.), *Social Security versus Private Savings,* Cambridge, Mass., Ballinger.

Capie, F., and Webber, A. (1985), *A Monetary History of the United Kingdom 1870–1982,* Vol. I, London, Allen & Unwin.

Cooke, W. P. (1985), 'Some current concerns of a banking supervisor', *Bank of England Quarterly Bulletin.*

Culbertson, J. M. (1968), *Macroeconomic Theory and Stabilisation Policy,* New York, McGraw-Hill.

Currie, D. A. (1981), 'Monetary and Fiscal Policy and the Crowding-out Issue', in M. J. Artis and M. M. Miller (eds.), *Essays in Fiscal and Monetary Policy,* Oxford University Press.

Cuthbertson, K. (1985), *The Supply and Demand for Money,* Oxford, Basil Blackwell.

Davis, E. P. (1984), 'The consumption function in macroeconomic models: a comparative study', *Applied Economics.*

―――― and Saville, I. D. (1982), 'Mortgage lending and the housing market', *Bank of England Quarterly Bulletin.*

Domar, E. D. (1944), 'The burden of the debt and the national income', *American Economic Review.*

Dornbusch, R. (1976), 'Expectations and exchange rate dynamics', *Journal of Political Economy.*

Dow, J. C. R. (1964), *The Management of the British Economy 1945–60,* Cambridge University Press.

―――― (1986), 'Trade unions and inflation', *Lloyds Bank Review.*

Drayson, S. J. (1985), 'The housing finance market: recent growth in perspective', *Bank of England Quarterly Bulletin.*

Duck, N. W., and Sheppard, D. K. (1978), 'A proposal for the control of the UK money supply', *Economic Journal.*

Easton, W. W. (1985), *The Importance of Interest Rates in Five Macroeconomic Models,* Bank of England Technical Paper no. 24.

Farmer, R. (1984), 'Bursting bubbles', *Journal of Monetary Economics.*

Fforde, J. S. (1982), 'Setting monetary objectives', in *Central Bank Views on Monetary Targetting,* New York, Federal Reserve Bank of New York: reprinted in *Bank of England Quarterly Bulletin,* 1983, and in Bank of England (1984).

Fleming, J. M. (1962), 'Domestic financial policies under fixed and floating exchange rates', *IMF Staff Papers,* November; reprinted in Fleming (1972).

―――― (1972), *Essays in International Economics,* London, Allen & Unwin.

Flood, R. P., and Garber, P. M. (1982), 'Market fundamentals versus price-level bubbles: the first tests', *Journal of Political Economy.*

Foot, M. D. K. W., Goodhart, C. A. E., and Hotson, A. C. (1979), 'Monetary base control', *Bank of England Quarterly Bulletin;* reprinted (without appendix) in Goodhart (1984).

Forsyth, P. J., and Kay, J. A. (1980), 'The economic implications of North Sea oil revenues', *Journal of the Institute for Fiscal Studies.*

Frankel, J. A., and Johnson, H. G. (eds.) (1976), *The Monetary Approach to the Balance of Payments,* London, Allen & Unwin.

Friedman, M. (1956), 'The quantity theory of money', in M. Friedman, *Studies in the Quantity Theory of Money,* Chicago, University of Chicago Press.

―――― (1980), Memorandum submitted to Treasury and Civil Service Committee, included in Treasury and Civil Service Committee (1980).

_____ and Schwartz, A. J. (1982), *Monetary Trends in the United States and the United Kingdom: Their Relation to Income, Prices, and Interest Rates, 1967–1975,* Chicago, University Press.

Gale, D. (1982), *Money: in Equilibrium,* Welwyn Garden City, James Nisbet.

Gardener, E. P. M. (ed.) (1986), *UK Banking Supervision: Evolution, Practice and Issues,* London, Macmillan.

Goldsmith, R. (1969), *Financial Structure and Development,* New Haven, Yale University Press.

Goodhart, C. A. E. (1984), *Monetary Theory and Practice: The UK Experience,* London, Macmillan.

_____ (1986), 'Financial innovation and monetary control', *Oxford Review of Economic Policy.*

Gowland, D. (1982), *Controlling the Money Supply,* London, Croom Helm.

Greenwell Associates (1980), *Special Monetary Bulletin: Monetary Base Control,* London, Greenwell.

Griffiths, B. (1979), 'The reform of monetary control in the United Kingdom', *Annual Monetary Review,* no. 1, London, City University Centre for Banking and International Finance.

Gurley, J. G., and Shaw, E. S. (1960), *Money in a Theory of Finance,* Washington, Brookings Institution.

Hacche, G., and Townend, J. C. (1981), 'Exchange rates and monetary policy: modelling sterling's effective exchange rate', *Oxford Economic Papers.*

Hendry, D. F. (1985), 'Monetary economic myth and economic reality', *Oxford Review of Economic Policy.*

_____ and Ericsson, N. R. (1983), 'Assertion without empirical basis: an econometric appraisal of Friedman and Schwartz's *Monetary Trends in . . . the United Kingdom', Bank of England Panel of Academic Consultants* Paper no. 22, London, Bank of England.

Hicks, J. R. (1937), 'Mr Keynes and the "Classics": a suggested interpretation', *Econometrica.*

_____ (1939), *Value and Capital,* Oxford, Clarendon Press.

_____ (1981), '*IS–LM*: an explanation', *Journal of Post-Keynesian Economics.*

Jaffee, D. M. (1971), *Credit Rationing and the Commercial Loan Market,* New York, John Wiley.

Kaldor, N. (1980), 'Monetary policy in the United Kingdom', in *Memoranda on Monetary Policy: Evidence to Treasury and Civil Service Committee;* reprinted in Kaldor (1986).

_____ (1986), *The Scourge of Monetarism* (2nd edn), Oxford University Press.

Kareken, J. H. (1986), 'Federal bank regulatory policy: a description and some observations', *Journal of Business.*

Keynes, J. M. (1930), *A Treatise on Money,* London, Macmillan.

_____ (1936), *The General Theory of Employment, Interest, and Money.* London, Macmillan.

_____ (1937), 'Alternative theories of the rate of interest', *Economic Journal.*

Knight, F. H. (1921), *Risk, Uncertainty, and Profit,* Boston, Houghton Mifflin; reprinted 1933, London School of Economics.

Kohn, M. (1981), 'A loanable funds theory of unemployment and monetary disequilibrium', *American Economic Review.*

Laidler, D. (1984), 'The "buffer stock" notion in monetary economics', *Economic Journal* (Supplement).

Layard, K., and Nickell, S. (1985), 'The causes of British unemployment', *National Institute Economic Review.*

Lerner, A. P. (1948), 'The burden of the national debt', in *Income, Employment, and Public Policy: Essays in Honor of Alvin H. Hansen,* New York, W. W. Norton.

Lutz, F. A., and Mints, L. W. (eds.) (1951), *Readings in Monetary Theory,* Philadelphia, Blakeston.

Matthews, R. C. O., Feinstein, C. M., and Odling-Smee, J. C. (1982), *British Economic Growth, 1856–1973,* Oxford, Clarendon Press.

Mayer, C. (1986), 'Financial innovation: curse or blessing', *Oxford Review of Economic Policy.*

Meade, J. E. (1934), 'The amount of money and the banking system', *Economic Journal.*

Meyer, L. M. (1980), 'Financing constraints and the short-run response to fiscal policy', *Federal Reserve Bank of St Louis Review.*

Modigliani, F. (1945), 'Liquidity preference and the theory of interest and money', *Econometrica;* reprinted in Lutz and Mints (1951).

Moore, B. J., and Threadgold, A. R. (1980), *Bank Lending and the Money Supply,* Bank of England Discussion Paper no. 10.

Mundell, R. A. (1968), *International Economics,* London, Macmillan.

Odling-Smee, J., and Riley, C. (1985), 'Approaches to the PSBR', *National Institute Economic Review.*

Okina, K. (1985), *Empirical Tests of Bubbles in the Foreign Exchange Market,* Bank of Japan Monetary and Economic Studies.

Poole, W. (1970), 'Optimal choice of monetary policy instruments in a simple stochastic macro model', *Quarterly Journal of Economics.*

Reid, M. (1982), *The Secondary Bank Crisis, 1973–75,* London, Macmillan.

Robinson, J. (1952), *The Rate of Interest,* London, Macmillan.

Rogoff, K. (1985), 'The optimal degree of commitment to an intermediate monetary target', *Quarterly Journal of Economics.*

Rose, H. (1986), 'Change in financial innovation in the UK', *Oxford Review of Economic Policy.*

Sargent, T. J., and Wallace, N. (1975), ' "Rational" expectations, the optimal monetary instrument and the optimal money supply rule', *Quarterly Journal of Economics.*

Saville, I. D., and Gardiner, K. L. (1986), 'Stagflation in the UK since 1970: a model-based explanation', *National Institute Economic Review.*

Sayers, R. S. (1957), *Central Banking After Bagehot,* Oxford University Press.

—— (1976), *The Bank of England 1891–1914,* Cambridge, University Press.

Spencer, P. D. (1986), *Financial Innovation, Efficiency, and Disequilibrium: Problems of Monetary Management in the United Kingdom 1971–81,* Oxford, Clarendon Press.

Spencer, R. W., and Yohe, W. P. (1970), 'The "crowding out" of private expenditures by fiscal policy actions', *Federal Reserve Bank of St Louis Review.*

Stiglitz, J. E., and Weiss, A. (1981), 'Credit rationing in markets with imperfect information', *American Economic Review.*

Tobin, J. (1963a), 'Essay on the principles of debt management', reprinted in Tobin (1971).

———— (1963b), 'Commercial banks as creators of money', in D. Carson, *Banking and Monetary Studies;* reprinted in Tobin (1971).

———— (1969), 'A general equilibrium approach to monetary theory', reprinted in Tobin (1971).

———— (1971), *Essays in Economics,* Vol. I: *Macroeconomics,* Amsterdam, North Holland.

———— (1980), *Asset Accumulation and Economic Activity,* Oxford, Basil Blackwell.

———— (1981), 'Money and finance in the macroeconomic process', Nobel Prize Lecture, Cowles Foundation Discussion Paper no. 613R, New Haven, Yale University.

———— and Brainard, W. C. (1977), 'Asset markets and the cost of capital', in R. Nelson and B. Belassa (eds.), *Economic Progress: Private Values and Public Policy,* Amsterdam, North Holland.

Treasury/Bank (1980), Green Paper on *Monetary Control* (Cmnd. 7858), London, HMSO.

Treasury and Civil Service Committee (1980), *Memoranda on Monetary Policy,* Session 1979–80, London, HMSO.

———— (1981), *Report on Monetary Policy,* Session 1981–81, London, HMSO.

Trundle, J. M. (1982a), *The Demand for M1 in the UK,* Bank of England Discussion Paper.

———— (1982b), 'Recent changes in the use of cash', *Bank of England Quarterly Bulletin.*

Tsiang (1956), 'Liquidity preference and loanable funds theories, multiplier and velocity analyses: a synthesis', *American Economic Review.*

———— (1966), 'Walras' law, Say's law and liquidity preference in general equilibrium analysis', *International Economic Review.*

US Federal Reserve System (1980), Memorandum submitted to Treasury and Civil Service Committee, included in Treasury and Civil Service Committee (1980).

Vines, D., Maciejowski, J., and Meade, J. E. (1983), *Demand Management,* Vol. 2: *Stagflation,* London, Allen & Unwin.

Wadhwani, S. (1984), *Are Exchange Rates Excessively Volatile?,* London School of Economics Centre for Labour Economics Discussion Paper 198.

Walters, A. (1986), *Britain's Economic Renaissance: Margaret Thatcher's Reforms, 1979–1984,* New York and Oxford, Oxford University Press.

Wicksell, K. (1898), *Interest and Prices: A Study of the Causes Regulating the Value of Money,* English version 1936, London, Macmillan.

Williamson, J. (1983), *The Open Economy and the World Economy: A Textbook in International Economics,* New York, Basic Books.

———— (1985), *The Exchange Rate System* (2nd edn), Washington, Institute for International Economics.

Wright, P. A. D. (1984), 'Funding the public sector borrowing requirement: 1952–83', *Bank of England Quarterly Bulletin*.

Index